COMPTON ON CRICKETERS
PAST AND PRESENT

DENIS COMPTON

COMPTON ON CRICKETERS PAST AND PRESENT

CASSELL

LONDON

CASSELL LTD.
35 Red Lion Square, London WC1R 4SG
and at Sydney, Auckland, Toronto, Johannesburg,
an affiliate of
Macmillan Publishing Co., Inc.,
New York.

First published 1980

ISBN 0 304 30685 1

Printed in Great Britain by
Richard Clay (The Chaucer Press) Ltd.
Bungay, Suffolk

CONTENTS

ILLUSTRATIONS

FOREWORD

A famous Australian once said to me that an infallible guide to a
man's character was his approach and methods on the cricket field.
I am bound to feel the prospect is too alarming to contemplate in
some instances! But with Denis Compton the cap surely fits.
Denis the cricketer and Denis the man were one and the same —
cavalier, dashing, exciting and compelling.

To attempt to name the top twenty-five players in a span of
almost forty years is a daunting undertaking in itself; but Denis
has never shirked a challenge, and if there is controversy in his
choice the result is entertaining. I am flattered to be included. If, as
he says, he found me a difficult bowler, I can honestly retort that I
was glad not to have to bowl at him every day of the week.

The trouble is that Compton the author cannot include
Compton the batsman in his book. He would, of course, walk into
the first twenty-five, and moreover be a strong candidate for any
World XI in any period. I only wish he had been playing in my
years as chairman of Test selectors. He would have lightened the
load.

Denis trod a glamorous path between Lord's and Highbury, and
but for the war there is little doubt that he would have added a
substantial number of official Soccer caps to his total of 78 Tests.
As it was he was a regular member of the international side during
the war when there was no shortage of brilliant players. It was
really schoolboy hero stuff for him to tour South Africa in 1948–9
as a Test cricketer and return to help Arsenal beat Sheffield
United in the F.A. Cup final. Someone described him as the
eternal schoolboy, and the public was enraptured by his exploits
and the manner in which he scored his runs.

Once, dashing down the pitch, he fell flat on his face and still hit the ball to the boundary while lying prone on the ground. Until his serious knee operation he was miraculously fast on his legs. He was constantly looking for runs, seeking to dominate; and when bowling to him one knew that anything but the tightest length and direction would be avidly punished.

With such nimble feet, an eagle eye and abounding confidence Denis was a master of improvisation. Unfettered by techniques and the restrictions binding an ordinary player he hooked and cut with deadly precision and his cover driving was a treat to the eye (unless you happened to be bowling). Then there was the sweep. Ah. . . the Compton sweep! I wonder just how many times in all parts of the world a bowler's heart leapt in exultation as Denis played his sweep at the very last second, and often to a ball arrowing straight at his stumps. And I wonder just how many times joyous anticipation turned to disbelief as the ball was turned to the boundary.

Yet when things were at their worst for the fielding side there was always Denis's running between the wickets to keep hopes alive. Let us say he was an eccentric runner and caller — an optimist, keeping his partner, his side, the opposition and the spectators in constant suspense. It was said that he was the inventor of the triple call — 'Yes! No! Sorry!' — that after making a call he would always wish his partner luck, and that his first call was a basis for negotiations. I took part in one or two profitable stands with Denis in the 1948 series with Australia, and I will content myself with the observation that my partner's calling and the bowling were equally taxing.

At Old Trafford Denis and I put on 121, which was only three short of the eighth-wicket record by England against Australia set up by 'Patsy' Hendren and Harold Larwood at Brisbane in 1928. Denis, who had returned after deflecting a no-ball bumper from Ray Lindwall on to his head, finished 145 not out and ended our two-and-a-half-hour partnership by running me out. I did pass a remark to him which is better not repeated here!

Basically Denis was a great player, character and entertainer. He gave a lot to the game, and the bars were never filled when he was at the crease. Crowds saw him as a happy player as well as supremely gifted. In 1947 he broke record after record, scoring

3,816 runs with 18 centuries. He ended a memorable career with 38,723 runs and 122 centuries, and, it can further be said, he scarcely played a boring innings. If he did I never heard it mentioned. For England he made 5,807 runs, including 17 centuries, with an average of 50.06. In addition he took in all first-class matches 617 wickets and 417 catches — it ought not to be forgotten that he was a dazzling slip. Developing his original orthodox slow-left-arm spinners with the 'chinamen' and googlies after some instruction from that grand Aussie Jack Walsh, he could have won the Headingley Test in 1948 if England's catching had been up to standard.

To play with or against Denis was a refreshing and warming experience. One always sensed an air of challenge without a trace of bitterness, and cricket would be much enriched today if his spirit of adventure and belief in attack returned.

ALEC BEDSER

INTRODUCTION

In presenting my gallery of greats within the compass of my experience as player, spectator, writer and broadcaster, I am acutely aware of the many truly illustrious batsmen and bowlers I have been obliged to leave out. I can imagine the coals of fire about to be heaped over my head, the exasperated disappointment of a reader discovering his favourite player is not included (I would have felt the same as a lad in finding 'Patsy' Hendren rejected), and the brickbats of the statisticians. What, I can hear their surprised disgust, no Jim Laker? After his 19 Australian wickets in the 1956 Old Trafford Test?

The absence of Laker, perhaps the finest off-spin bowler of all time, and of George Headley, who, with George Challenor, is often described as the father of modern West Indies batting, admittedly continues to worry me. I am the last to subscribe to the libel that Laker owed much of his success to the favourable pitches of the time. His masterly control and accuracy on his one tour of Australia — ye Gods, one tour! — should have banished that nonsense for all time. The Aussies were after him in 1958-9, hell-bent on revenge, but he was never collared and in a losing side earned their lasting respect. Figures were shown at the time to prove that the famous Laker – Lock partnership was even more successful away than it was at the Oval, but I sometimes wonder if they would have been as deadly operating on the pre-war pitches of their home ground.

Before Hitler's War, 'Bosser' Martin's pitches were a byword, and the outfield was like polished glass — on this subject Bill O'Reilly, the supreme leg-break bowler, is interesting. Jim would still have been a pre-eminent bowler, of that I have no doubt, but I believe he would have found it harder to get his wickets as cheaply as he did. Facing Jim I was certain of two things: if the surface gave him *half* a chance he would be a better off-spinner than I had ever met; or, if it didn't, he would nag me into submissive defence by sheer control. In intelligence Jim had no superior, and I am desperately sorry he could not be fitted into my gallery.

Nor could I find a place for Lance Gibbs, with more Test wickets than any bowler in history. As with Laker and Gibbs, so with George Headley. In all these cases I feel rather like a lawyer presenting a highly arguable defence plea; but, at the same time, arguments are the life-blood of cricket, and no two opinions are exactly alike. I played in the 1939 Lord's Test when George scored a century in each innings. For years he carried the West Indies batting with enormous courage and ability. When the West Indies were an emerging power he stood apart, and his record speaks for itself. At home Headley's admirers called Bradman the 'white Headley' — a pardonable patriotic liberty. But the more one delves into the achievements of the Don, the more one's mind boggles. I accept what George did for the West Indies, and his high status in world cricket history. Some of his early big scores were against good attacks, but not entirely the best England could send. No doubt many other bowlers would have suffered the same punishment had they gone to the Caribbean . . . but they didn't, and a tiny question mark remains.

It could be said that Headley proved his rare skill on his visits to England and Australia, and I only wish I could have seen him at the peak of his powers against the very top bowling. It is my misfortune that I did not. I also have a lingering memory of him recalled for the Test at Kingston, Jamaica in 1954. He was long past his best, and his supporters ought not to have submitted him to the ordeal. The Headley of the 1930s would no doubt have been more than equal to modern demands — demands which Sir Gary Sobers, the W's and Viv Richards have so brilliantly surmounted.

After the No. 1 choice of the Don many of the others were blindingly obvious. There was Wally Hammond, Sir Len Hutton (who I believe could have been even better than he was), Peter May, Ken Barrington, Gary Sobers, Alec Bedser, Bill O'Reilly, Ray Lindwall, Keith Miller and Freddie Trueman. And to my mind it would have been a cardinal sin to have split the unique trinity of Sir Frankie Worrell, of blessed memory, Everton

Weekes and Clyde Walcott.

Apart from Graeme Pollock and Arthur Morris there were left-handers like Martin Donnelly and Bert Sutcliffe I omitted with reluctance. Many might think I have grown soft in old age, or spent too much time under the Adelaide sun, to risk nominating David Gower, who still has to prove his greatness against the best bowling. Yet I declare I have never seen a better timer of the ball. Gower excites me, as does Ian Botham. There is something about both Gower and Botham which suggests the natural athlete, the born winner. Botham has the aggression which is so necessary at top level to sustain success over a long period. If they prove me wrong in the next decade I can be called a bad judge.

Mike Procter is one of my favourite players, but he and Barry Richards have largely been denied through no fault of their own the chance of parading their gifts at international level. Then there was Dudley Nourse — they don't come much better than Dudley. And the Indian Vijay Merchant, and the Pakistani run-machine, the redoubtable Hanif Mohammed. The New Zealander John Reid was another exciting all-rounder to cross my mind, as was Vinoo Mankad. The list grows with Clive Lloyd and Rohan Kanhai and Stan McCabe, scorer of that never-to-be-forgotten 232 out of 300 at Trent Bridge in 1938. I doubt whether I have ever been so punished as a fielder as I was for four hours during that majestic innings.

I include Neil Harvey because he was sheer genius, and whenever one saw his back retreating to the pavilion one felt things were not so bad after all. Tom Graveney came very close to inclusion, which may surprise some, yet to me Tom personified all that's graceful and charming in batting. To be at the other end while he was batting was to study a silken virtuosity. His movements were almost lazy, and his touch like thistledown. But suddenly he would strike with a cover drive which had a glorious pugnacity. Some critics insisted he lacked the temperament for the big occasion, or was placed in a straitjacket by captains too concerned with defensive measures. The latter is the more feasible explanation for some of his failures, but, to my eyes, his tall, willowy figure playing immaculate shots is a memory to cherish. Perhaps the sheer grind of Test cricket was not for him, and the lesson is that a player good enough to represent his country must be allowed to play his own way. Tom gave me some blissful hours.

Much the same can be said of Colin Cowdrey, a batsman endowed with unusual gifts, but seeming to lack the killer instinct. He could be quite masterful, even arrogant and dismissive of high-quality bowling. But he was known to lapse into broody and unproductive spells which did not measure up to my philosophy that it pays to attack and keep on attacking. Colin ranks high among post-war batsmen, and, to me, his finest innings was his superb 102 at Melbourne in 1954 which saved England from rout and laid the foundation for eventual victory and the Ashes. It was only his second Test, and maybe Colin set himself standards impossible to follow.

Trevor Bailey always earned my unstinted admiration. No one shared his level of determination. The pity was that he couldn't bat as well as he bowled. Otherwise he would have been a brilliant all-rounder. Nor can I pass without mention of Fazal Mahmood, a magnificent attacking bowler of the Bedser mould, the aggressive leg-break bowling and captaincy of Richie Benaud, and the batting of the Chappell brothers.

In my forty years there have been many wonderful players. To squeeze my list into twenty-five has made me realize the dilemmas often facing selectors, who can only put eleven players into the field for any one Test match. The problem is not with the self-selected, but those on the fringe.

Everyone is entitled to an opinion. During the English season of 1979 some people were good enough to express their indignation to me when Tony Greig was reported to have described me as a 'so-called great player'. It is for others to decide my possible status in a game I loved to play, watch, write about, talk about and discuss. But I will permit myself one indulgence: that I would love to have batted against Greig's bowling in my heyday — particularly those so-called off-breaks of his.

Maybe he would also have enjoyed bowling to me. It's all a matter of opinion, my masters!

No book of this nature could be compiled without scouring the library shelves to confirm facts and revive memories. *Wisden* was indispensable, and I would particularly like to acknowledge *Viv Richards*, an autobiography written in collaboration with David Foot (World's Books, Ltd.), Trevor Bailey's *Sir Gary* (Collins), Ray Robinson for his study in *Cricket: The Great Bowlers* (Pelham Books), Neil Harvey's *World of Cricket* (Hodder and Stoughton) and Pat Landsberg's *The Kangaroo Conquers* (Museum Press).

Denis Compton
GERRARDS CROSS
November, 1979

1

KEN BARRINGTON

Ken Barrington joined Surrey from the Reading club at the age of seventeen as a leg-break bowler, and ended a remarkable playing career with 20 centuries in 82 Tests for England, and an assured status among cricket's international elite.

The Barrington saga is both a romance and a confusing paradox: on the one side a brilliantly gifted stroke-player with a real sense of fun and a gift of mimicry; and on the other a stern accumulator of runs, frugal with his shots, and obeying an awesome dedication to his cause.

I never had any doubt of his considerable natural ability, but I admit to being at a loss fully to understand how it is possible for the same player to enthral as he did at Melbourne in 1966 and be dropped by England for taking seven and a half hours to make 137 against New Zealand at Edgbaston six months earlier. Sadly, to many, he emerged as dour and unattractive. Yet he had all the shots, and his record of 31,714 runs is an eloquent testimony to the success of his methods and intense resolve. When he seemed to be in sight of cornering most records he succumbed to the years of concentrated effort and suffered a mild thrombosis during a double-wicket tournament at Melbourne. Wisely he called it a day, and has become a successful· garage proprietor, Test selector, a manager of England overseas teams, a true friend and counsellor to many players, and a single-handicap golfer.

If greatness is measured by results against Australia, normally the fiercest of competitors, Ken was truly great. Only Herbert Sutcliffe (66.85) has a higher average than Barrington's 63.35, and only Wally Hammond's 1,553 (average 91.35) was more than Barrington's aggregate of 1,451 (average 85.35) in 1962–3. In 39 innings he took 2,111 runs off the Australians, including his highest-ever score of 256 at Old Trafford in 1964, and those who denigrate English skills against leg-spin bowling must not include Barrington in their strictures. Richie Benaud took his wicket only three times in 17 Test innings against him, when he had made scores of 83, 78 and 101.

Barrington, broad-shouldered, rugged and craggy, became the ultimate in the long innings of carefully compiled runs. He made a century against every Test-playing country, and a Test century on every Test centre in England — Lord's, Trent Bridge, Old Trafford, Headingley, Edgbaston and his home ground of the Oval.

From Bombay to New Delhi he was the scourge of India's highly skilled spinners. He made centuries against the bumpers at Port of Spain and Bridgetown, Durban and Auckland. A profusion of runs poured from his bat, and his Test average of 58.67 in 131 innings has been bettered only by Sir Donald Bradman, Herbert Sutcliffe, Eddie Paynter, South Africa's Graeme Pollock and the West Indian George Headley — a distinguished gallery if ever there was one.

Basically Ken played more off the back foot than the front, and it ought to be fairly well established now that I am much in favour of the back-foot exponent, because I believe it to be absolutely essential at the highest level to be a master of your own crease. I schooled myself to be on the back foot to the quicks like Ray Lindwall, Keith Miller, Brian Statham and Frank Tyson a split second before the ball was released — not in the course of the run-up, as I have often seen — in order to give myself the longest possible sight of the ball to defend, or to be in the right position to hook, pull or cut if the length was short enough. I hear it said that if a player is committed to the back foot it is not possible to hit the half-volley, but assuming he is properly balanced and quick enough on his feet, I do not see why.

As his career developed Barrington adopted a wide open stance to counter the rash of in-swing bowling, which meant that for all intents and purposes he had eliminated the drive between cover and extra. He was always a good cutter, which remained a prolific weapon, and strong on the leg side. His technique was ruthlessly effective and functional, and he added to it his natural courage and determination.

Never was there a better or more courageous fighter in a crisis. Players and public felt a growing mixture of gratitude to Barrington as the cornerstone of England's batting, and frustration that so much of his splendour was cloaked in drabness. The self-discipline was severe, the concentration nothing short of remarkable.

If I have a criticism of him, it is that he did not punish the bad ball enough. He was in position soon enough, which is the first necessity, but only around twenty-five per cent went to the boundary. For perhaps the game's best-ever 'percentage' player this was poor value. If the loose delivery escapes punishment it is a bonus for the bowler and makes batting that much harder.

Ken was always wary of making a mistake and, perhaps more than any batsman of his class, was inclined to drop into a mental groove of defence, so that he lost the habit of hitting the ball in his latter years. Frankly, to do what he did would have driven me potty. It was not in my character to be able to change my style. Equally, I would have been proud to save England as many times as did Ken. His endurance was phenomenal, and I think if the truth were known he must have hated the role he adopted.

Having said that, I jump to his defence: like Peter May and all his contemporaries Barrington played on English pitches in the Fifties and Sixties when the odds were stacked on the bowler, even the indifferent bowler. Only six of his twenty Test centuries were scored on home wickets, all in the period from 1964 to 1967, but he was getting them with deadly regularity on the Indian sub-continent in 1961–2, and in the West Indies in 1968. Had he spent his formative years on pre-war wickets at the Oval, or in Australia or South Africa, I believe a totally different Barrington would have emerged.

He had a dazzling array of shots, and there were several reasons why he became a Scrooge at the crease. The first was the disgraceful deterioration of the wickets; then there were the defensive techniques of bowlers who cramped batsmen on the leg stump. There was an epidemic of medium pacers (some taking excessively long runs) aiming at middle and leg, and sometimes outside the leg stump. Defensive leg theory was a blight on the game, and mostly the blame went on the batsmen.

The son of a serving regular soldier Ken was a realist, and right at the start of his career he had a sharp lesson on the penalty of failure. During his National Service from 1949 to 1951 he was still primarily a bowler in his few matches at first-class level, but he always nourished an ambition to be a batsman. On his return to Surrey his progress was so rapid that by 1955 he was chosen for his first Test, against South Africa at Trent Bridge. I have good cause to remember it well.

At 6.10 precisely on the first evening I was leg before to Neil Adcock. If I had hung on for a few minutes more there would have been a 'night-watchman' on duty, and Barrington would have been spared his entry until the next day. As it was he went in and survived only three deliveries. Though he made 34 and 18 at Lord's he was promptly dropped, which I thought was harsh treatment. If he was good enough to be selected he was entitled to a longer trial. The same applies to all young batsmen, and if I have a quarrel with some selectors it is their peremptory dismissal of players whom they themselves have adjudged to have enough class to play for their country. All deserve a thorough trial, for the transition from first-class to Test status can be painful even to the highly gifted. Unhappily selectors are sometimes forced into a position which precludes an extended run.

Barrington had to wait four years before he was recognized again, and for some time it was on my conscience that I might have been the unwitting cause of his long absence and his new philosophy on his return. But Ken, the soul of honesty, insists he realized after two Tests that he was too immature and had much to learn, so that he returned to his apprenticeship in county cricket with gratitude.

It can be truthfully said that Ken was never anything but the total team man, and his annoyance at a poor England display led to his amazing innings at Melbourne in 1966. England had gone ahead with a victory by an innings and 93 runs in the third Test at Sydney, but surrendered with defeat by an innings and 9 runs in the next at Adelaide. Barrington, the ultimate in professionalism (which is intended as a compliment), was grossly offended by what he thought was a thoroughly irresponsible performance. He himself top-scored with 60 and 102 out of the England totals of 241 and 266.

When he went to the wicket at Melbourne he was further dejected because there had been a silly run out, and his friend John Edrich was having a sticky time. 'I remember telling him that things would come right and to stick around,' he says. 'The crowd was barracking, and I felt right down in the dumps.' Something must have rebelled and snapped in his ordered mind for he suddenly drove Keith Stackpole into the members' stand at least ten rows deep. A six at Melbourne is a prodigious hit, but to go as far as it did made it a shot to remember for all time.

For once Barrington discarded caution and dazzled with the range, power and timing of his strokes. He reached 102 off 122 balls in two and a half hours, which was comfortably the fastest hundred of the series, and was eventually out for 115, after an innings I recall with a glow. The stand with Edrich produced 178 in even time.

In contrast the 'other' Barrington was dropped for his innings at Edgbaston in 1965, which included 62 minutes when 20 overs were bowled with his score staying at 85. In effect he was suspended for one Test, but returned at Headingley to make 163 and set up a record second-wicket partnership against New Zealand of 369 with John Edrich, who made 310 not out. The stand was only 13 below England's best-ever for that wicket against all countries, and at one stage Barrington needed only 15 scoring shots to take 53 out of 89 runs. Once again he showed he was fully capable of cutting loose when he wanted to, and now and again he savoured the taste of surprising all and sundry.

Who else, for instance, has completed *four* Test centuries with a pulled six as he did at Melbourne, Adelaide, Durban and Trinidad? For one given to protracted periods of defence he had a singular habit of doing the unexpected. And who could be more courageous against the bouncer than Ken? No one stood up to Wes Hall and Charlie Griffith and hooked their barrage of short pitchers with truer skill or more steadfast determination. In the 1959–60 series in the West Indies he answered a whispered campaign that he was 'chicken' — a stupid campaign — in the most effective possible way with centuries in the first two Tests. In 1967–8 he took another, but he made big headlines when he made public his private feelings and refused to play in an end-of-season match at home against Griffith.

Barrington's exploits on the dead pitches of India and Pakistan are legendary, and if he did not have to contend there with short and fast bowling he proved a consummate ability to play subtle spin. He was always an excellent reader of the googly. In India he averaged 96.28 in Tests and in Pakistan 76.33 — and indeed, as if to give practical support to criticisms of English pitches in his time, he averaged almost 20 runs an innings better overseas than in Tests at home. In South Africa in 1964–5 his Test scores were 148 not out, 121, 49 (when he 'walked' to end a string of incidents involving batsmen who had stood their ground), 14 not out, 93, 11 and 72, and in all matches he took 24 wickets at 7.25 each to head both batting and bowling averages.

On his Indian tours Barrington achieved a popularity which only Bradman could match. In 1961–2, when Ted Dexter's side had to play twenty-four matches in India, Pakistan and Ceylon — and there are now complaints that the present tours of three months or so are too long! — Barrington's progress was like that of an immensely popular Viceroy, and it said much for his patience and good humour that he accepted the adulation in good part. If he was imitating one of his team-mates or the opposition, or the Australian Ken Mackay's Groucho Marx walk, Ken was a wow, and he had the post-bag of a film star. Not often was he seen without a smile. After the Test with Pakistan at Lahore, in which he made 139 and 6, his successive Test scores were 151 not out, 52 not out, 21, 172, 113 not out, while an England side below full strength held its own. Then when defeats were suffered at Calcutta and Madras — and incidentally he changed his methods — he hit only 14, 3, 20 and 48. His average for the Indian series was 99.00, and he was in such total command that he could have played with a broomstick.

In many ways it was an inspired choice to send him to India as manager, a position he held again the following winter in Pakistan and New Zealand; and as assistant to Doug Insole in Australia in 1978–9 he was virtually responsible for the cricket side. At the end of the series, in which strong criticism had been made of the batting of both sides, Ken made the honest declaration that he could not have made the runs he did in Australia on comparable pitches. He is not one of the old type of player who cannot see any good in contemporary cricket and is for ever harking back to the past. It is one reason why he is so popular with players.

Ken has never held a grudge in his life, and is a sportsman to his fingertips. The query against him is simply: did he make the utmost use of his wonderful ability? Despite his incredible record the answer is probably no. And again: would he have scored as many runs if he had been bolder and used more strokes? Possibly not, on the wickets of his days in county cricket.

His record for Surrey from 1953 to 1968 is infinitely poorer by comparison; his highest aggregate was 1,498, with an overall average of around 20 lower than in Tests. At home he was over-worked, and overseas I think he benefited from the rests which come in the gaps between matches, and the occasional match off. I know it helped me.

There was no doubt that Ken had the ability to become a leg-spinner of high quality, and on eight occasions he took five or more in an innings. He was occasionally very useful to England in this role: of his 273 wickets 29 were in Tests, and it is an eye-opener to find the class of his victims. Gary Sobers appears twice, and there are such famous names as India's 'Polly' Umrigar, who took some getting out, Alan Davidson, Seymour Nurse and Conrad Hunte. I always thought it fun to bowl, and Ken too looked as if he would have relished more opportunities. In the nets in Australia, India and Pakistan the new generation of England players were surprised that he bowled so well, including in his repertoire a hard-to-spot googly.

At slip Ken was more than reliable; in short he was the complete and accomplished cricketer, who never shirked his responsibilities and will be for ever remembered for his prolific scoring and his indomitable courage and skill. The late Wally Grout summed him up with his words: 'Whenever I saw Ken coming to the wicket I thought a Union Jack was trailing behind him.'

Those who criticized him most fiercely now look for his type of successor. When he went it was as if the centre pillar of strength had suddenly collapsed, and England was defenceless and exposed. If only he had hit the bad ball harder and more often . . .

2

ALEC BEDSER

Without hesitation or reservations I rate Alec Bedser the best medium-pace bowler I ever faced. On good wickets he was difficult enough with his eternally accurate swing; on a surface giving him the barest encouragement he was a veritable terror with his famous leg-cutter.

Bedser, born at Reading within a few minutes of his identical and inseparable twin Eric, comes of sturdy, independent-minded yeoman stock, and his stamina was undoubtedly a prime factor in his success. He took justifiable pride in his fitness, and a racehorse noted for its staying powers was fittingly named after him.

In all the years he toiled both at home and overseas he left the field only once, in the more than excusable circumstances of a heatwave at Adelaide. Alec, as usual, was bearing the brunt of the attack and had completed almost twenty overs with the temperature at 105. At one point Doug Wright, a brilliant but erratic leg-spinner whose art was endangered by overwork, stopped in his run-up to be sick.

Eventually even Alec's iron constitution rebelled and he had to race off, lumber up the stairs in the members' pavilion, and enter the dressing-room to be sick. Once it was over he was back on the field.

I am bound to compare that attitude with that of modern pace bowlers, who are often unfit and tend to leave the field so often that a regulation had to be introduced to cover the temporary absences. Yet on the whole cricketers are much fitter; and I think the daily exercises started under England's physiotherapist Bernard Thomas are much to be commended and will be taken for granted by all in the future.

Early on in his international career Alec was asked to do so much that some hasty and entirely wrong impressions were formed of him as little more than an honest, willing, hard-working stock bowler. Such critics did not have to bat against him, nor did they take into account the perfection of the pitches in Australia in 1946–7, the savage demands made on him and the fact that he was virtually a novice with only one full summer of county cricket behind him.

I vaguely remember seeing a grinning newspaper photograph of the Bedser twins joining the Surrey staff in 1938, and I played in one or two war-time matches with them. Up to the war Alec had made only two first-class appearances, against the universities, before he and Eric disappeared into the R.A.F. for six years.

Both lost vital years and virtually began new careers in 1946. With only twelve games behind him Alec had his Test baptism against India and enjoyed the instant success of eleven wickets in each of his first two Tests.

When England went to Australia in the following winter the average age was 33, and only Bedser (28), Jack Ikin (28), Godfrey Evans (26) and myself (28) were under 30. Alec had to share the new ball with Bill Voce (37) and Bill Edrich (30) and he ended bowling 246.3 6-ball overs with 16 wickets for 54.75 each.

Australia's leading batsmen were Sid Barnes, Arthur Morris, Don Bradman, Lindsay Hassett and Keith Miller; and in addition Colin McCool and Ray Lindwall hit centuries during the series. Rarely can an inexperienced bowler have had such a daunting initiation, but the Don was the first to proclaim Bedser's high talent, and though his wickets were expensive by and large he had a reasonable tour. On those pitches it needed something special to get wickets — the average or bad bowler had little hope. Tough though it was the experience was invaluable.

Originally Bedser was compared to Maurice Tate, which seemed nothing short of sacrilege to many, but as his ability was enriched he was given his own rightful place among the immortals — not a second Tate but an original Bedser.

The Don described the delivery which bowled him for a 'duck' in the 1947 Adelaide Test as about the best he ever received. It was delivered on the off stump and, swerving very late, pitched on the leg stump and finally came back to hit middle and off.

At Trent Bridge in 1953 the whimsical Hassett, who had scored

115, was bowled by Bedser with a ball which both swung in the air and moved off the pitch. 'I must be a fair bat,' he quipped. 'I tried to play three shots at one ball and almost made contact the third time it moved!'

Bedser's model action began with a purposeful, rhythmic approach and ended with a high arm and the left shoulder pointing straight down the pitch. There was almost a threat in the economy of his movements, and he walked back to his mark as if he could hardly wait to bowl the next ball.

He had style and stamina in abundance, but the gifts which lifted him to the heights were most appreciated by his fellow players. There was his uncanny accuracy: in all the overs I saw him bowl — and he completed over 16,000 in his time — I honestly cannot recall a rank bad ball. He regarded it as a pointless exercise to be wide of the stumps, and his simple maxim was: 'If you are straight and the batsman misses you have a wicket.'

The trouble for the batsman was that his straight ball swung at the very last second. It would come in a dead straight line until it was almost at the batsman and then dip very late and decisively. The lateness of swing is, of course, the hall-mark of true class. An in-swinger detected the moment it leaves the hand presents no problem to a good batsman, and even less for the top-quality player.

To get his swing Alec cut inside the ball at the moment of release, but an extra hazard was that occasionally on pitching it would straighten or, as it is said in the trade, 'hold its course'.

The leg-cutter, which brought the downfall of so many top-class internationals, was invariably delivered on a perfect length and was equivalent to a fast leg-break. A slow leg-break is often hard enough to keep out, but a fast one can be almost unplayable. It was Alec's most potent weapon, and even if it did not move back on a really good pitch it would still bounce disconcertingly. On a wet or damp surface it would whip back with the venom of a cobra's strike.

Normally for his leg-cutter Alec cut the ball across the seam, but when he fancied the conditions he favoured the orthodox leg-spinner's grip and cut the ball off the second and third fingers. Often this produced lift as well as moving the ball away from the bat. For the left-hander the inswinger became the outswinger, leaving the bat at the last possible moment, and I did not envy the task of even the best of the fraternity like Arthur Morris and Neil Harvey. I was once in the slips at Melbourne in 1950 when hard as he tried Harvey could not make contact for ball after ball. Everyone is familiar with the flat moments when an ordinary bowler can't get out an ordinary batsman, but here was an extraordinary stalemate caused by one of the finest players of the generation being unable to lay a bat on Bedser. Harvey eventually snicked a catch to Godfrey Evans.

It was also at Melbourne that Ron Archer, after opening for Australia and doing quite well, told me afterwards that he could not believe bowling could be so good. In this generous testimony Bedser shared the praise with Trevor Bailey, whose bowling developed into a significant feature of England's strength under Len Hutton and Peter May. I always had the highest regard for Bailey, who as well as being a highly accomplished all-rounder was the type of cricketer who knew exactly what he was doing.

After some experience I could pick Alec's leg-cutter by his action, accompanied by a fractional reduction in pace, but I never attempted to play him off the front foot. My theory was that if I was on the back foot I had a better chance of seeing the full period of the swing. In short I could watch the ball longer — which is often the difference between a good and a very good player. Also by playing back I hoped to play my shot when the swing was more or less completed. But as I have already stressed the danger from Bedser came from the last-second dip and movement. His was a very great art.

Playing forward increased the odds of being caught at leg slip, as the Don was by Len Hutton in three successive innings in 1948. In fact Bedser dismissed Bradman five times in consecutive Test innings that year, a distinguished 'rabbit' if ever there was one! The fact that Bradman went in the same way three times in a row naturally provoked endless discussion. It had never happened before, and some argue that this vulnerability to in-swingers pitched just around the off stump was evidence of the decline of a titan. In his prime, it was said, he would have been in position so quickly that he would have placed the ball just past mid-on. True, Bradman was on his last tour, but by any yardstick he was still Bradman, and finished the series with an average of 72.57, compared with my 62.44, which put me on top of England's averages. In all modesty I mention these statistical facts to put

Bedser's performance in perspective. The two salient factors to emerge in my mind both reflect to Alec's credit. First, the memory of that delivery at Adelaide was in the back of Bradman's mind. He knew Bedser was capable of more than straightening the ball pitched middle and leg, and felt he was obliged to play an inswinger in that area. His problem would not have arisen if he had felt certain the ball would continue its flight path and miss the leg stump. Therefore Alec had raised some doubts in the Don's mind by the pure skill of his bowling. Second, Bedser's accuracy meant the ball pitched fractionally outside or on the off stump had to be defended. The Don naturally and instinctively played with the flight towards mid-on but because of the movement in the last yard the ball found the inside edge of the bat and went to backward short leg.

How the pre-war Bradman would have dealt with this type of delivery is hypothetical, as the fact is he never faced one (to the best of my knowledge). Perhaps it was never tried, but the more probable explanation is there wasn't a bowler able to control an inswinger with such devastating lateness. Before or after the war, I certainly never batted against the equal of Bedser, who, remember, twice dismissed Bradman for 0 in Tests. Bedser was one of the very few bowlers Bradman respected, realizing there were no liberties to be taken or cheap runs in the offing. Every batsman has his favourites, but I always knew before I went out to bat against Bedser that I was in for a real contest. If the honours fell to me there was genuine satisfaction.

As I loathed being tied down one of my favourite ploys was to advance down the pitch as the bowler was about to deliver the ball in the hope he would panic and make me a present of runs. On one of my more hot-blooded stampedes 'Roly' Jenkins, the Worcester-shire leg-spinner who was seldom at a loss for words, stopped in his tracks and said, 'I don't object to you coming down the track, Denis, but I don't expect you to shake hands with me when I am about to bowl.'

Going down the wicket to Alec was more than I normally dared to try, but there is an exception to every rule, and a wet pitch at the Oval caused me to throw caution to the wind. I fancied there was no future in batting from the crease so I ventured forth. The gods were with me, and I managed around half of Middlesex's total with 60. Yet even on that occasion Alec did not bowl me a bad ball.

In 1949, when Middlesex were joint champions, Alec caught us on a drying pitch at Lord's with 8 for 42. Twice later he took 8 wickets in an innings at the Oval, against Nottinghamshire and Warwickshire. He also had 14 wickets in a match on two occasions — his major triumph in the first Test with Australia in 1953, and against Glamorgan in 1956 when Surrey were in the middle of their record seven successive championships. Playing against Surrey in those years with an attack led by Bedser, Peter Loader, Jim Laker and Tony Lock was infinitely harder than many a Test.

One of Bedser's most sterling qualities which stands out in my mind was his hatred of being taken off, even if the pitch was made for batting. He was never one of the fraternity who take one look at the wicket and, having decided it's not for them, seek every excuse not to bowl. Alec wanted to bowl and bowl, and was for ever turning over in his mind how he could get a batsman out. I have been at the other end wondering what he was up to, and what he would try next. His meticulous field placings showed how much thought was put into his bowling.

I have heard captains ask how he felt, and inevitably the answer was, 'I'm fine, I can keep one end going.' Sometimes, particularly on those gruelling days on his first tour of Australia, he knew the odds were against him. He would be undeterred; the answer to every captain's prayer.

When he passed the then record of 216 wickets held by Clarrie Grimmett he had bowled 14,573 balls for England — a truly Herculean effort. What put him on a pedestal was the high proportion of wickets he gained in the upper batting order. In the 1950–1 series against Australia he had 16 out of 30 wickets from No. 1 to 5, and 24 out of 39 in 1953.

Further proof of his standing at the highest level is furnished by the division of his 236 Test wickets in 51 matches: 104 v Australia; 54 v South Africa; 44 v India; 13 v New Zealand; 11 v West Indies; 10 v Pakistan.

Unlike most successful bowlers Bedser achieved his records without a settled partner; indeed from 1946 to 1955 he had no fewer than seventeen. Bedser was more fortunate with his wicket-keepers, whom he insisted stood up to him. If ever a wicket-keeper was put to the acid test it was by Bedser's late flight, and he is always generous in his praise of Godfrey Evans for England and Arthur McIntyre for Surrey.

In some ways it was a pity that Alec, who had given so much from the days when England scratched for a side to hold Bradman's Australians, did not bow out when the Ashes were recovered at the Oval in 1953. For fate was to play him a scurvy trick. Almost on arrival in Australia in 1954 he went down with shingles, and he was a long way from being fit when he played in the first Test at Brisbane. The whole match was an unmitigated disaster. Len Hutton, influenced by the behaviour of the Brisbane wicket in the previous match with Queensland, put Australia in to bat. Starting with one off Bedser catches galore were dropped, and I broke a finger in the boundary railings chasing a slice to third man. I batted No. 11, scoring 2 not out and 0 — not one of my happiest memories.

Australia scored 601 for 8 declared, and Bedser had 1 for 131 off 37 overs. Frank Tyson took 1 for 160 off 29, but Alf Gover, the ace coach who fortunately for England was in Australia, worked on his action. It is history now that Tyson and Statham formed a series-winning fast bowling combination in the rest of the series after Bedser was dropped. Bedser could take that disappointment in his stride, but he was understandably hurt when he discovered his omission by reading the team sheet in the Sydney dressing-room. After all he had done for England, and as a senior member of the party, he was entitled to be told in advance of the intention to exclude him. No doubt Hutton had a score of pressing captaincy problems on his mind, but he should have spared a moment for a word of explanation and sympathy to Alec. No player whatever his past record has a divine right to automatic selection, and in the end the retention of the Ashes justified Hutton. There was also a question mark against Alec's fitness — indeed, he said it took two years for the effects of his illness to disappear. But the gesture should have been made.

The lesson was not lost on Alec, and when in the course of time he became an outstanding chairman of selectors he made a point of telling a player personally or by letter why he was being dropped, before the side was made public.

Bedser is the type of man more eager to give a pat than a kick, and as well as being an earthy realist, he is kindly, absolutely sincere, a willing tutor to the young, and punctilious in his correspondence. Though he learned to pace himself he did not know how to give anything but his best, and his part in Surrey's glorious years was considerable both as a bowler and a dedicated team man. With Alec as vice-captain to Peter May Surrey had incomparable leadership, and Peter's question to him, 'What do you think now?' became part of the county scene. In 1960 when May spent the summer recuperating from illness Alec stepped up — he was 42 in the July of that year — and, as was to be expected, showed what a fine captain he could be.

Thinking back it's amazing that because of the wealth of pace bowling talent at the pre-war Oval the twins tossed to see which of them should carry on with that form of attack. Eric, the loser, turned to off-spin and was distinctly unlucky to fall in Jim Laker's shadow. He got as far as a Test Trial, and was a fine bowler and an opening batsman; he might have furthered his career as an all-rounder by going to another county. But that would have been unthinkable for twins so close that when Alec lost seven pounds one day bowling under the Adelaide sun, Eric, sitting in the stand, also lost seven pounds. If they batted together the scorers had a devil of a time, and in a charity game at the Oval Alec bowled the first three balls of an over and Eric the last three without it being noticed.

The twins have shared everything from the start, including hours of bowling to each other. They started life in a solicitor's office in Lincoln's Inn Fields together, tossed again when only one could be promoted in the R.A.F., and, at the end of their playing days, were still side by side in their highly successful business careers. They dress alike, write with the same hand, and think alike.

Alec's devotion to the game he adored so much was evident when he threw himself wholeheartedly into administration. In 1962, the year he became a Test selector, he was assistant manager to the late Duke of Norfolk in Australia and New Zealand. The premier Duke and the bricklayer's son could not have had a happier alliance. In 1974–5 Bedser progressed to the post of manager, and on a difficult tour did not put a foot wrong. He was always intensely popular in Australia, where they relish a fighter and recognize a man for what he is. His second tour as a fully fledged manager was in Australia in 1979–80, and his tact and diplomacy were invaluable. Bedser has been a marvellous servant to the game.

3

IAN BOTHAM

He has been described as a second Keith Miller (which made me blink), careless and irresponsible, and cricket's most compelling entertainer. His English team-mates playfully dubbed him Guy, after the late occupant of London Zoo, and the story goes that his reaction to some anti-Pommie spite in a Melbourne bar was to put the critic on his back. Somewhere between the extreme views is the concrete fact that Ian Terence Botham reached the 'double' of 1,000 runs and 100 wickets in the record space of 21 Tests, against Vinoo Mankad's 23 matches for India.

It can be justly argued that Botham was the lucky child of circumstances, picking up wickets and scoring runs while the cricket world was split in divided camps; that he would never have been as successful against Australians of the might of Bradman, Morris, Barnes and Harvey, the West Indies of the W's, and so on. The fact is he had the uncommon ability and strength of purpose to succeed, and I see in Botham's skills and pugnacity all the signs of one of life's winners. Adverse predictions have been with him from the start, for I remember that when he was sent by Somerset to the Lord's staff I was told by a knowledgeable coach that his bowling wasn't up to much.

In Australia in 1978–9 Bill O'Reilly took one look at Botham's batting and dismissed it as of little consequence, though it was the first time he had been to the crease on the tour. Having been injured with a cut wrist suffered on the eve of departure Botham had waited like a caged lion for his release to enter the fray, and O'Reilly's strictures were at least premature — though never withdrawn or modified. Unwittingly Bill did the England side a good turn, for in moments of crisis when the last ounce of effort had to be squeezed from Botham the players would pass such comments as, 'O'Reilly was right!' That was all the incentive needed. Actually I see in Botham, born at Heswall, Cheshire, on 24 November 1955, much of O'Reilly's own aggression and attitudes. Both represented that amalgam of talent and fighting quality so necessary to emerge on top in the highest company. It's a truism that character is the X factor in separating the very good from the stars.

Botham's father, a regular in a twenty-year career in the Fleet Air Arm, set his son the arduous target of a county place at eighteen, and England at twenty-five. Both aims were comfortably, almost arrogantly achieved, and by 1979, when only twenty-three — younger than Wally Hammond was when he first appeared for England — he was England's linch-pin, the indispensable, unchallenged all-rounder. I borrow an assessment of him from Ken Barrington, assistant manager in Australia in 1978–9, which aptly illustrates Botham's value to any side: 'A tower of strength whether batting, bowling or fielding. Always in the thick of the game, and prepared to accept a challenge. Even if he is knocked down, he comes back for more. Inclined to be impetuous at the start of an innings. Like Gower, he has a great future.'

Of course the incredible fact is that after two years of sensational achievement he already had a great past, a saga of decisive performances in every department of the game. He is every captain's dream of a hundred-per-cent trier, who takes it as a personal affront to be second, and excels batting, bowling or fielding in any position. His personal strength is a decisive factor, so much so that in the Perth Test in December 1978 he was able to bowl into the teeth of a stiff wind which others found intolerable. A mighty man is 'Both' in every sense.

Yet when he went to Australia under the excellent and invaluable Whitbread Scholarship Scheme — not all sponsorships are designed purely for self-publicity — Botham accomplished little in Melbourne Grade circles, and even the more sober judges thought little of him. Perhaps he was too impatient for the big time, or did not apply himself as he should have done. The debt he owes to his first county captain, Brian Close, is acknowledged with sincere appreciation. Again, like O'Reilly, he shared with Close a common determination to succeed. His fierce spirit, harnessed to considerable natural ability, comes through again and again.

Courage is the close companion of determination, and when only eighteen Botham gave a remarkable demonstration that nothing on the field frightens him, nor is there an opponent able to shake him. The occasion was a Benson and Hedges Cup quarter-final at Taunton against Hampshire, whose attack was spear-headed by Andy Roberts, then the fastest bowler in the game — a real frightener. Facing a total of 183, Somerset were in the unpromising position of 113 for 8. Botham, a mere fledgling with minimal first-class experience, was hit in the mouth by a bouncer from Roberts. It wasn't a pretty sight, and it cost him four teeth in the end. Though the bleeding would not stop he resolutely refused to quit; and in the time-honoured style of schoolboy fiction hero-ically won the match with 45 not out, including two huge sixes. As he was presented with the Gold Award Somerset must have glowed in the sure evidence that they had struck gold. I always maintain that my old colleague Bill Edrich, a war-time flyer with a distinguished R.A.F. record, was the gamest batsman I ever saw, but I link Botham, a fearless young lion, with Bill. I cannot offer higher praise.

At one stage he was at a sporting crossroads and after a concrete offer from Crystal Palace had to choose between cricket and soccer as a career. Before the football season was prolonged at both ends it was possible to play both, and I must say I have pleasant memories of my days with Arsenal. I enjoyed my football, but times have swiftly changed and Botham, a centre half, or central defender in the modern jargon, could not enjoy two careers, as many were able to do in the past. One can imagine Botham as a strong-tackling, uncompromising footballer, as enthusiastic and powerful in the last five minutes as in the first. He would certainly have measured up to soccer's demanding fitness standards. After he had bowled England to victory over India in the first Test in the 1979 series with a typical 4 for 10 in five overs with the new ball, he said his shoulders had broadened. I suppose with constant exercise this is not to be wondered at, but he was always built 'like a battleship' — a phrase I remember Len Hutton using to describe a young Freddie Trueman.

Physically powerful as he is, the last thing I want to suggest is that his brains are centred in his shoulders and feet. On the contrary. In Pakistan — where he was introduced in all good faith at a reception as Mr Iron Bottom — he once surprised a local scientist with an articulate discussion on the subject of nuclear waste disposal. I doubt if he relaxes as David Gower does with classical and contemporary music — Beethoven or Tchaikovsky, Bach or extracts from the Baroque period, according to mood. Botham's scene is more likely to be a lively disco.

Ever since boyhood he has set himself the stiff pace of one in a hurry to the topmost rung of the ladder. He would not understand any other way. His family moved to Yeovil when he was two, and both at school and with the Boys' Brigade he was outstanding at all games. He would haunt playing grounds before he was ten years old in the hope of finding a team short, and when he did there was never a more eager volunteer to make up the number. Progress to youth and county representative teams was formality with his precocious talent. The period at Lord's was vital to his apprenticeship, as were the matches for Somerset Second XI. His deeds did not so much attract attention as shriek to high heaven that here was ability extraordinary. He went to Lord's largely on his own efforts, and was just as keen to join the regular Somerset coaching sessions. Nothing could stop him, and nothing did. The only disappointing results were in Melbourne, an exception in an otherwise continuous and upwards climb in his career.

In 1973 he put a toe into the waters of county cricket with two John Player League matches. The following season he was displaying his gifts, while in 1975 he made 584 runs and took 62 wickets. In 1976 there was a brilliant first century, and 66 wickets in addition to 1,022 runs. His maiden century at Trent Bridge is worth recalling as it followed a score of 80 in the first innings and included six sixes and twenty fours in a match-winning 167 not out.

Aged twenty-one he took 5 Australian wickets, including those of Greg Chappell and Doug Walters, for only 74 on the first day of his first Test at Trent Bridge, and has for ever set himself new Everests to climb. With experience the diversification of his bowling became apparent in his clever exploitation of conditions, or his appreciation of the tactical needs of the moment, cutting down his speed in the cause of accuracy or to make the ball swing more. In addition to having Close as captain he had Tom Cartwright as coach, and it was logical that his technique should expand. There was so much natural material to exploit. If anything, I sometimes believe he experiments too much, and like many pace bowlers is too fond of the bouncer (there speaks the voice of a batsman!). Botham delivers his bumpers at different speeds and heights, which is a difficult art, and I would not quarrel with Mike Brearley — who as first slip is in the best of positions to judge — when he says Botham swings the ball more than any contemporary bowler. The inswinger darts and dips, and the outswinger, which he unaccountably lost for a time, is equally effective. When he pulverized Pakistan in the 1978 Lord's Test with 8 for 34 in 20.5 overs it was said he had no real opposition, but those behind the wicket were amazed how he was able to swing the ball on a cloudless morning. Apart from his wickets he regularly beat the bat with late outswing, and, far from denigrating his achievement, I believe that on the day any batsman would have struggled against him. In my experience overseas players find swing harder to overcome than spin, and I was left in no doubt on that day that Botham was a bowler of supreme class, mediocre opposition or not.

Botham also hit his second successive Test century, and his 8 for 34 were the best figures by an England bowler since Jim Laker's 9 for 37 and 10 for 53 against Australia at Old Trafford in 1956. There had not, in fact, been a comparable all-round feat to Botham's century and eight wickets in an innings at international level; and in seven Tests up to that time he had scored three centuries and taken five or more wickets in an innings five times. Incredibly he was to improve even on that record.

After taking five wickets on his Test debut he followed up with five more in the next match with Australia at Headingley — when Geoff Boycott reached his century of centuries. In eleven overs he took 5 for 21, and with Mike Hendrick collecting 4 Australia were put out for 103. Botham missed the last Test of the series with a foot injury. It also could have cost him a 'double' as he scored 538 runs and took 100 wickets in that season.

None could say he did not fulfil the highest expectations. England went to Pakistan and New Zealand in 1977–8, and *Wisden* picked Botham out as the find of the tour. It was at Christchurch that his star quality first emerged. Starved of combat on the paceless, bounceless pitches of Pakistan, he came sensationally into his own in the second Test against New Zealand, still only his fourth. *Wisden* enthused, 'He batted, bowled and fielded with the style and confidence of a titan.'

The story of that Christchurch match centres around Botham. England, dismayed by a first-ever defeat at the hands of New Zealand in the first Test, were in bad shape in the second when Brian Rose, Geoff Boycott and Derek Randall were out for 26. Botham, who had already made 126 not out on the ground against Canterbury — reaching 100 with 4, 4, 6 — hit 103 with the most impressive and powerful range of strokes possible to imagine. In the second innings when England were going for a declaration Botham answered with 30 off 36 deliveries, and he was equally aggressive with his bowling, taking 5 for 73 and 3 for 38. Then there were his three catches, two of which were quite spectacular. As *Wisden* said, 'an inspired cricketer in everything he did'.

These were heady words and heroic deeds for a virtual beginner. In 1978 he headed the batting averages against Pakistan with 70.66 — almost 20 runs an innings more than Gower — and the bowling figures against New Zealand with 24 wickets at only 14.04 apiece. In the 5-1 defeat of Australia he was always in the thick of the fray, taking 23 wickets, the same tally as Geoff Miller, whose off-spin twice bowled England to victory on responsive pitches at Sydney. At Adelaide he rescued England's batting with a brilliant 74 out of 169 and then took 4 for 42.

Now, after Australia, he scented a record ahead in the home series with India. Andy Roberts had taken 100 wickets for the West Indies in the space of two years and 142 days. Botham, starting on 28 July 1977, was well within that period of time and he was able to pass the old record at Lord's in two years and 9 days — and at an earlier age than any other England bowler. In terms of the number of Tests taken to reach 100 wickets, neither Botham nor Roberts (each in his nineteenth Test) touched the sixteen-match record of the Surrey fast bowler George Lohmann in the last century. England's Sydney Barnes and Australia's C.T.B. ('The Terror') Turner needed seventeen games, and Colin Blythe, the Kent left-arm spinner killed in World War I, also had exactly 100 in his nineteen Tests.

Broken down, Botham's 100 came this way:

1977 v. Australia (2 Tests)	10 for 202
1977–8 v. New Zealand (3 Tests)	17 for 311
1978 v. Pakistan (3 Tests)	13 for 209

1978 v. New Zealand (3 Tests)	24 for 337
1978–9 v. Australia (6 Tests)	23 for 567
1979 v. India (2 Tests)	13 for 232

By any standard it was a notable achievement, particularly as Botham soon afterwards reached 1,000 runs in 21 Tests. Typically he arrived at his target with a savage square cut off his second ball at the Oval, having reached 997 in the previous match at Heading-ley with the most exciting innings seen for years.

Until Botham's arrival it had been a drab, wet affair with contro-versies over the fitness of the pitch and other niggling problems. Then with four sixes and twelve fours Botham set Headingley alight, and missed by one run the rare distinction of scoring 100 runs before lunch. Even the more sober critics maintained that it was the most entertaining and daring innings seen in Test cricket for twenty years. Maybe a little exaggeration, but I am content to say any young player able to manhandle bowling as he did is a player to cherish. In the end he had five sixes and sixteen fours, and Headingley was a far happier place. Only five English bats-men have managed a hundred before lunch — Ranjitsinhji (1896), Phil Mead (1921), Jack Hobbs (1924), Wally Hammond (1932–3), and Leslie Ames (1935) — and Botham, who began with seven overnight, didn't even know he so narrowly missed a distinction until he watched the television news in the dressing-room!

I have written of the increasing range of his bowling, and it was fitting that in the gripping end to the final Test at the Oval Botham should once again be the centre point of the English action. It was his dramatic intervention with the ball and as a fielder which probably denied India the greatest victory in the history of Tests. India were set to make 438, and that remarkably fine opener Sunil Gavaskar took them to the very brink of triumph with an innings of 221. When it was touch and go and the nation was glued to tele-vision sets, who should turn the tide but Botham? In the heat of the crisis he captured three crucial wickets, including Gavaskar's, took a catch and dropped one which might have destroyed a lesser spirit — and ran out skipper Venkataraghavan. Botham was made Man of the Series, and I am left wondering what worlds the young cricketing Alexander has left to conquer.

Botham's season finished with Somerset scooping the Gillette Cup and the John Player League within forty-eight hours, and I am inclined to believe Brian Rose to be one of county cricket's luckiest captains ever, to lead a side containing Viv Richards, the fast bowler Joel Garner, and Botham, who is three brilliant players in one — and with a personal physique and a powerhouse ambition to match.

There will be some troughs as well as peaks to his career. That's inevitable. That's part of the absorbing fascination of cricket. But he is a player after my own heart. Talented, adventurous, combative, and throbbing with life. It's good to be around when Botham is on the hunt!

To underline his records Botham scored 114 and had match-bowling figures of 13 for 106, another record all-round performance, in the Jubilee Test at Bombay. 'Quite remarkable by any standards,' said Alec Bedser, who was soon to name Botham as captain for the Prudential Trophy internationals. Only time can determine Botham's fitness for such exalted rank, but such is his belief in himself that I put nothing beyond his powers.

4

SIR DON BRADMAN

Future generations may, I fear, become slightly sceptical about the legend and achievements of Donald George Bradman, and dismiss such scribblings as mine as exaggerated hero-worship, or a judgement warped and coloured by time. No single player, I can imagine it being said, could have been so impossibly gifted, or endowed with a temperament to match his extravagant ability. Or, it may be thought, the bowling of his age must have been ordinary — spanning twenty-one years? — and the field-placings naive.

The late Sir Pelham Warner was once asked by a group of players if W.G. Grace was as good as history made him out to be. His answer was: 'Only those who played with and against him could have appreciated his true greatness and his impact on the game.'

As with Grace, so with Bradman, who played havoc with all types of bowling, created records never likely to be surpassed, and fascinated all with the psychology of his make-up. He was unique, a batsman appearing not just once in a lifetime but once in the life of a game. His like will not be seen again, and I count it as my privilege that I was able to study his technique and methods from the closeness of slip and gully. I also came to know him as a man and in my experience the Don was far from 'a solitary man with a solitary aim', as an eminent critic claimed.

If any should doubt the crushing power of his strokes please, I beg you, take the word of one who fielded on the boundary to him and watched a round red bullet repeatedly pass at unstoppable speed, and placed with such precision that I had no earthly chance of getting within reach.

When I first played against the Don I was a precocious twenty-year-old. My mind was flooded with mixed sensations of awe, respect and plain curiosity — one could imagine a recruit to Winston Churchill's war-time Cabinet undergoing the same emotions. The mere presence of the greatest cricketer the world had known on the same field as myself was unnerving, and after encountering Bradman in two home series and one in Australia, I never lost the sense of being in contact with history.

Far from breeding contempt, familiarity nourished my wonder at everything Bradman did. He was a living miracle, defying comparison with any other player before, during or since his time, and an early description of him has stood the test of time. Jack Ryder, a former captain of Australia, was asked how Bradman played. He replied, 'He just belts the hell out of anything within reach.' He did just that, and, unlike Jack Hobbs and Victor Trumper, never threw his wicket away when he thought he had had enough.

I suppose my attitude to Bradman had its roots in my sporting background and my immersion in the game. My father and I once took a No. 13 bus from our home at Hendon to Lord's in 1930 to watch the phenomenon everyone talked about, but I am ashamed to admit that my memory of the occasion is blurred and I remember nothing of the Don. At least I didn't suffer the disappointment I had on a Bank Holiday at the Oval when Hobbs, my idol, was bowled for a modest 22, though there was a wondrous exhibition of cutting from his partner, Andy Sandham, the memory of which excites me to this day.

In 1934 Bradman was back in England, and I had been a ground-staff boy at Lord's for two years. Sometimes the leading players of Middlesex might stroll to the Nursery to cast critical eyes on young hopefuls like me, and the conversation inevitably turned to Bradman, who seemed to score at will and at a fantastic pace. Bradman was the constant subject. His very name was magic, and the inimitable 'Patsy' Hendren, who had played in the Don's first Test at Brisbane in 1928, fed me with every scrap of detail. 'Patsy' scored 169, England won by 675 runs, and the way Australia were ground in the dust was said to sour and fashion Bradman's attitude to the way a Test had to be played.

Unfortunately contact with the foremost players was seldom possible for groundstaff boys — the lowest form of cricketing life! — and I was able to see Bradman in action only briefly as I sold scorecards during the famous second Test, when the late Hedley Verity took 14 wickets in a day and 15 all told. Frank Chester, the umpire, told me an overnight storm left a patch at one end no bigger than the circumference of a frying-pan. It was enough for Verity.

Bradman had been out when the game was resumed for a small but brilliant 36, but, oddly, he served as an inspiration to me even in failure. Australia followed on, and I was at once fascinated and impressed at the way Bradman met aggressive bowling with a counter-attack. Though he gave a skied catch to Les Ames at the wicket I could not forget his positive approach in what was really a hopeless situation, and there can be no doubt that a firm Compton philosophy which was to serve me well throughout my career was conceived on that occasion. He made me realize that in the final analysis attack is the best form of defence, and it is better to take the fight to the enemy than be dominated by him. I have never changed my opinion that the successes gained by intelligent assault far outnumber the failures.

It was invariably held against Bradman that, in contrast to Hobbs, he was not a master in all conditions and was vulnerable to the turning ball, particularly with his unconventional grip if it was leaving the bat. Aren't we all? Verity did not share the conventional view, and I am inclined to agree with his opinion that the Don's attitude on sticky pitches was a form of protest.

He was never one to hold a weak belief on any subject, and he was very much against uncovered pitches. The argument was that Lindrum and Davis would never be expected to perform on a lumpy billiards table, and it was wrong to play cricket on a pitch open to the vagaries of the weather besides being grossly unfair to one side. As a batsman I agreed, and for my part I find it inconceivable that the Don, who batted with ultimate perfection and saw the ball on the bat as late as it was possible, could not have devised a technique for wet conditions if he had put his mind to the problem.

It seemed a matter of principle to him not to overcome a bad wicket, and he shrugged his shoulders like a renowned actor enduring bad acoustics at a one-night stand. Nor did I pay much attention to the criticism that he would hold himself back and expose his less fortunate and less talented team-mates to the torments of a drying surface. To me that would be simple logic, and totally in the interest of his side.

Even a cursory look at his fantastic record defies the imagination. In 338 innings he made 117 centuries, or one in every three innings, and 28,067 runs. To put his overall performances in perspective I mention that in 839 innings I aggregated 38,942 runs. He averaged 95.14. The nearest an England batsman can get to that astronomical figure is Wally Hammond with 56.10, and Sir Len Hutton with 55.51. Geoff Boycott could eventually overtake both Hammond and Hutton.

For Australia he hit 6,996 runs in 80 innings with 29 hundreds and an average of 99.94. In 63 innings against England he scored 5,028 runs — including 974, average 139.14, in 1930 — with an overall average of 89.78. He scored 1,000 runs before the end of May twice, and 1,000 runs in a season on sixteen occasions. In 1938 he made thirteen centuries in England, and in 1938–9 made six in succession. At Headingley he made 309 in a day. Nothing was beyond him, and his achievements needed not only unmatched genius but the mental capacity to sustain it. In four tours of England his Test average was 139.14, 94.75, 108.50 and 72.57. No wonder no one could touch his achievements.

To the Don there was no mountain high enough. His cricket was planned to the last detail, and I confess that on the occasions I bowled to him I was in near-despair. Every basic requirement of batting was there in abundance — the lightning reflexes of brain and eye, footwork which would not have come amiss in the Bolshoi ballet, a delicate balance and the self-confidence springing from a belief in his own dazzling ability.

He had a marvellous gift of getting into position quicker than any batsman I have ever seen, played the ball very late, and was never off balance, or stretching out of control. With his judgment of length he would make his quick decision and play either back or forward without hesitation. Brain and body were in perfect harmony. I could understand the temptation to regard him as simply a run-machine with such built-in powers of concentration and personal drive as to be incapable of human error. Certainly he lacked the charm at the crease of an Alan Kippax or a Tom Graveney. He was not in that sense a stylist. But he was fallible to the occasional error for the simple reason that he made his runs at a fantastic rate and never refused a challenge. Often I would look at the scoreboard and be surprised to find he had twice as many runs as I figured he had scored. He was for ever finding the gaps and taking the singles and the twos.

Modern bowling and field placings might have crabbed and confined him to a degree, but would not have finally defeated him. It might have taken him longer to make his scores, but he would not have been utterly shackled or have allowed the bowlers to dictate their terms. Instead of being 300 at the end of that remarkable day at Headingley he would possibly have been 220 or 240 not out. In any case with the slow over rates of the Sixties and Seventies he would not have received anything like the number of deliveries.

With his uncanny ball sense Bradman could master a ball game. He flirted with lawn tennis for a time and doubtless would have become a champion. Within weeks of starting billiards he made century breaks, and he had the same success with golf and squash.

His cricket was uniquely Bradman. No coaching manual was intended for him, and despite what is said to the contrary I am sure that had he been born English no coach would have dared to interfere with him. His grip would have doubtless caused some consternation. Both hands were turned over the handle with the fingers of the left hidden from the bowler. The swift answer to those who said it was wrong was in his murderous hooking and cutting. The only doubt raised by his unorthodox grip was his cover drive and his defence against the ball leaving the bat.

But I cannot honestly recall him as an ineffective cover driver, and his record scarcely suggests that he was ever technically handicapped! If he once reached 30 or so the fielding side were thankful if he was satisfied with a single century.

He gathered runs at such a speed that it was impossible to set a field for him, and it occured to me at times that he had a private game with a slow-moving fielder or with the opposing captain. His placements were so exact that he could have a fielder moving backwards and forwards from one position to another. There was, in fact, no precise field setting for the Don because he was able to improvise brilliantly as I found to my cost at Sydney in the 1946–7 series.

Bradman's hook was pure magic. There has not been a batsman I have seen able to match his special skill with a shot that gets so many able batsmen in difficulties. Today's batsmen, plagued with the obsessive use of the bumper and the short-pitched delivery, ought to study every action picture and film they can get of Bradman playing the hook. Never once did I see him hook in the air, and, unlike even the best who aim for deep square or fine of square, Bradman whacked the ball in the direction of mid-on. Bradman was different because he was fractionally quicker in picking up the ball, and was in position faster. His secret was to pick up the flight path and pitch of the ball so soon that he actually seemed to be in position and waiting for it from the moment it left the bowler's hand. He was unsurpassed in his timing and execution, and I am certain bowlers would have been disinclined to use the bouncer too often against him.

Bradman was the unwitting cause of the so-called bodyline form of attack. If ever there was a back-handed compliment to genius it was the invention and employment of bodyline. Douglas Jardine and his ally Harold Larwood roughly halved Bradman's output and average to 396 runs at an average of 56.57. By Bradman's standards a failure, but even with seven fielders on the leg side and the ball screaming at his head at a speed of ninety miles an hour or so Bradman improvised with shots placed on the off side. He also had a tennis-style smash back over the bowler's head.

The cut was one of the Don's favourite shots. As with his hook, the ball was kept on the ground. Anything fractionally short of a length or over-pitched was murderously assaulted, and his moral ascendancy over the bowlers was enough to give him an advantage before a ball was bowled. Understandably Bradman's reputation was enough to send a chill down the spine, and bowlers knew they had to pitch an immaculate line and length or they were set for merciless punishment. I suffered a definite sense of inferiority on the occasions I bowled to him. I admit I was an unpredictable slow-left-arm spinner with an inclination to experiment. But precisely because I felt I must not bowl a bad ball to Bradman, I invariably ended up doing so. And he never failed to hit a bad ball.

When he made his last Test appearance at the Oval in 1948 I was more emotionally affected than by my own last innings at Lord's — and I admit to a mist before my eyes on that occasion. The crowd stood and cheered Bradman's every step to the wicket, and the players gathered and gave him three rousing cheers as years before the Australians had for Hobbs. I was at cover and the nostalgia could almost be felt. I can imagine how Bradman felt and it did not over-surprise me when he got an inside edge to a googly from Eric Hollies and played on second ball.

He had need only a boundary to average a century an innings in Tests — just think of that! — a fact which he did not know at the time. 'Had I known I would have been a bit more careful,' he told me years later. Nevertheless it must be hard to spot a googly when tears are in the eyes.

I sometimes wonder if Bradman would have stayed on in Test cricket had he been given out when Jack Ikin caught him off Bill Voce in his first innings after the war. To play at all he had won a battle with his health. He had been invalided out of the Army, and at one time I am told he could barely shave himself. In my opinion the Don was legitimately caught, and at the end of the over Hammond said to him, 'What a way to start a series!' He went on to make 187, remain as captain for two winning series, and complete his record of never losing a rubber. It is all hypothetical now, but he was 28 at the time and for the first hour or so of that first trial-and-error comeback he struggled as he had never done in his entire career. Snicks went over slips and to fine leg without going to hand, and he could have been out half a dozen times before reaching double figures.

On the field we began to feel sorry he had made a decision to resume his career, but later we were sorry for ourselves as his confidence and form surged back the longer he batted. By the end he was as dominating and as irresistible as ever, and the massive crowds of 1946–7 and 1948 saw a Bradman only marginally short of the pre-war Bradman. For my part I was glad for him and the game at large that he survived his personal crisis, but it was touch and go. There had been a long gap during the war years, his health, never robust, was suspect, and, as he was the first to acknowledge, England had a new champion bowler in Alec Bedser.

Bradman could be a hard and relentless competitor, and some of his team-mates insisted that he was not aware or appreciative of the performances of others. His relationships with his fellow players were not always harmonious, and it was natural that he should arouse some jealousy, that most common of all human failings. My personal dealings with him could not have been happier, however, and he emerged as a good friend in my troubled tour of 1950–1.

As for his not appreciating others, I found the exact opposite to be true. When I reached my century in my maiden Test against

Australia at Trent Bridge in 1938 he ran from the covers, shook my hand, and said, 'Well done, Denis, this is a great start for you, and you have played brilliantly.'

If he had been as hard and as ruthless as many would have he would have contented himself with a polite perfunctory clap. But in those more innocent days the courtesies of cricket were cherished, and the deplorable practice of 'sledging' — violent abuse of opponents — was yet to blight the scene.

I was even more touched in the second Test at Lord's when I made 76 not out on a drying pitch, and England passed from a dangerous position to an outside prospect of victory — scotched by Bradman's 102 not out. To this day I believe that innings was one of the peaks of my career, and my euphoria was increased by the arrival of the Don in the England dressing-room at the end of the match. His words are entrenched in my memory: 'All things being equal you have a great career ahead of you,' he said. 'But you will look back on today's innings as one of the greatest innings you have ever played even if you score many hundreds — which you are going to do.'

When life tourned sour following an operation to my right knee, injured playing football, I hit a personal rock bottom in Australia in 1950–1. There were several reasons why I wanted to do well. I was tired of being on the receiving end against Australia, I had been made vice-captain under Freddie Brown, and there was a young side needing my experience and runs. Though I had 1,095 runs in Australia and New Zealand with an average of 52.14, second only to Hutton, I could not do a thing right in the Tests. In eight innings I made 53 and was thoroughly in the dumps.

One evening Bradman, now knighted for his services to the game, a top administrator and an Australian selector, invited me to his hotel room. When I went I expected a few words of consolation but not his priceless advice. He told me, 'You are doing one or two things wrong that you are not even aware you are doing. You don't normally do them, and they are getting you out.' He went on to explain where and why I was going wrong, and though his advice did not bring immediate results, it was an exceptional gesture and one which I more than appreciated.

So much for the image of the tough, ruthless man concerned only with his own affairs!

Only once did we have a difference of opinion. It was during an intensely hot Test at Adelaide, when Arthur Morris the affable left-hander and I had the distinction of scoring a century in each innings. On the fourth afternoon Ernie Toshack put England in serious danger with a sudden destructive spell. Godfrey Evans and I were left with no alternative but to defend with all the skill we could muster. Evans, the No. 10, played his part manfully staying for 95 minutes without scoring and holding on to lunch on the final day.

Obviously Bradman wanted to get at Evans, and we tried to manipulate the bowling so that I had as much of the strike as possible. Bradman put the field back so that a normal two was reduced to a single. Many runs were refused, and inevitably a stalemate developed. I was wearing spikes and played Colin McCool by going down the pitch — as I always did leg-spinners. During a particularly dull patch Bradman, now somewhat frustrated, complained about my running down the wicket. 'We have got to bat on this pitch after you,' he said.

My answer was that that was the way I always played leg-spin, and would continue to do so. He countered with 'Why are you not taking runs?' I said, 'I will if you bring the field in. I am playing for England, and you can't expect me to give the strike to Godfrey, or risk being run out going for a second. I am only going for a two when it's a safe two. As for roughing up the pitch, you do the same when you go down the wicket to a slow bowler.'

As if by mutal consent the matter was then closed.

Few people unburdened by fame can appreciate the well-nigh impossible pressures imposed by Bradman's cricketing genius. He became the property of a nation. There was no escape; no expectation of a normal life. I wonder how many tens of thousand times he was asked for his autograph, how often unwanted attention was forced on him, and how many hurtful words were written by sniping critics. (The Aussies have an unfortunate tendency to knock their heroes and Bradman was no exception.)

How much cash he brought into the game is beyond calculation. Wherever he played he drew huge crowds, and when he was out spectators tended to drift from the ground. What his commercial value would rate today I dare not guess — particularly when I read of the contracts offered to second- and even third-rate players engaged by World Series Cricket. I would even go as far as to say that a Kerry Packer would not have dared to compete with

Bradman playing in the traditional game.

Bradman's opinions are strong and fair, and once his playing days ended — even in his testimonial match in 1948–9 he hit a century — he threw himself into administration and selection. He who had given so much was prepared to give even more. Without doubt he could have named his own fees as a writer and commentator. After his coverage of the Test series in 1953 for the *Daily Mail* he earned the praise of a fourth leader in *The Times*.

As a captain he was the shrewdest and most perceptive in my experience. Untypically he made a cautious start, no doubt because of his fast-bowling limitations at the time. Tactically he was a deep thinker, an infallible judge of a wicket, a long-term planner with an encyclopaedic knowledge of his opponents as I know to my cost. Probably there has never been a better captain, and he never lost a rubber. It was his special pride that he went through England undefeated in 1948. England's recovery from the war was necessarily slow, but no England side I have been associated with could have held his post-war side. I have never played against any side of comparable class and strength.

Bradman was a magnificent fielder at cover or in the deep. If the miracle happens and another Don should rise my prayer is that I shall be around to see him.

5

B.S. CHANDRASEKHAR

Broadly speaking, it can be said no game more faithfully character-
izes a people than cricket. The Aussies play it with tough aggression, the West Indies with colourful abandon, the English with
caution, and the Indians with charm and subtlety. India's batting
is of a gracious touch, and a Dennis Lillee or a Jeff Thomson
would be as strange in their attack as a performance of the rope
trick on the Adelaide Oval.

For a vegetarian land of steamy heat and parched slow pitches to
produce fast bowlers would be incongruous, asking too much of
providence, but there has always been an ample compensation in
slow bowling. Spinning a cricket ball comes naturally to Indians,
and the decade of Chandrasekhar, Bedi, Venkataraghavan and
Prasanna illuminated the pages of Test history. Each is a star in his
own right, with Bedi and Chandrasekhar comfortably topping 200
Test wickets each.

I choose Bhagwat Subramaniam Chandrasekhar — truly a name
to conjure with! — as one of my personal gallery of greats, not only
for his record, ability and status but because he is so different. To
use a modern term — an original. There has been none like him.
Bishen Singh Bedi is a classical slow-left-arm bowler, one of the
best of all time; Erapalli Prasanna and Srinivasaraghavan Venkataraghavan are distinguished off-spinners and as good as they come
— especially Prasanna with his model loop and variations. But to
my mind Chandrasekhar stands apart.

Mention Chandra's name to Ken Barrington and he waxes lyri-
cal in his praise of the spinner who presented endless problems.
Rather like Hedley Verity and Derek Underwood, Chandra is
difficult to categorize as he is a law unto himself. For a start, he is

not in the strict sense a slow bowler. His pace is distinctly medium, and with a low trajectory from a high arm supplemented by a liberal wrist action, he whips wickedly off the pitch. His leg-break turns sharply, and he has been known to unleash bouncers in Test matches. Above all he is an attacker, a belligerent bowler giving the harassed batsman the minimum time to play his shots, and to discover, either by reading the hand or playing off the pitch of the ball, whether he has to counter leg-break, googly or top-spinner.

Chandra says only three batsmen have played him with real assurance — his old adversary Barrington, Colin Cowdrey and Gary Sobers. So there were many top-line batsmen who never succeeded in working him out. If India's catching had been as consistent as the best of Australia, England and South Africa, and he had not spent the best part of his career toiling on drugged pitches, Chandra's international tally would assuredly be higher. Also for some unaccountable reason he was consigned to the wilderness for four long years — broken by a triumphant return in England in 1971 — and at other periods he was reduced to the status of a workhorse stock bowler.

The ups and downs of his career suggest a partial waste of brilliant talent or at least a failure to recognize it to the full, but his stars seem to have consigned him to an erratic course. At the age of five he contracted polio, the legacy of which is a withered right arm — his bowling arm. After coming out of hospital in his native Bangalore (where he was born in May 1946) he was wisely taught to lead a normal life, and as D.J. Rutnagur wrote in *Wisden* 'turned his deformity into an instrument of success'.

I never played against Chandra, but those who have believe the very thinness of his arm gives a spring-like flexibility. Like Sonny Ramadhin, the mystery spinner from the West Indies, Chandra has his sleeves buttoned at the wrists, and the dark hand flicks over at such a pace that it is extremely difficult to follow, particularly in England's sometimes dubious light. With slow bowling, obviously, the longer the ball is in the air the more time the batsman has to deal with spin. My policy was to advance down the pitch to leg-spin, but Chandra's pace, accuracy and trajectory made it hard to get at him. He could keep the batsman tied to worried defence, which in itself is a prime asset for a bowler. Speed and bounce were his potent weapons. Short legs were placed to pounce on the slightest mistake, and he arrived so fast that it was often hard to punish a delivery other than of a good length.

True to his unorthodox style, Chandra did not come to light through school and university as do most Indian Test players, but was only seventeen when he first played for his State, Mysore, in the Ranji Trophy. Two months later, on the strength of twenty-five wickets in only four games, he was playing in a Test against Mike Smith's 1964 England. Beginning brightly with five wickets in the Madras match he was later defeated by Cowdrey, who joined the side from the third Test. Even so he took ten wickets, and England returned to talk of a new and awkward customer with a long and unpronounceable name.

None of Smith's party were very surprised when the Australians later that year were just as mystified during their three Tests in India on the way home from England. Chandra played twice. At Bombay, where a new foundation of bricks had given the pitch some much-needed bounce, he had 4 for 50 and 4 for 73. Bill Lawry, Bobby Simpson, Brian Booth, Peter Burge and Tom Veivers, four of the first five, fell victim to him in the course of a match which India won by two wickets. The key wicket of Burge went to a trimmer pitching leg stump and hitting the top of the off, and Burge paid tribute by tapping his bat. He was by no means the last to be beaten by a virtually unplayable delivery.

The West Indies of 1966–7, led by Sobers, were the next to be puzzled by his variations. Although he was badly let down by poor fielding Chandra took 18 wickets. In the first innings of the first Test at Bombay he took 7 for 157, being obliged to bowl over 61 overs, and followed with 4 for 78 in the second. Once again, it was leading batsmen of the class of Conrad Hunte, Rohan Kanhai, Basil Butcher and Clive Lloyd who fell to him. The rubber was also notable for the introduction of Bedi in the second Test and Prasanna (who had played two Tests five years earlier) in the third.

Chandra's first overseas tour was to England in 1967. In the three Tests he ended with 16 wickets, more than twice Bedi's haul, while Prasanna's 9 cost 47.77 each. Again the fielding let him down, but his 57 wickets in all made it plain to everyone that he was in the top flight of bowlers. Then, before the triumph of 1971, Chandra was to experience one of those depressing ruts into which the best can fall. Many contend that he was bowled into the ground; and certainly it did not appear clever to overwork him even on a non-prestigious tour of East Africa immediately after the visit to England, particularly with Australia in the offing. Within two months he was off to Australia, where it was widely assumed he would be a trump card on bouncy pitches.

From the very start, however, it was evident that Chandra had been asked to do too much, and he took part in only two unsuccessful Tests before he broke down with a foot injury and returned home with a stern medical warning to rest. When one's luck is out nothing goes right, and uncharitable fate next arranged a fall from his motor scooter on his way to work at a Bangalore bank. Recovery was slow, and he missed the entire domestic season of 1968–9 and the following rubbers with New Zealand and Australia. At least his injury in Australia had forcibly brought it home to India not to abuse high talent with overwork, and the policy of using him more sparingly was made infinitely easier by the success of Bedi, Venkataraghavan and Prasanna. Once the lesson was digested Chandra returned to his — and India's — greatest hours, when England were beaten for the first time on their own soil by India.

Victory by four wickets in the last of the three 1971 Tests also gave India a first-ever series victory in England, and ended England's run of twenty-six Tests without defeat. Chandra, who most judges on and off the field proclaimed was better than ever, was the match-winner. There was something in the pitch for him; he took 6 for 38 and England were dismissed for a paltry 101. Edrich was bowled by a similar delivery to the one which defeated Peter Burge at Bombay, and the hard, plain fact was that England succumbed to a genius. I would have given a lot for a magic carpet to transport me from the Oval to Bombay, where the result was hailed with unrestrained joy. Garlands were placed over radio sets bearing the news, dancing began in the streets and the whole city gave itself over to all-night celebration. If Chandra had accomplished nothing else in his illustrious career, that one performance was surely enough to put him on a pedestal at home and confirm his international status.

I have wondered what might have happened if Chandra with his pace and bounce, his top-spinner and googly, had operated on matting, as the South African googly bowlers did in the early part of the century. The effect was venomous and must have made batting terrifying. The Indian spinners in England in 1971, surely the most fearsome spin quartet since England were able to choose from Laker, Lock, Wardle and Appleyard, actually took 197 of the 244 wickets falling to bowlers on the tour. In the Tests Chandra, Bedi and Venkataraghavan, who was preferred to Prasanna as a superior batsman and fielder, shared 37 compared with 11 by the two pace men, Abid Ali and Solkar. And India could afford to leave out Prasanna, once described by Sobers as the world's finest off-spinner.

Chandra's unusual bounce into the rib-cage proved both pronounced and disconcerting, and was equally puzzling to a new generation of world batsmen. In 1975–6 he took 6 for 94 in India's first Test victory over New Zealand at Auckland, finishing an innings with three wickets in his last fourteen balls. From New Zealand, India undertook a sixty-two hour journey to the West Indies, and incredibly were committed to open their programme just over a day after arriving. I cannot believe cricket authorities can appreciate the time it takes to acclimatize from one hemisphere to another. Before a tour of the West Indies I asked Worrell, then domiciled in Manchester, how long it took him to readjust to the light and conditions of his native Caribbean, and he reckoned three weeks to a month. And he was born and bred in Barbados!

In the four Tests Chandra took 21 wickets, to 18 by Bedi and 7 by Venkataraghavan. Six other bowlers were nowhere, collecting four expensive wickets between them. Chandra had a brilliant spell in the second Test at Port-of-Spain, 6 wickets for 120 in the third at Kingston, and 5 in the fourth. Back home he added 17 wickets in three Tests with New Zealand, playing a decisive role in India's two victories, and 19 in five against Tony Greig's England, who comfortably won the series. During the third match Bedi became the first Indian to reach 200 Test wickets, but Chandra was well below his top form, perhaps because the pitches, in the main, were soporific, slow and bounceless. At Calcutta all the surface grass was scrubbed away with household brushes!

But in the fourth Test at Bangalore, which started with England 3–0 ahead, Chandra's ability suddenly erupted with 6 for 76 and 3 for 55, and the menacing short leg, which always tormented batsmen and was part of his potency, collected catches like picking ripe apples from a tree. Chandra again took some time to warm up in Australia in 1977–8, when he had a series tally of 28 wickets to Bedi's 31.

The third Test at Melbourne in the early days of 1978 added another page to his distinguished personal triumphs. As in England in 1971, Chandra was the main instrument of a first victory on foreign territory. On this occasion it was India's maiden success in Australia in twelve attempts and Chandra, bang on form, had 6 for 52 in each innings — a match aggregate of 12 for 104, the best figures of his career. There will be some prepared to scoff at a performance against the weakened Australia of 1978, but in my view the old enemy were on the decline before the ranks were plundered by Kerry Packer. It was significant, however, that Chandra claimed Bobby Simpson, Craig Serjeant (a much-hailed prospect) and Gary Cosier, who began his Test career with a century off the West Indies, in both innings. In the next Test at Sydney he again put India firmly on the path to victory with 4 for 30. Adelaide, the scene of the final Test, with its plumb pitch also yielded another 5 in the first innings . . . and, for those interested in bizarre statistics, Chandra's first runs of the series! In eight innings his only runs were 2 and 2 at Adelaide and he ended with an average of 0.66.

Joke the Aussies might over Chandra's number eleven batting efforts, but they were unanimous in their praise of Chandra and the orthodox left-arm spinner Bedi. Undoubtedly they complemented each other, the tigerish bite at one end and the gentle coaxing to self-destruction at the other. How high does Bedi rank among the classical-style spinners? I would answer: very high indeed. His action could serve as the ultimate model for all bowlers of his type — smooth rhythm, perfectly balanced, unhurried and with an uncanny accuracy. Everything comes so naturally to him that it would seem an unnecessary affront to suggest he was ever coached. Once again we come back to natural gifts, happily beyond the rigid control of orthodox coaching and supervision. But Bedi's development, as with Alec Bedser, Bill O'Reilly, Ray Lindwall and other great bowlers, was nourished by hours of practice in his native Punjab. He was born at Amritsar, the spiritual home of the Sikhs, and did not begin to play until he was thirteen, but he was a born spinner and an industrious pupil.

Watching Bedi I have always admired the instant way in which he drops into his rhythm. One ball and he is away, and if his action is mechanical it is because every fibre of his body and his mental philosophies are at once beautifully blended. And because everything is so right he is able to wheel away for hours without strain or worry, whatever the fortunes of the game. Before play he meditates — he is an exponent of yoga — and I have never seen him upset or ruffled if things go wrong. In the 1976 Gillette Cup final he bowled what could have been a disastrous last over for Northamptonshire, when David Hughes slogged 24, including two sixes over mid-wicket and long on. Bedi joined in the enthusiastic Lancashire applause, and when he was afterwards asked how he felt he said he had enjoyed Hughes's batting! The point was that all believed him. I cannot remember seeing him bowl defensively to a split field, and if a batsman accepted the challenge Bedi would be the first to be appreciative.

His orthodox ball is the delivery spinning away from the right-hander. Some spin more than others, as he deceives by relaxing the grip and sliding the ball under his wrist. The batsman must also expect slight but highly effective pace variations, and a seamer floating towards his slips. Of course some of his tricks were exposed in the years he bowled for Northamptonshire, but it is a striking tribute to his skills and versatility that he remains, year in year out, a classic spinner at the highest level.

With his coloured patka, beard and glistening bracelet, he would have been a distinctive figure even as a moderate performer; but he is far removed from mediocrity. When he became captain he enjoyed a popularity in India which the Western world might find it hard to understand fully. During England's tour of 1976-7 an early fixture was being played in the city of Ahmedabad against the President's XI. England were in the field when suddenly the packed ground erupted — it was as if a popular emperor had arrived, or the Beatles at a pop festival. Bedi was taking his place in the stand! Unhappily for India and Bedi some of the euphoria vanished as England built up a 3-0 advantage, and there was the so-called 'ointment row' — as nonsensical a protest as I have ever heard. Bedi was an independent captain, going his own way and making his protests at excessive bumping. In Australia he was immensely popular, but he paid the price of losing in Pakistan and the captaincy in England in 1979 passed through Sunil Gavaskar to Venkataraghavan, who had some experience with Derbyshire.

Venkat had a more orthodox passage to the top, via High School at Madras and an engineering college. He was helped on by Ghulam Ahmed, formerly an off-spinner for whom I had the utmost respect, and by then a Test selector. When Chandra was ill Venkat took 8 New Zealand wickets for 72 at Delhi in 1965, and won a duel with the brilliant Bert Sutcliffe.

For almost a decade India had an embarrassment of riches, and before then Vinoo Mankad and the leg-spinner Subash Gupte were undoubtedly world class. Indeed Mankad was an all-rounder of uncommon distinction, and few have bettered his Test figures of 2,109 runs and 162 wickets. I played in the 1952 Test at Lord's in which Mankad, released from the Lancashire League club Haslingden, scored 72 and 184 as India's opening batsman, and bowled 73 overs in the first innings to take 5 for 196, and 24 overs in the second. I have seen some all-round performances, but Mankad's on this occasion was unforgettable. Apart from his physical endurance and mental stamina in taking on an opposition including Hutton, May, Graveney, Evans, Laker, Bedser and Trueman, he was a giant both as batsman and slow-left-arm spinner. I made the point at the time that he did not cover up or allow one delivery to pass without offering a shot which must have been a record in contemporary cricket. He pulled 'Roly' Jenkins's first ball for six, and on one day, thanks to Mankad and Evans (who scored 104), no fewer than 382 runs went up for seven wickets. It was a really refreshing exhibition, and Mankad's reputation, particularly among his fellow players, went ceiling high.

Wisden regretted that Mankad played in the League while his country toured, a sentiment I shared. I doubt if such an anomaly would be allowed in these times.

India's finest have always compared with the best in the world. They contribute a special charm, and, for me, the jewel in the bowling crown is Chandra — unusual, brilliant and an attacker. Great qualities all!

6

ALAN DAVIDSON

They called him 'the Claw' or 'Davo the Demon'. I understood why on an August evening at the Oval in 1956, when Alan Davidson was the cause of the most disappointing moment of my career. I had lived through eight months of personal hell after the operation on my football-damaged knee, not knowing whether I would ever walk properly again, let alone play cricket.

Exactly twelve months before on the same ground the knee, originally hurt in a collision with Sam Bartram, the Charlton goal-keeper, at Highbury, finally gave way while I was batting with Peter May in a Test with South Africa. I hobbled around while 62 rather important runs were added, but I couldn't field. The upshot was, I was told, that my only chance was for my right knee-cap to be removed. What with the pain and anxiety I was desperate, and the operation was duly performed at University College Hospital, London. By a sad coincidence Tom Whittaker, my old Arsenal trainer and later manager, was ill at the same hospital. None of my knee trouble would have happened if I had accepted an invitation to tour South Africa with M.C.C. in 1938–9, but I felt I owed something to Arsenal.

After the operation my knee would not bend properly, and, despite intensive treatment, the weeks went by without improvement. April arrived, and at the Cricket Writers' dinner to the Australians I was told of a new treatment. Back I went to the operating table, and under an anaesthetic the knee was manipulated into bending positions. After the third manipulation there was seventy-five per cent flexion, which was enough for me to play cricket again. First there were short spells in the nets, then one-day matches, and finally in July I returned for Middlesex against

Lancashire at Lord's, starting on a Saturday. There was a crowd of 17,000.

Unfortunately I spent the whole of the day in the field, and perhaps unwisely I bowled seven overs — though there was the consolation of Alan Wharton's wicket and three catches at slip. By the close of play I was limping badly and wondering if I had been too optimistic. On the Sunday I rested, and by Monday I was more confident; though Middlesex had to struggle on a rain-affected pitch and my scores were 4 and 1, I was inwardly rejoicing.

Gradually my form returned and I made two centuries off Kent and Somerset. Godfrey Evans was behind the wicket for the first and was marvellously encouraging, even laughing and joking with me as the bowler was running up. Fielding was my worry, but at Glastonbury I took two catches jumping to my left. Before the Oval Test 'Gubby' Allen, chairman of selectors, sounded me out. England had retained the Ashes under the new skipper Peter May, who was to take M.C.C. to South Africa that winter. Deep in my heart I realized I was only sixty per cent fit. The knee-cap, which the surgeons said looked as if it had been gnawed by rats, had taken its toll, but I said I was fit to play.

When I went into bat I was determined to retire if I should fail. Miller was bowling, and his first ball to me was described as the fastest of the day. For fifteen agonizing minutes I struggled for my first run, but I went on to make 94 out of 156 with May, in a deperate battle.. Bradman was kind enough to tell me it was the best innings of the series.

I apologize for a somewhat lengthy recital of my personal history of the time in what is intended to be a tribute to the substantial all-round contributions to Australia by Davidson. But my misfortunes serve as an example of his remarkable catching ability — as good as I have ever seen. When I turned Ron Archer off the meat of the bat I instinctively looked for a boundary only to see the ball end in those bucket-sized hands at backward short leg. For a moment my mind blazed at my cruel luck in having 'the Claw', capable of clutching anything above the ground, in that position at that moment. That evening I was a guest at a private dinner party at the Savoy given by Sir Arthur Sims, and attended by Sir Robert Menzies, then Prime Minister of Australia, Sir Don Bradman, Sir Jack Hobbs, Sir Pelham Warner and Sir Len Hutton; one of the topics of conversation was that catch and

Davidson's fielding in general.

Between 1949 and 1953 'Davo' played in 44 Tests, made three visits to England, scored 1,328 runs and took 186 wickets. But, important as those figures are, they cannot include the matches he influenced by his catches, or the number of runs he saved as a dynamic fielder. He was an extremely hostile and clever left-arm fast-medium over-the-wicket bowler, able to use the new ball with great intent, rated by many as the world's best in the late fifties, and a highly dangerous left-handed batsman with an ability to hit that matched his six feet in height and burly strength.

His bowling action did not belong to the classical school, with no discernable use of his right arm, but he swung the ball, especially if it was new, very late either way. Slant bowling across the right hander can be extremely awkward, and there was always the chance of the ball nipping back. If he had a weakness it was being injury prone, which seemed unnatural for a whole-hearted player of impressive-looking fourteen-stone physique, who trained hard with a Rugby League club and was spectacularly fast and agile as a fielder in any position, either close or far from the bat. I remember in South Africa in 1948 Allan Watkins superbly catching that fine batsman Dudley Nourse round the corner. Not only was it a crucial catch in the context of the situation of the Test, but from then on Nourse hesitated to use one of his favourite and most profitable strokes for fear of a similar dismissal. Davo had the same effect. His very presence in a close-catching position made me wary, and I support the contention that he was the most exciting and capable Australian all-rounder in my time after Keith Miller.

Even as a boy he practised fielding for hours on end by throwing stones or oranges — they must be cheaper in Australia! — at targets to improve his accuracy. How often he was to turn an innings with a bull's-eye throw! In New Zealand with an Australian second team he once ran out a batsman from the boundary with only one stump at which to aim, and in another match on the same tour he took all 10 wickets for 29 runs and followed with a dazzling 160 not out. At the tender age of eight he fielded for a team run by his father at a small country town named Lisarow in New South Wales, and took two catches, the second winning the game with the opposition six runs short.

At nine he was playing second-grade cricket, and was a star at both school and junior representative level. What constantly surprises me in delving into the backgrounds of top players is the early age at which promise emerges. Davo also dug himself a wicket on the side of a hill to help his bowling, which began in the Fleetwood-Smith style of 'chinamen' and googlies. As he was obliged to chase the ball downhill if he missed the stumps it can be assumed that his dedicated endeavours at least improved his accuracy. He did not begin to bowl fast until his uncle needed an opening bowler at Gosford; Davo took four cheap wickets and abandoned spinners for all time. It was in the role of fast bowler that he started with New South Wales in 1949–50, getting a wicket with his second ball, and graduating to the national side in four years.

With Bradman's sides breaking up it was a time of opportunity for the up-and-coming player, and until 1963 he served Australia splendidly — only Richie Benaud, Graham McKenzie, Ray Lindwall and Clarrie Grimmett had taken more wickets — and gave infinite pleasure to crowds in England (where he played his first Test), South Africa, India and Pakistan. His capacity for devastating spells brought him five or more wickets in an innings fourteen times, two more than Lindwall, and his best, at least on figures, was 7 for 93 against India at Kanpur in 1959–60. Davo was particularly proud of that performance because he bowled 57.3 overs in a temperature of over 100 degrees. I know from personal experience how cruel the Indian sun can be. In another Test at home he bowled over fifty overs in two days and had two big innings.

His career bowling of 672 wickets at 20.91 each compares with the best, and in addition there were 6,804 runs, with nine centuries, at the respectable average of 32.68. But again I stress that mere arithmetic cannot accurately reflect his influence and the exhilarating way he played at any level. I remember two gigantic hits off Colin Cowdrey at Sydney — a pull which seemed to drop from the clouds on the roof of a stand, and a straight drive going smack into the wall at the Hill which must have been among the biggest hits ever seen on the ground. The 76 he scored in his second Test at Lord's in 1953 was the clue to his future, though understandably he began as the bowling support to Lindwall and Miller. Strong forearms and wrists gave his batting distinction, and bowlers had cause to fear the sight of his right foot advancing down the pitch. He was, in my opinion, an immeasurably better bowler and fielder than a batsman; but England were always relieved to see his broad shoulders retreating towards the pavilion.

Several times he came close to achieving a Test century, and many a century has been of less value to a side than some of his innings. Notably there was the match-winning 77 at Old Trafford in 1961, which set up Richie Benaud's six-wicket triumph and Australia's 2-1 victory in the series. When Davidson went in to bat on the fourth evening Australia were in a precarious position, but 'Slasher' Mackay and Davidson still added 35 in the last hour. England's hopes were high on the last morning when David Allen, the off-spinner from Gloucestershire whose accuracy was a by-word, took the wickets of Mackay, Benaud and Wally Grout in fifteen balls. With one wicket left Davo, who had been defending grimly, suddenly shattered Allen's dominance with two massive sixes, and an over which was to prove decisive cost 20 runs. One six went over cover's head like a rocket, and the other met the brickwork by the railway line. Davidson and Graham McKenzie put on 98 for the last wicket, and Australia won by 54 runs. Without that even Benaud's historic bowling — leg-spin into the bowler's rough — would not have been enough.

In the stormy 1958–9 series Australia banked on the fast left-arm over-the-wicket new-ball attack of Davidson and Ian Meckiff, whose action caused so much trouble. Never, I hasten to add, was Davidson involved in any of the controversies, though I remember four years earlier Hutton objecting about his fellow-through marks to his opposing captain Ian Johnson. Johnson countered by asking, 'What about Tyson's rough for our left-handers?' It was an argument, I confess, that I had never heard advanced before, and while the exchanges went on Keith Miller intervened with the playful admonition, 'Now, now, children, no harsh words.'

Davo got Australia off to a winning start on the last day of the old year in 1958 in the second Test at Melbourne with as electric an opening burst as it was possible to offer. Moving the ball extremely late away from the bat he had Peter Richardson caught behind, beat and bowled Willie Watson by sheer pace and deceived Tom Graveney with a swinging yorker, all in one sensational over. Indeed, though Peter May scored a century, England never recovered from that third over of the match. The only runs Davo had conceded at that period were four taken in the first over.

Finishing with 6 for 64 from 25.5 8-ball overs he also had 3 for 41 in the second innings, and was top scorer among the last seven batsmen.

In the series Davidson had 24 wickets at only 19.00 each and a batting average of 36.00; moreover, I doubt if any would quarrel with the contention that he was the outstanding fielder on either side. Davidson was always capable of new-ball havoc because he used it with skill and intelligence. In England in 1961 he emerged as the leading bowler in every sense, with 23 Test wickets at 24.86, far outshining McKenzie and leaving his stamp on the game when it really mattered. At Lord's three of his 5 wickets for only 42 were opening batsman Geoff Pullar, and the two most prized catches, Peter May, with a lifter, and Ken Barrington, with a ball which left him at the last moment and earned a snick to second slip. Barrington, whose judgement I profoundly respect, maintains that the two bowlers to give him the most trouble were Davidson and the unorthodox medium-paced spinner Chandrasekhar. Davidson not only had pace from a wheeling action, late swing, and the deceptive angle common to left-arm over-the-wicket bowlers but also showed the ability to cramp the batsman in the vicinity of the leg stump. Essentially Davo was an attacking cricketer, and in his element when carrying the fight to the enemy. But no individual, captain or team can attack all the time, and tactical know-how is judging when to attack and when to defend. I thought it out of character and uncharitable when Davo criticized Ted Dexter for developing what he described as a run-saving phobia at the expense of bowling efficiency.

In the four Tests in which he played in 1961 May fell three times to Davo, including the Old Trafford Test, and there was another contribution of 24 wickets at 20.00 against Ted Dexter's side in Australia in 1962–3. At Melbourne he had 6 for 75, and at Sydney he played the major part in squaring the series with 9 wickets for 79, including 5 for 25 in the second. In the course of the match, in which he was well-nigh unplayable, he dismissed Geoff Pullar, David Sheppard, Ted Dexter and Ken Barrington — all among the first five in the order – at least once each.

England, South Africa, India and Pakistan had suffered at Davo's hands at one time or another, but the whip of his ability was most keenly felt by Sir Frankie Worrell's powerful West Indies team in Australia in 1960–1. If he had accomplished nothing else in his career Davidson's achievements in that fabulous series entitled him to a special niche in the annals of Australian cricket. Beyond dispute he was the man of the match in the first tied Test in history at Brisbane, taking 11 wickets for 222 runs and having two excellent innings of 44 and 80 — the latter his highest score for Australia. The next highest score was Benaud's 52, and after that Mackay's 28. Davidson gloriously hooked and cut Wes Hall, whom few of the other batsmen could manage at all let alone take apart. With 7 wanted Davo was called for a risky single, and was run out side on by Joe Solomon, who entered history a minute or two afterwards when he hit the last wicket to run out Lindsay Kline off the last ball and tie the game, in which each side scored 737.

In the first West Indies innings Davo completed 30 8-ball overs and his five victims were Cammie Smith, Rohan Kanhai, Frankie Worrell, Conrad Hunte — four of the first five again — and Sonny Ramadhin, No. 9, for 135. In the second from 24.6 overs he had Smith, Kanhai, and Worrell again, plus Gary Sobers, Peter Lashley (another accredited batsman at No. 7) and Hall, who had clouted 50 in 69 minutes in his first innings, for 87 runs. On the first day a heavy atmosphere helped Davo's swing, and his tactic was to move it away from the right-handers and deprive the West Indies batsmen of the chance to use one of their favourite shots, the on drive. The only pair he could not curb was Sobers and Worrell and, heaven knows, he could be forgiven for that!

Davidson remained the sharpest thorn in the West Indies flesh. Although he missed the fourth Test with a muscle injury he had 33 wickets at 18.54 — 27 coming from the first three Tests. In each match he had five or more wickets in an innings — 6 for 53 in the second at Melbourne. Benaud, the next most successful Austalian bowler, had ten fewer wickets at the far more expensive rate of 33.86.

For the most part, as against England, his line was towards the off stump, tempting the flash and the catch to the slips or at the wicket. Several of his West Indies victims were caught off their gloves, to prove he could make the ball lift sharply from a length. In my experience against him I discovered he could move the old ball almost as much as the new, and, unlike some of the foremost fast bowlers, could control the swing with the shine on the ball. I rated him as a remarkably fine attacking bowler and admired his spirited venom. It was fitting that he should be the first to take 10 wickets and score 100 runs in a Test match.

Davo certainly left his mark at the highest level of the game, and after all these years I have just forgiven 'the Claw' for what he did to me at the Oval in 1956! His M.B.E. was richly deserved for the pleasure he gave, and he took his much-needed enthusiasm into administration and became President of New South Wales.

7

GODFREY EVANS

Cynics may sneer and say that Godfrey Evans made the difficult catches look easy and the easy appear difficult, but I cannot believe it possible that a better wicket-keeper ever donned gauntlets at Test level. The international qualification is deliberate, as Evans of England and Evans of Kent could be a class or two apart. To spark the Evans vitality, the incentive had to be there. If the situation of a match or even a crowded ground fired him, Evans would come alive and exhibit a glorious talent.

I judge my wicket-keepers not by their acrobatics standing back — though Godfrey could take the diving catch with the best — but in the arts of standing up. Alec Bedser, who insisted his wicket-keepers stood up, provided the acid test with his late swing and fast leg-cutter and he is the first of Godfrey's advocates. Bedser acknowledges with gratitude the brilliance of Evans, who combined a remarkable agility with needle-sharp reflexes.

He was also the ultimate morale-booster, whose perpetual mood of cheerfulness and vivacity was communicated to the team both on the field and in the dressing-room. No matter how grim the outlook or how long and tiring the day — and there were some in Australia in the first two post-war tours — Godfrey would be urging, cajoling and driving his team-mates. He could be the gentle bully, but always he was the fulcrum of the fight.

Even on the second day in the field he never gave up, and at the end of a tea interval his cry was, 'Let's get at 'em. Let's give them the full treatment and pick up three or four wickets.' There was never a despairing, 'Oh God, we've got another session to go.' He was an eternal inspiration, and you felt you could not make a mistake in the field for Godfrey's sake. The chores of county cricket were clearly less inviting and challenging, and there could have been finer keepers in the championship. But put the England cap on his head and there was none to touch him.

The greatest catch I ever saw by a keeper standing up was from my position at backward short leg when Evans held Neil Harvey at Brisbane in 1950. Harvey turned Alec Bedser to leg with a perfect deflection off the middle of the bat, but Godfrey's anticipation started him moving towards the correct position possibly even before Harvey's initial movement. My first instinct was to wonder if the deep fine leg could cut off a four, and, accustomed as I was to Godfrey's wizardry, I was dumbfounded when he took the catch.

Harvey was thrice unlucky with Evans. After Brisbane, where he was on the way to a century, there was Godfrey's decisive full length dive to his right at Melbourne in 1955 off the seventh delivery of the morning from Frank Tyson. Australia had started needing 165 runs to win with eight wickets to go, and lost by 128. And at Lord's in 1956 Evans got Harvey again, this time with Trevor Bailey bowling.

If Evans was not a classical stylist in the mould of Bob Taylor or Bertie Oldfield, he was inspiring and capable of the highest brilliance. I can vouch through experience that if you have a Godfrey Evans or a Don Tallon behind you a warning lurks at the back of the mind not to take liberties, which, of course, is to your own disadvantage.

The only time I saw Godfrey down in the dumps was after Australia's victory at Headingley in 1948 — the victory that should never have been. For once he was off form and made some disastrous errors, some against my googlies and chinamen to Arthur Morris and Don Bradman after I had caught and bowled Lindsay Hassett. Another trouble was that Jack Crapp at slip could not read my googly. Anyway, Australia scored 404 in the last innings to win by seven wickets.

Godfrey returned to the dressing-room and apologized; he genuinely thought it might be his last Test for England. He was dropped for the last two Tests in South Africa in the following winter when he was jaded, but his one disappointment when he retired at the age of thirty-nine was that he did not make his 100th Test appearance. Still, he played in 91, and his record of 219 dismissals is surpassed only by Alan Knott, with 252 from 89 Tests. (As evidence of the changing bowling methods, Evans made

46 stumpings to Knott's 19.)

Against Australia Evans stands second to Warwickshire's Arthur Lilley, who had 84 victims in 32 matches to Evans's 76 in 31. I was fascinated to listen one day to the great England and Surrey wicket-keeper Herbert Strudwick. In the 1903–4 tour of Australia 'Struddy', who had gnarled hands to prove his trade, was understudy to Lilley. He placed Evans, Oldfield, Lilley and the South African H.B. Cameron equal top. Frank Chester would not be budged from his opinion that Oldfield was unbeatable. 'Struddy', who bridged the generations, told me of Lilley in his second Test at Lord's in 1896. W.G. Grace put him on to bowl, and he dismissed the Australian captain Harry Trott. Lilley also took nine catches in his first two Tests, and when he helped in the runouts of Clem Hill and Frank Iredale, Ranjitsinhji presented him with a gold tie-pin.

Evans never bowled for England, but my brother Leslie and Arthur McIntyre both bowled the opening overs before putting on the pads in the Surrey–Middlesex match at the Oval in 1948. A versatile lot, we Comptons!

Brilliant as he can be, I do not place Knott in the same bracket as Evans. Indeed in the real science and art of wicket-keeping I would rate Bob Taylor well in front of Knott. Long before Knott went to World Series Cricket I thought Taylor was desperately unlucky to be the permanent understudy on tour. The reason for Knott's precedence could be understood, with the selectors looking to bolster the batting, but Taylor's form in Australia in 1978–9 was so revealing that one wonders if he could have been almost as useful with the bat if he had enjoyed an earlier opportunity. In one calendar year Taylor not only claimed a record number of Test victims, with one polished display after another — he was the Player of the Series against New Zealand at home in 1978 — but won the fifth Test at Adelaide with his batting, when his innings of 97 out of 204 took England from seeming defeat to the launching pad of victory.

In contrast to both Evans and Knott, the Derbyshire wicket-keeper is quiet and almost self-effacing. His movements are of silken stealth, of feline grace and economy of movement, but clinically effective. He is the swift executioner, and he shares with Evans an in-built instinct of anticipation with the brain directing feet and gloves to be in exactly the right place at the right time.

And, as with Evans, his ability to spot chinks in the batting armoury of opponents is of inestimable value to his captains. I also believe Taylor would have been equal to Alec Bedser's demands.

In the late seventies there was no doubt in my mind that Taylor was the world's number one wicket-keeper, but I also pay tribute to Pakistan's Wasim Bari, who maintained a high level of performances for over a decade. Agile, active and safe he missed little and frequently gave his side the bonus of reaching a wide snick, which at one time in the game would have been conceded as runs. 'Struddy' said it was common-place for a wicket-keeper to chase a deflection to the boundary as normally there would be only two fielders on the leg side, and his impressive speed in cumbersome pads was one of the reasons why Surrey originally engaged him!

Lancashire's George Duckworth, dubbed 'Quack-Quack' in Australia, was not only a loud appealer, but is given credit for widening the area of the wicket-keeper's responsibility on the leg side. Batsmen of his era say he increased his catching arc by twenty-five per cent, and what was once a safe deflection became a dangerous exercise. I can appreciate this development, as I always went wider at first or second slip or leg slip to Evans. With his jack-in-the-box dives and incredible anticipation he could get to catches few other wicket-keepers could reach. To stand too fine at slip with Evans behind the wicket was to court misunderstandings.

Alec Bedser rightly insisted on having his field placings exact to an inch, and clearly there are better chances of catches if every gap is covered, or is as near to being covered as possible. I have seen first slip in some games so fine that he was virtually hidden by the wicket-keeper and became a wasted fielder.

Was Evans guilty of playing to the gallery? At times his sheer exuberance and vitality gave the impression of an act, but even if it was the crowds were thrilled and it did not impair his efficiency. Evans's style, as distinct from Taylor's as it was possible to be, was his own. At worst it did no harm; at best it enlivened many a tedious hour.

Modern Aussie wicket-keepers have tended to be aggressive, loud in their appeals, and consciously busy and challenging. The late Wally Grout was a highly efficient performer with a string of records, without in my opinion matching the dazzling perfection of Don Tallon in the first two series against England after the war. Tall and lissome, Tallon was lightning in his movements, and for twenty-one Tests he was an important part of Australia's success.

After putting Evans on a pedestal I name Taylor, Tallon (for two series) and South Africa's Johnny Waite as the foremost keepers of my time. The order of the last three is unimportant, because at his best each could be the perfect wicket-keeper. Evans had a little something extra in his ebullience, and was probably a degree superior with his anticipation. He had an incredible ability to make the really difficult chance look absurdly simple, as did Wally Hammond at slip. I was often surprised to find certain catches he had made dismissed as easy by the watchers. Only those close to the wicket could know that his deceptive casualness hid the fact that it was a stunning catch.

Waite was easily the best batsman of my four keepers, indeed one of the best bats among regular keepers since Les Ames took over from Duckworth, and started in earnest the cult of the wicket-keeper who was also a specialized batsman. As a tactical policy this had its failures, if the roles were reversed and a batsman was turned into a makeshift long-stop with gloves. Jack Hobbs firmly believed the wicket-keeper to be so important that he should be the first choice of every side and the remaining ten built around him — if he *could* also bat, so much the better.

South Africa were fortunate in that Waite could have been a Test batsman in his own right. In 50 Tests he scored 2,405 runs, including four centuries against Australia (at Johannesburg and Durban), England and New Zealand. His maiden Test hundred at Old Trafford in 1955 was part of a record sixth-wicket stand of 171 with Paul Winslow. In a previous series he had 23 dismissals against New Zealand, and later he surpassed even that achievement with 26, also against New Zealand. Rodney Marsh needed six Tests — one more than Waite — to equal the figures. All Marsh's 26 victims in the series with the West Indies in 1975–6 were caught — yet another example of the modern predominance of pace bowling.

Evans and Tallon were certainly no mugs with the bat. Tallon, one of the many Australian Test players from small country towns, hit 92 against England at Melbourne in 1946–7, and Evans could adapt his mood to the occasion. There was his grim defence as my partner at Adelaide in 1947 when he went for a record 95 minutes without scoring, which must have been absolute hell for him. Then there was a 47 in 29 minutes off Australia at Old Trafford and a joyous century off India at Lord's in 1952, when in a stand of 159 in 130 minutes with Graveney Evans made 104. At lunch he was 98, and when he came in he dismissed all the commiserators at having so narrowly missed a rare distinction by saying, 'Those kinds of records are meant for the real batsmen, and not the likes of me.'

As he had already hit a superb century on a hopeless pitch at Old Trafford in 1950 I was inclined to think Godfrey was either inordinately modest or underrated his batting. His cover drive was a real punch, and at Old Trafford his 104 came out of 161 with Trevor Bailey for the sixth wicket, a stand which knocked out the West Indies.

In his youth Evans, who was born in the London borough of Finchley, was a boxer and had three bouts as a professional lightweight. At thirty shillings a fight he was on the bill on the pier at Herne Bay and Plumstead Baths. His third 'purse' was twenty-five shillings, and he gained two second-round knock-outs before he was persuaded that cut eyes might end his cricket career, which had just started.

Perhaps some of Godfrey's speed and footwork was inspired by his boxing, and perhaps his flamboyance followed his desire to draw attention to himself when he was striving to become established with a county that had Harold ('Hopper') Levett to call on when Les Ames was absent on Test duty. Evans felt his need to be spectacular, and spectacular he remained.

Tallon inspired him on the first of his four tours of Australia, and Evans still looks to Tallon as the greatest. Evans liked nothing more than the quick stumping on the leg side, and often what appeared as spontaneous genius was a planned trap. Alec Bedser and Godfrey would agree before an over that, say, the third or fourth ball would swing down the leg side. Godfrey would be ready if the batsman missed the ball, and often a stumping would result.

Godfrey never lost his high spirits. On board ship on the way to South Africa and Australia he would perform his 'German Band' act that he learned from a Canadian soldier during the war. He was the most noted Carmen Miranda outside South America at the fancy-dress ball, and he was the natural bookie at the ship's race meetings.

Nothing kept Godfrey down: he bubbled with effervescent life, and his sparkling spirits allied to his natural gifts made him the wicket-keeper I would want for any Test side.

8

DAVID GOWER

Watching David Ivon Gower smash India's bowling all over Lord's in the 1979 Test, Sir Len Hutton leaned over and offered one of his sage asides. 'He makes batting look as easy as drinking tea,' he said, with the appreciation of a fellow artist. As I clearly remember the great man himself at a similar age treating the West Indies with much the same disdain on the same ground I thought it was high praise indeed. Len is too shrewd and jealous of his judgements to risk flattering the ordinary.

Perhaps it is too early to talk of Gower in the same breath as Frank Woolley or Graeme Pollock, and I shall understand it if there is surprised reaction at my choice of a callow left-hander whose number is scarcely dry in the international sense. Surely, it might be argued, the presence of Gower in the company of such as Bradman, Hutton, May and Hammond is premature. It is true he started for England in 1978 at a time when the cricket world was split and England's opposition was moderate to say the least. Moreover he is prone to carelessness, plays mostly from the vicinity of the crease and slashes with dicey abandon outside the off stump; and his record for Leicestershire in his early years left much to be desired.

All the searching criticism is accepted, but I will also be so bold as to declare that in all the years I have played and watched I have never seen a batsman anywhere with such exquisite timing. For me Gower positively bubbles with natural ability and vitality; he is my kind of batsman, happy to challenge, unwilling to be shackled, and a brilliant entertainer. Unlike the bulk of my gallery of greats Gower has his career stretching in front of him, and I see no reason why he should not tread a path of gold provided he learns from experience. If I am proved wrong I feel mine will not be the only judgement called in question, for I have not seen any young batsman in the modern game to share his natural ability. He is the one to excite; to set the pulses racing. So often when he arrives at the crease it suddenly becomes a totally different game, and the spectators are left wondering why the batsman before him found it so difficult. Whether in success or failure he doesn't bore me as Geoff Boycott does with his play-safe technical methods.

One of the curious features of English cricket is the attitude to talented youth. In Yorkshire too many swans become geese. Over-praise retards progress. Too much is expected too soon. Yet in other parts of the land there seems to be a guarded pessimism and a slow reluctance to accept unusual gifts. Even Gower has a few detractors and wiseacres ready to predict his decline — and particularly when he ended the Indian series in 1979 with scores of 0, 0 and 7. All too often it needs time to fashion genius. From my own experience I understand the pitfalls and how quickly and astutely your fellow pros detect technical strengths and weaknesses. The grapevine is soon alive with the best way to get young so-and-so out — that is why the second and third seasons are often more diffi-cult than the first. It's not jealousy on the part of the older players, but professional shop, and it is understood that if a young batsman is made of the right stuff he will profit from mistakes. This is one reason why I have qualified opinions about coaching. Your best tutors are out in the middle, trying their best to get you out!

If Gower has any little grey cells under his angelic mat of hair — which I am sure he has — he will build steadily and crea-tively on his vast natural ability. Consider his advantages. First a good middle-class background, an education at King's School, Canterbury, and a year at London University studying law, which he gave up because he said it was interfering with his cricket; second, uncommon balance, eye, splendid footwork — the basis of all batting; third, composure and confidence, and the knack of being able to 'switch off' and enjoy music or whatever. All add up to the most elegant young batsman since Tom Graveney or Colin Cowdrey. He is probably more relaxed than either of them. Cowdrey was nicknamed 'Kipper' because he was able to sleep at any time and exercised his talent with enthusiasm, but for no logical reason I always felt he was slow to make up his mind. With his towering ability he should have done even better than he did, and most certainly should have made the captaincy position his own.

Those who travelled with Gower in Australia in 1978–9 were taken aback by his outward calm, and his insistence that it was part of his philosophy to keep cool no matter how trying the circumstances. It is one thing to acknowledge the benefits of an even temperament, but it is another matter to put theory into practice. In Australia Gower slept a lot — shades of Worrell, Compton and Cowdrey! — and his skipper Mike Brearley granted him the status of virtuoso, better to be left alone. Gower appreciated the tacit compliment.

Like most of the select few born with a flair Gower's technique is devoid of fuss or flourish, complications or mannerisms. His ballet-light movements are swift, sure but minimal and can be a poetry of co-ordination. If you ask him the secret of his extraordinary sense of timing he merely answers, 'The ball just seems to go off the bat,' as if surprised by the question. If genius is the perfection of simplicity Gower has it, and I doubt if he understands the meaning of the word 'temperament' — that final hurdle to be cleared by every quality performer. Truly he is a big-occasion young man, and it was not surprising that he bridged every tier of the game without effort, from school to Young England player through to county level and on to full England status. Hard though it can be for the modern youngster to master the many forms of competitive cricket from the forty-over fiesta to the five-day Test he at least has the considerable advantage of extensive travel never open to my generation.

My first official tour did not come until after the war, due to my Arsenal allegiance and to something that happened between 1939 and 1945. But by the time Gower was ready to step on a jet plane on behalf of England he was an experienced traveller, having gone to South Africa with an English Schools XI, to the West Indies with Young England, to Canada with a private team, and to Perth in Western Australia for a season's Grade cricket. Wisely, in my view, Alec Bedser and his selectors held him back from the official tour of Pakistan and New Zealand in 1977–8, arguing that his development would be more rapid with the experience of batting at Perth than on the dead pitches of Pakistan, where he would not be guaranteed many matches. The far-seeing decision, far from appreciated by the public at the time, paid handsome dividends when Gower eventually returned to Perth to score a century and participate in a partnership with Geoff Boycott which paved the way for a famous Test victory.

The conditions at Perth were daunting for batsmen. In the State fixture Western Australia had been dismissed by Mike Hendrick and Ian Botham for totals of 52 and 78, and when England were put in to bat Graham Gooch, Derek Randall, whose batting technique amazes me, and Brearley were out to Alan Hurst and Rodney Hogg for 41. Australia were close to a complete breakthrough when Boycott's defensive skills and Gower's youthful audacity took the total to 199. At one point Hogg hit Gower in the neck; far from being unsettled he hit the next ball to the boundary.

In the sixth Test at Sydney, where runs were hard to come by, he was second top scorer, and Brearley, with his customary scholarly reserve, was acknowledging Gower as a minor genius capable of becoming a major genius. Even the hard-to-please Aussies sat up after a remarkable 101 not out in a one-day international on the vast Melbourne ground. With the last ball to be bowled and seemingly every possible scoring lane sealed off with practically every fielder on the boundary he still found a way through. The next highest score was 33, and England had been put in in conditions most favourable to the bowlers. Gower finished the Test series with the best figures on either side, and on pitches which, by general consent, were nothing like as good as they had been in my day. Indeed the assistant manager Ken Barrington put it on record that he could not have made the runs he did on his Australian tours on such surfaces.

Gower arrived in Australia with a Test century to his name off New Zealand, a score of 114 not out against Pakistan in the Prudential Trophy and a reputation in these days of advanced publicity which would have scared the wits out of many senior players. I suppose for one who hooked the first ball he received in a Test for four it was nothing to be perturbed about, but I have experienced the secret nagging fears that assail a young player expected to do well. He took to Australia in the manner born, starting off with 73 and 50 against South Australia at Adelaide. The first knock, I am told, was inclined to be careless, but the second was of genius quality. That 73 taught him a lot — of what he could and could not do. He scores heavily to third man and square on the off side, which means his selection needs to be good, and his early Test innings caused some misgivings with air shots in the direction of mid-on because he was inclined to lean back.

Back home from Australia, his form for Leicestershire was so indifferent that a well known umpire, who shall remain nameless to spare his blushes, argued that Gower would be a useless choice for the first Test against India at Edgbaston. He scored 200 not out, the first double-century by an England batsman since Dennis Amiss's 203 against the West Indies at the Oval in 1976. Only Hutton has made 200 for England at an earlier age — when he was on his way to his 364 at the Oval in 1938. Gower also completed his 1,000 runs in his twentieth Test, a feat bettered only by Herbert Sutcliffe (in the astonishingly brief period of twelve Tests), Hutton and Hammond. Since Gower was also the youngest Englishman to make a Test century since Peter May his name is constantly associated with exalted company.

In the last two Tests of the series Gower lapsed with two second-ball ducks to Kapil Dev, one of the fastest bowlers to emerge from the subcontinent, and a 7. Disappointing, but it happens to the best, and a levelling-off of performance tends to take the heat and pressures away, at least for the time being.

The way Leicestershire plucked Gower from under the nose of his native Kent — he was born at Tunbridge Wells on 1 April 1957 — will surely become one of the legends of English cricket. When Mike Turner, Leicestershire's admirable secretary-manager, wrote to Canterbury seeking permission to offer terms to Gower, he fully expected a curt brush-off. Instead, to his surprised delight, Kent replied almost by return of post offering no objection. Whatever the reason, Kent allowed a future Test player to slip through their fingers, and Kent's loss was immeasurably Leicestershire's gain. It was not as if Gower was unnoticed at school, for he was in the first XI for three years and made two centuries in his last season. His uncommon talent was spotted by an opponent playing for the Stragglers of Asia who notified Leicestershire. Before going to King's School, Gower went to Marlborough House preparatory school at Hawkhurst, Kent. Apart from Kent he could have ended with Sussex as his father, who had been in the Colonial Service in Tanganyika, preferred a post as registrar at Loughborough Colleges to one at Eastbourne.

During school holidays Gower naturally joined his parents in Leicestershire and began to play in the Second XI and in the

Under 25 competition. In 1975 he made three championship appearances and six in the John Player League, but at the time he had no clear intention of making cricket his career. Though he had three 'A' levels and eight 'O' levels he was rejected by Oxford University — in a more enlightened age he would surely have been welcomed with open arms! The law course at London University ended after a year, and again, I suspect, his heart was in cricket though he might not have known it at the time.

Luckily for him Ray Illingworth was captain of Leicestershire, and if he is not everybody's pin-up Ray was a good captain to help a fledgling to feel his way. There was lots of sound advice for Gower from his mature colleagues and the side was successful. That means a lot; if things are not going well pressures build and the dressing-room atmosphere becomes tense and strained.

Soon Gower was tagged cricket's 'Golden Boy', which has something of a familiar ring to my ears. To have such a good reputation has both advantages and disadvantages, and David Gower carries it all with a common sense which augurs well for the future. I am sure he will emerge as a true champion in every sense, and that is why I rate him as one of the finest batsmen I have ever set eyes on. His disappointments in Australia in 1979–80 suggested at times a lack of application rather than of ability, and he should be all the wiser for the experience.

9

WES HALL

Ever since cricket took root and flourished in the West Indies — if nothing else the English presence left one worthwhile legacy — they have had a record of producing high-class fast bowlers. Long before the granting of official Test status in 1928, George John took 100 wickets on a tour of England, and once he bowled a form of leg theory at the batsman's body.

There was George Francis, who was engaged as a practice bowler at Kensington Oval, Barbados; Learie Constantine, one of the most magnetic personalities ever to step on a cricket field; Manny Martindale; and many others. Constantine, the son of an overseer in a cocoa estate near Port-of-Spain — himself a noted player who toured England in 1900 — was a much respected name when I went into the Middlesex dressing-room. Even though his spectacular performance — 86 in less than an hour and 103 in an hour, as well as taking 7 for 57 — had been accomplished almost a decade before, Constantine's name was used in hushed tones at Lord's.

According to Sir Pelham Warner both Constantine and Martindale, against whom I played in the 1939 series, were at least two yards slower and with far less control than Larwood when they gave Douglas Jardine a dose of his own bodyline medicine in the Old Trafford Test in 1933. Jardine responded with a century, and Hammond was hit on the chin. By all accounts it was an easy-paced wicket. Earlier, in 1930, England batsmen in the West Indies had accused Constantine of intimidation, which seems totally out of character. Walter Robins, a superb cover himself, put Constantine as the most dazzling all-round fielder he had seen, and in his prime he must have been a formidable pace bowler.

After the war Hines Johnson, who preferred to shelter under the covers rather than leave the field in a Test at Trent Bridge, Roy Gilchrist, Wes Hall, Frank King and Charlie Griffith preceded the 1976 era, when the West Indies had no fewer than four authentic speed bowlers in England — Mike Holding, Andy Roberts, Wayne Daniel and Vanburn Holder, who owed much to his skipper Tom Graveney when he went to Worcestershire.

In my playing days it was bad enough for the opposition to have two fast bowlers, or 'frighteners' as they have become known, like Lindwall and Miller, the deadliest pair of my experience, South Africa's Heine and Adcock or any combination of Tyson, at his peak, Statham and Trueman.

For once speed took a secondary place when Ramadhin and Valentine span the West Indies into a new era of success. In 1954 my personal belief was that King bowled too many bouncers, and Hall and Griffith overdid it again on Ted Dexter's tour. That was perhaps a matter of opinion, but no fair-minded spectator could have enjoyed the liberty allowed the West Indies for ninety minutes on the third evening of an Old Trafford Test. John Edrich and Brian Close were subjected to a constant barrage of short-pitched bowling which was not only bad cricket but, in my view, totally unacceptable.

Holding emerged as one of the most impressive of his type for many years, and his feat of 8 for 92 and 6 for 57 on a lifeless Oval pitch in 1976, when the other bowlers of both teams could manage only five between them, was an epic. Yet a year before he had captured only 16 wickets in three seasons at 51 each and, understandably, had not been thought of as Test match material. Suddenly, like a snap of the fingers, he clicked. But he was still pretty much of a gamble when he was chosen for Australia, where his form decline corresponded with the team results.

In the next series at home against India he took 19 wickets in four Tests, and what he did in England is history.

Roberts — Anderson Montgomery Everton — was arguably as fast as Holding, but, in my view, became overworked playing in his native Antigua (also the home of Viv Richards), for Hampshire and for New South Wales. Daniel has had lightning bursts of speed for Middlesex, but I am afraid Charlie Griffith had a questionable action at times. Long and furious were the debates over Charlie, who took 94 wickets for the West Indies, some way behind Hall in striking rate. Colin Croft and Joel Garner were the latest in a seemingly endless line of genuinely fast West Indies bowlers.

After a good deal of thought I give the palm to Wesley Winfield Hall for his consistency over a longer period. There can be no argument about his high standing, and his awesome run up to the wicket — the very earth trembled — was one of the magnificent sights of the sixties. With a gold crucifix flying out from a gold chain around his neck, his six-foot-two and fourteen-stone frame soaked in sweat, he epitomized all that was best in West Indian fast bowling. Summed up, that can mean deadly pace, accuracy and superhuman strength allied to the sheer joy of the release of a God-given uninhibited power. Little wonder he was called the Black Panzer of the West Indies attack.

His run-up was of such ideal co-ordinated power that it suggested a monstrous smouldering anger. But he was the gentlest of giants, full of humour and fun. He could move a sightscreen, normally needing the combined effort of at least three able-bodied volunteers, with one heave of his massive shoulders. To preserve his prodigious strength he remained both teetotaller and non-smoker. In fact he never even touched tea or coffee. On match days he had steak for breakfast and dinner, and fruit, sugar and a glass of milk at lunch.

At school he was a batsman and wicket-keeper, and took to bowling for fun. 'It is still fun for me,' he said at the height of a run of forty-two Tests. 'I just bowl.' Reduced to such simplicity, this seems to mean that anyone with the right physique could run thirty yards or so and hurl a cricket ball towards a set of stumps at around ninety miles an hour. But even Hall, with his unusual gifts, did not burst into the Test scene. At nineteen on his first tour of England in 1957 he was very raw and hardly had a look in. Not only did he fail to make the Test side and complement the speed of Gilchrist, but he was given only 292 overs in all first-class matches. He took only 27 wickets at over 33 each, and he finished ninth in the bowling averages, below all the recognized bowlers.

Few destined to climb to the very top have had such a discouraging start, and he might have dropped out of the reckoning but for one of those happy accidents of fate. The West Indies toured India and Pakistan in 1958–9, and when Worrell was unable to go Hall was given a second chance. A fast bowler on India's slow pitches and in the dehydrating heat might have misgivings, but Hall was anything but dismayed, and by the end of the visit it was evident that a new fast bowling star had arisen. In five Tests in India he captured 30 wickets at only 17.66 each, and 16 in Pakistan at 17.93 each — a total of 46 wickets, and a different story from the disappointments of England. Hall and Gilchrist were a fearsome combination to the Indians — Gilchrist did not go on to Pakistan — and were described as the most hostile from the West Indies since Constantine and Martindale.

The knowledgeable, mindful of India's record against speed, needed confirmation of Hall's qualities, and it came in the home series with England in 1959–60. I was, by then, out to pasture, but my batting successors May, Dexter and Barrington soon found Hall excessively difficult to handle. After one or two bruising experiences most of the top batsmen devised and wore padded vests as protection — this was long before the arrival of the helmet. *Wisden* complained there was an abundance of short-pitched bowling, but Hall was never one of the several West Indian bowlers of the period at whom the finger of suspicion was pointed for doubtful actions. *Wisden* praised him as the biggest threat to England, a tremendously hard worker with a lovely action, genuine speed and remarkable stamina. His 22-wicket haul was the highest by either side, and his 7 for 69 in the third Test at Sabina Park — including 5 for 35 at the end of the first day — was one of the most sustained spells of accuracy in gruelling conditions of post-war fast bowling.

He was to give an even more sterling example of his superb stamina at Lord's in 1963 — the Test with the nail-biting finish when Cowdrey (who had denied Hall a complete triumph at Jamaica) went to the wicket with a broken arm.

Hall bowled at top speed unchanged for forty overs in England's second innings, conceding only 93 runs for the wickets of Mickey Stewart, John Edrich, Fred Titmus and Fred Trueman. In terms of time that represented three hours and twenty minutes of actual bowling, and 240 deliveries at a speed of between eighty and ninety miles an hour. The cricket scribes had to turn back to the last century for a comparable feat of endurance, by Tom Richardson in the Old Trafford Test with Australia in 1893.

The vital point was that Hall was as fast in the last historic over as he had been in the first, and on that evidence alone I believe he is entitled to be regarded as one of the world's best and fastest bowlers. I certainly would not have enjoyed facing him as the ball reared and kicked and thumped against the body, arms and fingers. England's heroes, Barrington and Close, were black and blue.

In the opening Test of the series Hall dismissed Edrich, Barrington and Cowdrey inside fifty minutes with as devastating a spell as it is possible to see, which played a considerable part in his side's victory. And in the last Test he rounded off with 4 for 39, which killed off England. At home it was said that Hall had 'pace like fire', a colourful phrase. He had the Aussies equally at his mercy in 1960-1, with 21 wickets, including 5 for 63 in the second innings of the Brisbane tie. He also slogged 50 in the first innings, an invaluable contribution as it turned out.

Such a dominating figure could hardly fail to catch the imagination and the Aussie public took him to their hearts wherever he played on that astonishing tour. Without doubt the mighty man was *the* personality of a party brimming with dazzling crowd-pleasing individualists like Worrell, Sobers and Kanhai. To capture the public's affection from such gods needed something extra special. The crowds adored his very largeness, his verve and vitality, his glorious menace, the thrill of his speed, and his boyish enthusiasm reflected in the field where he chased every ball as if his life depended on saving a run.

I always felt criticisms of over-rates to be out of place and not seriously relevant when Hall was in full cry, as every delivery was a separate drama. You needed time to catch the breath after each ball, and while the tempo might have been slow in arithmetical terms it could not possibly be dull when Hall was bowling. Wes had the extra yards to excite, and every delivery was designed to get a wicket. He was all attack, all action, and willingly responded to every call his captain might make. Batsmen, having survived the first onslaught, knew he had the capacity to come back without loss of speed or heart, and many a wicket was lost by going for runs when the 'Big Fella' was about due to return. How many wickets Wes gained for other bowlers is of course incalculable, but it must have run into scores.

In Australia the wickets became surprisingly slow after the second Test. When they were faster he took 15 in two matches. I am rather inclined to the view that he was guilty of too many bouncers, a criticism which can be generally levelled at West Indian bowlers. In the Caribbean I have had endless friendly arguments on what constitutes a short pitcher. England and the West Indies have a fundamental difference of opinion on what the accepted length of a short pitcher might be, but there cannot be any argument that Hall had the ability to make the ball lift off a good length. That can be a wicked ball, a flyer, and a sure wicket-taker. His general length did not give him much chance of moving the ball. The subtleties of Lindwall, the prime example of a fast bowler using pace changes and variations of swing and movement, were not for Hall. He was an out-and-out speed merchant bowling fast for the sheer hell of it. 'I never once deliberately tried to hit a batsman,' he once said, 'and when it happens I am upset for days.' I believe him entirely, as I do his next words, 'When I'm walking back I sometimes think I'll try a bouncer. Then I just bowl it. My idea is to unsettle the batsman and let him know I'm a fast bowler.'

Personally I would never have had any doubts about that! In 1962 he was timed at 91 m.p.h.; and around the same period a time check in which the ball was photographed over its flight was made with Hall, Trueman and Alan Davidson. The cameras were capable of 16,000 exposures a second, and a neon lamp, flashing away every 100th of a second, enabled the ball to be timed as well as photographed. Trueman's maximum speed was 84.6 m.p.h. through the air and 73.5 off the pitch, Davidson's 71 m.p.h. and 62.4, Hall's 85.2 and 71.4. Davidson was shown to be more accurate, though if Hall's length was less consistent than the other two he did hit a single stump five times in six balls, and once the stump was sent careering over the back of the net. The tests were made on a cold morning with an old ball, and Hall, with justification, claimed he would have been at least 5 m.p.h. faster with the sun shining and a new ball.

One of his strongest recommendations as the third highest wicket-taker for the West Indies was that his 192 wickets from 48 Tests cost only 26.38 each, a better average and striking rate than Lance Gibbs (309 wickets) or Gary Sobers (235). Hall bowled 10,415 deliveries to Gibbs's 27,115 and Sobers's 21,599. Gibbs played in 79 Tests and Sobers 93. Figures can present a distorted picture, but I think these point to Hall's greatness.

I would have given a lot to have been at Lahore when he performed his hat-trick on the 1958–9 tour, and I cannot resist quoting the account by the late Qamaruddin Butt, umpire and author. The game signalled Mushtaq Mohammad's entry into Test cricket at the alarmingly tender age of 15 years 124 days — actually a year older than was claimed at the time. Butt wrote:

Mushtaq won the motherly instincts of every woman on the ground by going to the crease in his first Test match. The whole crowd wished him well, but not the fielders who tried to crowd him out as he was hemmed by the cluster like vultures. With Mushtaq's advent to the crease Hall was beckoned to bowl to intimidate the tiny boy, which Mushtaq is. The crowd rose to its feet as Mushtaq neatly cut Hall for four . . . then in five minutes Hall got rid of Mushtaq, Fazal Mahmood and Nasimul Ghani almost in the same breath. An extra fast one struck Mushtaq on the foot and the pigmy was out l.b.w. — the batsman limped towards the pavilion in agony of pain. From now on the journey became rough.

The ship began to sink, was holed by Hall and finally sunk. Fazal was caught in slips by Sobers, and Nasim, guilty of playing a straight on a cross bat, saw his wicket uprooted. Hall danced a fandango to complete his first hat-trick. He was applauded by his colleagues at the end of a telling piece of bowling. Hall, one feels, should have chosen a more distinguished trio of batsmen as his victims but such things are not made to order. It was a culmination too of a high-class piece of fast bowling.

I can picture the incongruity of Hall, of the rippling muscles, one of the most perfect specimens of manhood it is possible to imagine, bowling to Mushtaq, 'the pigmy', who was presumably at that age still growing!

If Hall's bowling was fun to him, his batting was exhilarating to the spectators. A wide grin accompanied every scoring stroke — and, to be truthful, there were not all that many — but in 1963 he reached a maiden century at Cambridge in 65 minutes. Everything within reach was hit with joyous abandon. Earlier Trueman had also scored a hundred, and Hall received a congratulatory telegram addressed to 'Wes Trueman Hall'.

A car crash, which necessitated a knee operation, ended Hall's run of 42 Tests — itself a tribute to his strength and enthusiasm — and he was reluctantly dropped by the West Indies in March 1968.

He became Senator Wes Hall, a member of the Barbados Government, and a senior executive of the biggest brewery in the island. For me there is an enduring memory of a wonderful personality, a whole-hearted and tireless fast bowler of very high class. There have been few faster, and none able to keep going for so long or with such an even temper. I rate Wes very highly indeed.

10

WALTER HAMMOND

As a groundstaff boy at Lord's I revered the names of Hobbs, the perfectionist, Bradman, the prodigious record-breaker, Hammond, the prince of classical elegance, and Hendren, who was a big influence in my early Middlesex years. I still do. I addressed 'Patsy' as 'Mr Hendren' and it was a red-letter day when he told me it was to be 'Patsy' from then on. I felt I had been accepted.

My one regret is not seeing Hammond, still recognized as the most cultured and powerful off-side batsman of all time and second only to Hobbs, at the zenith of his powers. By 1938 when I joined him in the England team he had abandoned the hook and the drive wide of mid-on in deference, so it is said, to the wishes of his captain Douglas Jardine during the bodyline tour of 1932–3. As likely as not Hammond, regarded as a dasher in his first years, adjusted his technique in his maturity.

Also it seemed to me that as time went on he did not relish very quick bowling, though, before his maturity, the best fast bowlers of the day had been destroyed with the same facility as the spinners — and Hammond and Len Hutton were the best against the turning ball it has been my fortune to see.

I seldom went to Old Trafford without some of the older members recalling an innings of 187 by Hammond, then twenty-eight, played against the legendary Australian fast bowler Ted McDonald, then with Lancashire. Hammond drove the morning's first five balls from McDonald to the boundary, and scored his runs in what would now be regarded as the ridiculously fast time of three hours.

Hendren used to talk of a match on a dry and dusty pitch at

Bristol in 1924 when Middlesex put Gloucestershire out for 31 and in turn were bowled out by Charlie Parker, the slow left-arm spinner, for 74. The twenty-one-year-old Hammond went in at the fall of the first wicket and, in conditions which doomed every other batsman to failure, hit 174 not out in a total of 294, with a masterly display of cover driving and pulling to leg. Gloucestershire went on to win by 61 runs, with Parker completing his second 'hat-trick' in three days.

Hammond began his 85-match Test career in South Africa in 1927, and with Percy Chapman in 1928–9 — still arguably the strongest England party to tour Australia — scored 44, 28, 251, 200, 32 (run out), 119 not out and 177 in the same match at Adelaide, 38 and 16 — an average of 113.12 in the series. His aggregate of 905 remained an England record by 1979, though six Tests are now played instead of five. If I may say so my record of 562 runs, the highest for a home series against Australia, seems positively puny by comparison.

Only 'the Master' Hobbs and Hendren scored more than his 167 centuries, and included in his 50,493 runs were nine centuries off Australia, six off South Africa, three innings over 300, including 336 not out against New Zealand. He is one of the seven — Bradman did it twice — to reach 1,000 runs before the end of May, a feat not now possible with the advent of one-day competitions.

Records are one thing; the way runs are compiled is another. It was the grandeur and majesty of his stroke-play, his poise and almost regal assurance, that put him above all others. If he made a comparatively meagre score he would still charm and captivate by the flow and instinctive grace of his movements. If his innings was bigger, as it often was, he was the most thrilling adornment the game has known. His 240 against Australia at Lord's must have been vintage Hammond, the Hammond who evoked ecstatic praise from even the most hardened pro.

He made the deepest impression on me on that occasion, not for his unsurpassed cover driving — the shot the gods must have invented — but for a manner none could emulate. On a green pitch with the ball lifting England lost Charlie Barnett, Len Hutton and Bill Edrich for 31 to Ernie McCormick, the Melbourne fireman. It was a decidedly sticky position. Due to bat No. 6, I already had my pads on when from the balcony I watched the captain make his entrance. I was fascinated, and all my fears were put to rest.

Someone wrote that he went to the crease like a galleon in full sail. To me he had an emperor's tread, and everything to happen in the next six hours made me realize what a supreme artist he was, and that composure was as much a gift as a good eye or balance. He looked a cricketer from cap to toe, and I cannot help thinking it was a tragedy that he should have had one too many tours to Australia and blemished his record with an apology for his greatness.

In fact not only Hammond 'but English cricket suffered some humiliation for responding to Australia's plea for a tour in 1946–7, so soon after the end of hostilities. Hammond was forty-three, ten years above the already too high average age, perhaps a little bored, and with such thin resources realistically unable to match Australia's strength and Bradman's intensity. No longer was he able to marry the timing and effortless ease which sent the ball screaming through the covers; the reign of a champion ended with 168 runs from four Tests and an average of 21.00.

I preferred to remember the Hammond of Lord's 1938, the finest of all off-side players. His batting somehow epitomized the best dressed cricketer I ever saw on or off the field. With his silk shirt, pressed trousers, his blue handkerchief protruding from his right hip pocket to add a splash of colour, and his always whiter than white pads and boots, he was immaculate. Even his gloves were part of his dress, and it made one wonder if they were handed to him on a silver platter by a butler before he left the dressing-room. When some wrote of the charisma of Tony Greig I used to think of Hammond . . .

At the end of play Hammond was the same sartorial figure, looking as if he was tailored by Savile Row, which he well might have been. It was thought his attention to his appearance was a legacy of his father's military background. Wally was born at Dover, and was taken to Malta and China before he was eleven. He was lost to Kent, despite their understandable struggle to keep him, when he attended Cirencester Grammar School.

If time demanded a modification of his early dashing, corin-thian-style brilliance his eye remained true, his balance perfect and his judgement of length, which gave him so much time to make his shots, unimpaired. His wrists were steel-strong and his forearms powerful, and the criticism which sometimes crept into discussion about him — that he was inclined to be one-sided — was something of a fallacy. All things are relative, and if he was so powerful on the off side that did not render him impotent on the other side of the wicket. I can vouch for the ease with which he dismissed the ball off his legs, but I would agree that modern bowling techniques with the emphasis on the leg and middle stumps could well have restricted him. Bill O'Reilly bowling in that line was inclined to tuck him up, but the 'Tiger' was exceptional and made the ball bounce prodigiously.

In all probability Hammond would have made just as many runs, but like even the Don, it would have taken him longer. I am not enamoured of post-war bowling methods, which have restricted batting freedom and taken a lot of the joy and entertainment away from the game.

I can imagine a pre-Test tactical talk in these days starting with the question: how can we stop Hammond? At one time it was: how can we get Hammond out? Before the war bowlers attacked longer before turning to discreet defence. Nowadays as soon as a boundary is hit the captain moves the field to block the shot. Fielding sides are disinclined to bait a trap with runs. Clearly cricket has lost much by attritional tactics, ultra run-saving fields and slow over-rates — a ploy for which its originator Hutton must take much of the blame. My admiration for Hutton runs deep, but not for dreaming up this policy of deliberately slowing down the flow of the game.

Much of modern cricket with its varied one-day competitions, restrictions on the length of the first innings of a county match, and general defensive attitudes would have been anathema to Hobbs, Hendren and Hammond. They needed the full stage to display their artistry, which, in Hammond's case, extended to opening the bowling for England and slip fielding nothing short of wizardry. Had he not been the batsman he was there was little doubt he could have made a reputation as a bowler alone. Again he was a bit over the hill when I saw him, but he had a lovely, lithe action and was highly dangerous with the new ball.

He took 15 inexpensive wickets in his first series in South Africa and 83 in all for England. Everything came so naturally to him — he was also good enough to play professional football — that had he felt the inclination I am sure he could have taken many more wickets than he did. When I played with and against him it seemed as if he put something into his bowling only if he felt like it. Once

for Gloucestershire in 1946 he became impatient at the failure of
his main bowlers to part two stubborn opponents. 'Give me the
ruddy ball,' he said, and immediately broke the partnership with a
googly!

As a slip fielder I rate him with Bobby Simpson of Australia as
the best. When fielding near to him I was constantly amazed at the
ease with which he took the most difficult chances. The catch
phrase of the day was: 'Wally could catch a swallow in flight and
not blink an eye-lid.' Always it looked so absurdly easy that one felt
almost an impostor to be by his side. With legs widely straddled to
give him comfort throughout a long day he might to the casual
spectator have seemed slightly indifferent to the proceedings, but
no slip fielder was ever more alert, could exercise such uncanny
anticipation, or took the hardest chance with less fuss. He was
never flurried, and often pocketed the ball before many had
realized the catch was taken.

In 1928 he held a record 78, including ten against Surrey at
Cheltenham — another record for a match — and 819 in his career.
Slip catching was never made to look such a comfortable occu-
pation. He seldom spoke, made a field placing with a gesture of his
hand, and, I confess, he gave me the impression of silent boredom
and unfriendliness. Those with more erudite insights into human
nature thought his cricket was sometimes an escape from his own
complex nature.

When I am asked what Hammond was like as a person the
answer is a frank, 'Really, I don't know.' I never came to know
Hammond, which remained an acute disappointment. To become
England's captain he changed his status from pro to amateur —
that was the way of the English cricket set-up before the war — and
as a leader he lacked the ability to communicate. He was too non-
committal, and exceedingly difficult to talk to, particularly for a
young player.

Les Ames, his closest friend, clearly found a way, but he was
very reluctant to pass on the wealth of his knowledge and experience. I had an early example of his failings to find a rapport with
his team. In my first Test against Australia at Trent Bridge I was
caught at deep square leg for 102, made in the good time of 135
minutes. With Eddie Paynter I helped to put on 206 for the fifth
wicket. If I had hit my last ball from Fleetwood-Smith just a little
higher it would have been a six. Admittedly it was a rush of blood

to the head, an impulsive moment, but old heads can't be put on young shoulders. I was only twenty, and the total was 487 for 5 — hardly a crisis.

When I got back bubbling with inner satisfaction Hammond took me aside and gave me a schoolmaster's wigging. 'Don't you ever do that to me again,' he said referring to my last stroke. 'You will remember, I hope, that when you play against Australia and you make a hundred you take fresh guard, start again and rub it in.'

His words, given with chilling directness, were a real dampener, though well intentioned and sound advice in the ways of Test cricket between England and Australia. No matter how justified his criticism, I still think he should have waited until I had cooled down. A more compassionate nature would have realized I was in the clouds, and shown more understanding.

Hammond's aloofness also came through when you were his batting partner. Again I was disappointed, for there was practically no communication. It goes without saying he was a superb craftsman, an object lesson in all the true arts of batting. The ball would be sent to the boundary as if child's play, so exquisite was his timing and selection. Like Bradman he was so soon in position that he had all the time in the world to make his shots.

Without too much hero-worship on my part I felt it a privilege to be with him. But help a young partner? No. I cannot remember him coming up to the wicket to advise me on how to play a bowler, tell me what to look for or warn me of a trap being set. The silence was a new experience for me — Hendren was absolutely marvellous at making you feel relaxed and confident.

Unlike Wally, Hendren was no introvert and wanted to share his humour and know-how with his partner. The tightest situation became less grim, and I felt a better player for his guidance. 'There's an enormous amount of class talent watching today, and I hope that will be an incentive rather than a distraction,' was his greeting when I arrived for a Whitsun match against Sussex before a packed Lord's. The 'class talent' was a reference to the female spectators, and Hendren's way of not only putting me at my ease but warning me to concentrate. It was far more effective than being greeted with an admonishment to 'get your head down and don't give it away'.

Knowing I was a bit vague, Patsy's warning of the speed of two fast bowlers as I arrived was, 'I hope you've got your box on?' I got the message loud and clear.

I would have loved to have shared a dinner with Wally just to soak up the aura of the great man, but in Australia in 1946–7 when the opportunity for some fraternization was best, the only time I saw him off the field was at the pre-Test tactical talks.

There can be no arguments that he knew the game inside out and was a master strategist, but a captain has to offer more. The liaison never started. In fact the tour got off to a terrible start because Hammond and manager Rupert Howard, the Lancashire secretary, travelled separately in a Jaguar instead of being in the train — the most favoured mode of getting from place to place in those days. Norman Yardley, the vice-captain, looked after the team, which was met at the next destination by the captain and manager. On the several tours I have made to Australia, South Africa and the West Indies it was the worst example of mismanagement from the top I encountered. The players looked to the captain for guidance and it was not there. The only time we saw him was at the grounds. Hammond was bad that way.

I preferred to remember him as the stately figure on his way to the wicket at Lord's, and demonstrating the cover drive as it has never been demonstrated before or since. The Hammond who at Cheltenham scored 139 and 143 though the Surrey captain posted a cover point, two extras and a mid-off.

Many of his contempories of the late twenties and early thirties swear he was English cricket's supreme all-rounder and athlete. I would not quarrel with that judgement, for in performance and stature he was truly immortal.

11

NEIL HARVEY

One of the most fascinating facts in the story of Neil Harvey, second only to Bradman as Australia's heaviest Test scorer, is his contention that he was not naturally left-handed. In everything but batting and golfing he is right-handed, and he is the only member of the six players in the well known Harvey clan to have batted left-handed. Yet from the moment he picked up and swung a cricket bat he instinctively felt that the right way to hold it was with the left hand at the bottom of the handle.

If nature intended him to bat 'the wrong way round' it was a beneficent gesture; despite the difficulties caused by the rough patches around the off stump, there are advantages. Most bowlers detest having to change their line of direction. Maybe it is an illusion, but left-handers do seem to get more opportunities to accumulate runs on the leg side, which is usually their strength. Harvey was distinctive as a driver, and owed his twinkling footwork to the splendid coaching method of making the pupil dance down to a chalked spot without the use of a ball. He was weakest outside the off stump, partly because his cavalier approach scorned the practice of leaving the ball alone. Harvey was apt to chase, with either spectacular success or prompt failure. The purists, bless'em, deplored his tendency to fall away when square-cutting fast bowling, but again, the result more often than not was a sizzling boundary. When he was at his best I do not think there was any Australian left-hander in my time to touch him as an entertainer, not even Arthur Morris, for whom I have the highest regard.

Bowlers feared Harvey, the brilliant improvisor, the dark, dapper adventurer with the lightning footwork, who faithfully followed his innate impulse to attack. He would dance down the pitch in the pursuit of runs to meet deliveries lesser batsmen would be content to smother. In short he was the type of batsman after my own heart, and for fifteen years was a tonic to international cricket not only with his philosophies at the crease but with his cover fielding. Arguments can go on for ever on whether Harvey was better than South Africa's Colin Bland, his compatriot Alan Davidson, England's Cyril Washbrook of the unerring return, or Derek Randall. To me when a fielder reaches their class of performance a favourite is a matter of personal choice. My contribution to the debate is based on the simple fact that no placement was guaranteed to pass the swift feet and safe hands of Harvey. He saved hundreds of runs to add to the 6,149 he scored in 79 Tests for Australia.

Bradman made 6,996 from 52 Tests, and had more than twice Harvey's average of 48.41, but it is pointless to compare any batsman with the Don, who stood apart from the rest of us ordinary mortals. What put Harvey, too, apart from most big scorers was the fact that records meant little to this shy Australian. Some players could reel off their figures to a second decimal point at the drop of a hat — I knew bowlers who kept their overs, maidens, runs and wickets in their heads and have challenged scorers — but Harvey played only for his personal satisfaction, and the needs of his side. In 1952–3 his aggregate in South Africa of 834 runs from nine innings follows the inevitable Bradman and Hammond as the third highest in a series. His average was 96.66, and the highest of four three-figure innings was 205.

The first of his 21 Test centuries was in his second match in 1947–8 against India, which sealed his selection as the 'babe' of Bradman's invincibles in England in 1948. In July of that never-to-be-forgotten season he hit the first of his six centuries off England at the age of 19, when runs were desperately needed. The last was at Adelaide in 1963, but I am inclined to believe his finest hour facing English bowling left him 92 not out.

Another and very revealing side of his character and ability was shown that day at Sydney in December 1954. England had taken a thrashing at Brisbane and were very down in hope and spirit. In the meantime Tyson had worked on his shorter run, and it was crucial for Hutton and his side to get a good result. I could not take part because of a broken finger, and after much heart-searching the decision was taken to leave out Alec Bedser, though the mottled pitch and conditions suggested everything was right for him. England gambled on Tyson, Statham and Bailey for pace, with Wardle and Appleyard for spin.

On the last morning Australia wanted only 151 with eight wickets left. In a low-scoring match in which only the superb Peter May had risen over the conditions, which included a stiff breeze down pitch from Botany Bay, Australia looked odds-on favourites. Then in the second over of the day Jimmy Burke and Graeme Hole fell to Tyson, who ended with 6 for 85. The only batsman on whom the fury of Tyson and Statham made no impression at all was Harvey. Those who have called him careless and too much of a gambler at the wicket ought to have seen his barn-door defence — though when given the slightest chance he would suddenly unleash one of those enthralling strokes for which he was justly famous. A nail-biting last wicket stand with Bill Johnston took Australia to within 38 runs of victory, but the next highest score to Harvey's undefeated 92 was 16 from the No. 1, Les Favell.

I remember that Tyson bowled with an egg-sized lump on the back of his head after being felled by a bumper from Lindwall — this was before the 'Typhoon' gained his reputation — and he did not take kindly to the dressing-room suggestion that he arrange some more bumpers to ensure he would bowl as fast again.

There was another occasion when Harvey was the valiant loser, at Headingley in 1956. Again the gallant tight defence, the grim self-discipline, punctuated by the flashing strokes; not this time against blistering pace but fighting the turn and twist of Jim Laker and Tony Lock on a spin bowlers' paradise. Understandably Harvey was incensed like the rest of Ian Johnson's team by the controversial pitches of that year, when he averaged a mere 19.70 in the Tests. Yet, once again, figures were impudent deceivers, and though he failed in both innings at Lord's and Old Trafford he had the technique for the dreaded Surrey pair in the other Tests. His 39 at the Oval looks insignificant on paper, but the rain-affected wicket was at its worst in the two hours of his partnership with Keith Miller. For those able to appreciate his problems it was a classical performance.

No less an achievement were his two innings of 73 and 53 on the chemically prepared Headingley pitch of 1961, when Trueman, reducing his speed and bowling off-cutters, enjoyed his most sumptuous feast in Test cricket with 11 wickets for 88. To play one good innings on that surface of bubbling uneven heights was a wonder; to play two was a miracle.

Then, too, there was his 96 against Fazal Mahmood, the 'Pakistani Bedser' — in Pakistan Bedser was known as the 'English Fazal' — on the villainous mat at Karachi.

Yet the same Harvey shared with Bradman and the peerless stylist Victor Trumper the signal honour of a century before lunch in England, and had for himself the distinction of the fastest Test century scored in Australia since the second war. The old timers said he played cricket in the tradition of Clem Hill and Jon Darling, which raises my respect for Messrs Hill and Darling!

In 1953 when he was less shackled by conditions the full flower of his stroke play and adventurous disposition was displayed for all to see, with 2,040 runs and ten centuries, four of which came in a golden flush up to the first Test and did not include his 202 not out at Leicester. Ironically he was dismissed for 0 and 2 at Trent Bridge by Alec Bedser, but the luck was with him at Old Trafford where he scored an outstanding 122. When he was 4, Godfrey Evans of all people missed him, standing back off Bailey. Maybe fate decreed that it was time for retribution — Harvey had had trouble with Evans before. As far back as 1946, though, Godfrey had told Harvey after a splendid innings for an Australian XI against M.C.C. that he would go to England. The thought had not occurred to a quiet, almost colourless lad, who did not often venture an opinion and, from the very beginning, preferred action to words. He had not seen a Test match until he was called up for one as a player, and reached his maiden century for Australia in the unconventional way with a 5, all-run with Ray Lindwall.

In 1948 he was surrounded by illustrious names like Bradman, Morris, Barnes, Hassett, Miller and Bill Brown (who I thought ten years before was the best Australian batsman after Bradman), and his chance came in the fourth Test only because Barnes had been injured. He started at a time when the match was in the balance: Washbrook and Edrich had scored centuries, Hutton 81, and Bedser, the nightwatchman, had gone on to make 79, so England had totalled 496. Morris, Hassett and Bradman were out — two to Dick Pollard — but in the next 90 minutes Miller and Harvey scored 121. From my position in the slips I marvelled at the stroke-range and confidence of a nineteen-year-old who was able to take over like a seasoned and extra-brilliant batsman. I guessed from the way he attacked that he had been raised on pitches he could trust completely, and I remember that when he was eventually bowled by Laker he was met by an enthusiastic Bradman, who had raced from the dressing-room.

Back in Melbourne one could imagine the Harvey celebrations. In 1946–7 I had been told about an eighteen-year-old Neil, the second youngest of a family of six boys and one girl. The eldest, Mervyn, opened as a substitute for an injured Barnes at Adelaide that year, scoring 12 (played on to Bedser) and 31, and he, Neil, Clarrie, who later opened for Queensland, and Ray all represented Victoria. Mervyn, Neil and Ray were in Victoria's side which beat New South Wales in 1947 by nine wickets. Some years later Clarrie, a solid opener who scored 49 against Len Hutton's touring side for Queensland, Ray and Neil all made Sheffield Shield centuries on the same day.

The other brothers, Harold and Brian, were also with Fitzroy, and at one time the Harveys occupied the first four positions with the club in Melbourne pennant cricket. I think Neil was lucky in two respects. First, his upbringing in a cricket-mad family and the excellent facilities at his disposal; second, for all his immense talent he was surrounded by marvellous players when he first entered Test cricket. It is doubtful whether his progress would have been unduly retarded if he had been in a less powerful team, but it could have been that much harder. He took to each new grade of cricket in the manner born, from his initiation in a school side at the age of nine to the international level a decade later. There was no doubt where Neil was going, with all the encouragement he got from family, school, club and State. From the time he could lift a bat he played with his brothers. One game consisted of bowling a marble along a stretch of concrete in the back garden, with the wicket defended by a small-sized bat. Another pastime to sharpen the wits and eyes was playing cricket in a lane paved with cobble-stones, with a tennis ball which would bounce off at all angles. After that basic training orthodox spin might seem pale by comparison!

The serious training was done with Fitzroy, and in one season he was promoted three grades. To me the important point was that Neil's enterprise was never restricted by smothering techniques, despite some inevitable failures, and the size of his cap was never altered in his triumphant years, of which there were many. In his four tours of England he slaughtered any bowling of less than the highest quality, and many of the best attacks too were left in disarray. At home and overseas on all types of pitches he took 2,416 runs and six centuries off England, and was no less successful in South Africa, at least on the first of his two visits, the West Indies and India.

Neil and I share a common love for South Africa, and even if there was a come-down in 1952–3, he had such triumphant scores in two series that his centuries deserve to go on record. In South Africa, 1949–50: 178 at Cape Town, 151 not out at Durban, which turned what seemed to be an inevitable defeat into a victory, 116 at Port Elizabeth and 100 at Johannesburg. In Australia, 1952–3: 109 at Brisbane, 190 at Sydney, 116 at Adelaide, 205 at Melbourne.

One of my South African contacts sent me a newspaper cutting from East London in 1953 which carried a banner headline reading: NO COMPTON, NO HARVEY, NO NOTHING. Apparently Neil, like me on a previous tour, was not chosen for the match with Border. I was flattered to be put on the same entertainment level. Apparently on the strength of the newspaper complaint Neil was included, but did nothing out of the ordinary. East London was unlucky. In 25 innings on that tour Harvey scored 1,526 runs, which is a record for an Australian in South Africa. Outside the Tests he hit four more centuries.

On his second visit, starting with an average against South Africa in excess of 100, he experienced one of those tours in which a malignant fate takes a hand. A twice broken finger ended a run of 46 successive appearances, and as I can personally vouch once things start to go wrong there is little the victim can do. Happier results came in the West Indies, where Harvey's exquisite timing and forceful methods led to a fine series in 1954–5 with centuries at Kingston, Port-of-Spain and Kingston again — the last a double-century and a record-breaking third-wicket stand of 295 with Colin McDonald.

There were four more Test hundreds against India, his maiden appropriately in his home town of Melbourne, and the others in distant Bombay, twice, and New Delhi. His runs in India, the home of the deft-fingered spinner, must have appealed to Neil's sense of humour since he passed through his career with a reputation of not being able to pick the googly. The fact was that, like so many gifted batsmen, he had no need to do so. He was so phenomenally light and quick on his feet that he would go out to the pitch of the ball before it did its work.

In his career Harvey had 67 centuries, a high tally for an Australian. Indeed only Bradman, with 117, has more. Unless an overseas batsman migrates to English county cricket he has no chance of reaching a century of centuries, Bradman excepted. I believe Harvey would have raced to the target and amassed a mountain of runs with a county.

Harvey was not appreciated enough in his home State of Victoria to be offered a job worth his staying, and in 1958 he moved to New South Wales, then under Richie Benaud. One of Neil's disappointments was his failure to get the Australian captaincy. As vice-captain in 1961 he took over in the Lord's Test when Benaud's bowling shoulder proved troublesome. Thanks to Bill Lawry, and the bowling of Alan Davidson and Graham McKenzie on a fiery pitch, he had the satisfaction of leading Australia to victory by five wickets. Neil was the victor in that 'Battle of the Ridge', and was a capable if straightforward captain. Maybe he suffered by comparison with Benaud's well publicized dynamism. The main chance probably slipped when Harvey was vice-captain to Ian Craig in both New Zealand and South Africa. There was no comparison between Craig and Harvey as cricketers — in fact Craig never lived up to his promise. But Australia made an early decision that he was captaincy material, come what may, and Harvey, more of a personality at the wicket than off the field, was overlooked. He had to wait ten years before he was given the chance to lead Victoria, for whom he played for sixteen years.

When I first played against Neil I thought he looked so boyish he might have been a truant from school. He always retained his mild, soft-spoken manner — though heaven knows he could be violent enough with a bat in his hands.

For his immense contribution to cricket Neil was deservedly awarded the M.B.E., and since 1967 he has been a Test selector, rising to the position of chairman.

12

SIR LEN HUTTON

One glance at Len Hutton's stance at the crease was enough to recognize the classical batsman. Perfectly positioned to go either forward or back, he was balanced, co-ordinated, comfortable and composed, and carried an aura of dignity. Alec Bedser's bowling action was sculptured, and it was a pity Hutton's still grace at the wicket was not also captured in this art form — or his cover drive which, like Wally Hammond's, I could watch for eternity.

Later, looking at the bolt upright stance with bat wagged above the ground favoured by Tony Greig and Mike Brearley, and Derek Randall's constant impatient movements, I thought of the contrast with Hutton, and of the fate that would have befallen them facing Ray Lindwall and his yorker.

Hutton's stance was symptomatic of a batsman who had cultivated his natural genius and mastered every technique. He was faultlessly correct to the last detail, particularly in defence, and he is unquestionably one of the immortals to be put alongside Hobbs and Hammond. Though, to my mind, Peter May emerges as the greatest English all-round batsman of my generation, until Peter's arrival in full maturity Hutton had strong claims to be considered the finest batsman in the world.

He has the figures to back the contention. Between 1934 and 1960 he amassed 40,140 runs from 814 innings, and hit 129 centuries, of which 19 were for England. But for the war, these figures might well have been a third as large again. Our careers ran parallel: we played in the 1937 series against New Zealand — I made my Test debut in the final match, after Len had scored 100 in his second at Old Trafford — and we toured together in Australia, the West Indies and South Africa. I played under his captaincy, and from first to last I had the utmost admiration for him both as cricketer par excellence in the way he fought with stubborn dedication for England — particularly in the West Indies in 1954 — and as a modest and decorous man off the field. Our bond was strengthened when we both scored centuries in our first Test against Australia, in 1938. But this does not mean I understood him, and least of all why he often did not make the utmost use of his towering gifts. I will at once be accused of Middlesex bias against all things Yorkshire . . . south is south, north is north, and ne'er the twain shall meet and all that. Temperamentally I suppose we are opposites in many ways, and it was sometimes said our differing styles were complementary. Yet it is my sincere belief that Len, who had every scoring shot in the book, for some reason kept his wonderful ability on tight rein.

There can be no argument that he was supreme (and the bravest) among all world-class batsmen since Hobbs and his own mentor Herbert Sutcliffe on sticky wickets. His concentration, unmatched skills and dead bat could defy the worst conditions and the best bowling. At Brisbane in 1950 he made 8 not out batting at No. 8 (but that is another story) and 62 not out at No. 6, when England lost by 70 runs on an impossible pitch after Bedser and Trevor Bailey had bowled out Australia for 228 on a blameless one. At the Oval in 1950 in almost equally taxing conditions, with England facing a 500 total and against Sonny Ramadhin and Alf Valentine (who spun the ball so much that blood oozed from his fingers), he carried his bat for 202. As I stayed for a while before being run out I can vouch for an innings which any leading batsman would be grateful to play once in a career.

His class was way, way above all but a tiny few in any era, but to me it was all the more puzzling that he remained suspicious and defensive and allowed all types of bowlers to dictate to him on good wickets when he should have been the boss. Trundlers who ought to have been shivering in their boots as they ran up would be treated with respect. When I batted with Len in one of our few big partnerships against the West Indies at Lord's in 1939 I was enthralled by his skill and attacking range, and as the years went by and I watched him plod against inferior attacks I could not fathom why.

In 140 minutes we put on 248 for the fourth wicket, including 51 in 25 minutes, and I remember Len driving the fast bowling of

Martindale and Hylton back over their heads. Learie Constantine was then past his best, but he was shrewd, and the leg-break bowler Cameron was by no means the worst around, but none could contain Len. Looking up the record I find he hit twenty-one fours and myself sixteen, and I could scarcely keep pace with his driving and cutting. He made 196 in that spanking innings.

During the intervals I remember appeals being broadcast for National Service volunteers, and by the last Test at the Oval, which was so often the setting for Len's triumphs, Europe was girding itself for Hitler's war. Depression and dread of the future were mingled with relief that the uncertainties were to end. But for a while we sat on the dressing-room balcony drinking the heady wine of Hammond and Hutton, who had a match aggregate of 238 for once out, and forgetting Hitler. At 88 an hour they put on a record 264 for the third wicket, and Hutton never lagged behind Hammond. Earlier in that ominous summer Hutton hit 141 off Somerset in 160 minutes.

My final example of what he could do to any class of bowling if the mood took him was at Sydney in 1946. By his own scoring standards it was only a tiny gem, 37 runs out of 49, but for 20 minutes the older spectators relived the glories of Victor Trumper. The Don said he wasn't too worried, as scintillation of that order could not logically last. He was, of course, right, but for once Hutton had escaped from the imprisonment imposed by the perfections of his own technique and allowed his unfettered talent to soar to the sky.

I wonder deep down if the restrictions he imposed on himself were the real Hutton; whether he was much handicapped by the war injury to his left arm, or if the growing responsibilities of England and Yorkshire rested too heavily upon him. In 1950–1 in Australia — my horror series — Len *was* England's batting. His Test average was 88.83, twice that of Miller, Australia's leading batsman. And he was on the losing side!

Now and again he would discard his workaday overalls and don glittering robes befitting his genius. At Adelaide in 1947 he and Cyril Washbrook answered a bumper onslaught by Ray Lindwall and Keith Miller with 87 in 57 minutes, of which Hutton made 50. Len did not often hook after the war, but he did so with a vengeance on that memorable occasion. Could he bat when he let himself go!

Hutton must be the pre-eminent Yorkshire batsman, and though my verdict may appear harsh in the light of his achievements and ranking, I honestly believe he could have been even greater than he was. What held him back on so many occasions to smother his genius? I have mentioned his accident in an army gymnasium, and the charges made on him, but in the final analysis I am inclined to blame a native prudence in his psychological make-up; an unjustified caution in the marrow of his Yorkshire bones.

A dash of adventure is seldom to be discovered in the hard school of Yorkshire cricket. It is fundamentally serious, and has many virtues which are passed on like treasured heirlooms. Hutton was made to feel conscious of his inheritance. Like George Geary and Peter May, Hutton at 14 was told by the Yorkshire coach George Hirst there was nothing he could be taught of batting techniques. At the same age Herbert Sutcliffe said he was good enough to play for most counties, which I believe must have been true. Also at fourteen Hutton watched the Don make 309 in a day at Headingley. What ideas must have gone through his mind as the bowling of Harold Larwood, Maurice Tate, George Geary and Dick Tyldesley was cut to ribbons! Eight years later at the Oval Bradman from cover beat Joe Hardstaff to be the first to shake the hand of the new holder of the world's record individual Test score.

Bradman made 334 in 383 minutes (the first 200 in 214), and Hutton 364 in 797 minutes, Hutton began at 11.30 on the Saturday morning and, taking in some interruptions for rain and bad light, was out at 2.30 on Tuesday afternoon when the total was 770 for 6. By then he had hit 35 boundaries, fifteen 3's, eighteen 2's and 143 singles, and shared in a record second-wicket stand of 382 with Maurice Leyland, 135 for the third with Hammond and 215 for the sixth with Hardstaff.

My contribution to England's declared total of 903 for seven and victory by an innings and 579 runs was to make 363 runs fewer than Hutton and take one catch in the two Australian innings; and I didn't get a bowl. But I did revel in Hutton's skills, wonder at the inexhaustible patience, discipline and concentration in only his second year of Test cricket. England had started the match one down and Hammond, on winning the toss, told Hutton to go out and stay there on a perfect batting pitch, which made tactical sense. Time did not come into the argument and much of the

praise for Hutton was stinted. It was all too easy to disparage his
feat on the grounds of a too-perfect pitch and Australia's indifferent bowling. But they had Bill O'Reilly; and it was still possible
to play over the top of a straight ball as I discovered to my cost!

Most batting records are set up in conditions favouring the
batsman; when Gary Sobers eventually passed Hutton's score
with 365 not out there was nothing wrong with the Sabina Park
pitch, and Pakistan were reduced to three bowlers. Old players
have told me that Percy Chapman, England's captain at
Headingley in 1930, persisted with an attacking field around and
behind the bat, though Bradman consistently scored in front of the
wicket.

Back at Hutton's home town of Pudsey the parish church rang a
peal of 364 chimes, and the delight of Hutton's fellow Yorkshire-
men in the England dressing-room — Maurice Leyland, Arthur
Wood, Hedley Verity and Bill Bowes — understandably knew no
bounds. I don't remember Len saying much. He had a droll,
quaint humour as was typified during one of our uncommonly few
stands for England. During a crisis period in Willie Watson's Test
at Lord's in 1953 Ray Lindwall and Keith Miller were giving us
hell with some of the best and most sustained fast bowling I ever
faced. We just couldn't afford to get out, and the Aussies were
sensing it — just one wicket and a breakthrough to victory.
Tension mounted to a point when you could almost feel it crackle.
When Len called me down the wicket I thought it was to point out
a trap being laid for me, or to watch for Lindwall's yorker, a word
of encouragement, or at least a tactical profundity from that
shrewdly analytical cricket brain of his. Instead I was surprised to
hear, 'What are we doing here? Surely we could have got better
jobs than this?' Typically Hutton.

When he became captain he gained a reputation among the
media for side-stepping awkward questions with a bland counter-
question. First there would be the pause while the point was given
serious thought, and at length would come something out of the
blue like, 'What car are you running now?' or, 'Have you had your
holidays yet?' More than one experienced correspondent, hotly
pursuing a line of questioning, would be thrown by this unusual
tactic, which might well have been envied by a harassed politician.
But it would be unfair to suggest that Hutton, the first England
professional captain, did not conduct his public relations well. If

unorthodox he could show tact and diplomacy, be frank and share a dry wit. And he could also bewilder.

As a captain he was more efficient than inspiring, a long-term strategist rather than a tactician. Once he had embarked on a planned course he followed it with single-minded determination. His fiercest critic could never justly accuse him of irresolution. The very fact that he was England's first professional captain put him in an invidious position, the object of microscopic scrutiny, and vulnerable to those unable to come to terms with the historic break with tradition. Undeniably there were times when an obdurate Hutton seemed to represent their worst fears, but he could reply that he was no tougher than Bradman or Jardine, and if they wanted England to win some flat periods would have to be endured as the grand design took shape. My major quarrel with his tactics was that he slowed the tempo and natural rhythm of the game down with a bad over rate, and preferred the batting grind to defeat the bowling before attack. He was inclined to have fixed ideas, but to the public he brought results and ended Australia's post-war dominance. And for that they — and I — were grateful. Deservedly he was the second to be knighted for his services to cricket, and the first professional to be elected to M.C.C. membership before his retirement.

He was fortunate in one vital aspect: his reign coincided with a golden age of English bowling. He had been on the receiving end of bumpers from Lindwall and Miller, but his dream of retaliatory weapons arrived with Trueman, Statham and Tyson. Bedser was still a potent force, Trevor Bailey was a significant all-rounder, and there was the devastating slow bowling of Laker, Lock, Wardle and Appleyard. In quality, depth and variety Hutton had the bowling resources to lay the cricket world at his feet.

Beginning with the relaxed demolition of India by 3-0 in 1952, he regained and retained the Ashes in the next two series, gained a remarkable draw in the West Indies, beat New Zealand twice, including their dismissal for 26 at Auckland, and somehow contrived to lose to Pakistan at the Oval and draw a series which should have been a formality. His record of 12 victories and 4 defeats in 24 Tests well satisfied England. To my mind his comeback in the West Indies in 1953–4 was as good as anything he did. Before the first ball he told us the West Indies before their own fanatical followers were the toughest side in the world to overcome. To begin with there were the three W's, Weekes, Worrell and Walcott, then Ramadhin and Valentine, Dennis Atkinson, Garry Gomez and Jeff Stollmeyer. A young unknown named Garfield Sobers was brought in for the final Test.

What we had not foreseen was the unbridled fervour the series would provoke, the rumours which flew around the islands like seeds carried by an unfriendly wind — and Trueman! In no time Hutton was engulfed by problems. Two defeats tore apart the team which had proudly won the Ashes the previous summer. Most captains would have given the situation up as beyond control, but that was not Hutton. He won the third Test in British Guiana, where there was a riot, drew the fourth, and went to Jamaica still one down and with the odds very much on the West Indies when Stollmeyer won the toss. On a hard, firm wicket the West Indies were astonishingly dismissed for 139. Candidly we had expected a 500 total when we took the field, but Trevor Bailey, making superb use of a cross breeze, took an unbelievable 7 for 34.

Hutton proceeded regally to score 205 out of 414, and finally England won by nine wickets and squared the series. In 532 minutes under a blazing sun against a splendid and balanced attack Len did not make a mistake, and his concentration was not even upset by one of the most unfair incidents it has been my misfortune to witness. Having batted for nine hours Hutton went in to tea eagerly looking forward to a cup of tea, his customary cigarette, and a complete change of his sweat-soaked clothing. Suddenly the dressing-room door was flung open and an official shouted to manager Charles Palmer, 'This is the crowning insult.' Asked what all the fuss was about he said that Len had insulted Jamaica's Chief Minister, the late Alex Bustamante. The burden of the complaint was that Hutton had passed the Chief Minister, who was among the throng applauding him on his return from the field, without acknowledgement. Believe me, at such moments one is exhausted and all that is seen is a sea of faces.

Hutton was accused of being 'ill-mannered' and a lot more and the atmosphere in the dressing-room during those twenty minutes was dramatic, tense and upsetting. The England players were incensed that an innocent Hutton should be pilloried, and he was so upset that he was out without adding to his score. Though Mr Bustamante denied he had been insulted, and later had a drink with Hutton, a version of the incident was front-page news the next morning. I believe that was one of Hutton's finest innings, and the stuff of his character. For all the turmoils of the tour he averaged 96.71 in the Tests, and I was a long way second with 49.71.

Hutton's records abound: he shared an opening stand of 359 with Cyril Washbrook in the rarefied air of Johannesburg in 1948; twice he carried his bat through an innings against Australia; and his career average of 55.51 from 40,140 runs exceeded Hobbs, Hendren, Cowdrey and, I might add, Compton. In June 1949 he scored a record 1,294 runs in a month, including three successive ducks!

Yet I still believe Sutcliffe was right when he said at the beginning that Hutton had as many shots as Bradman or Hammond. To me it will be an eternal mystery why he did not use them more often, and end as the undisputed champion.

13

DENNIS LILLEE

Cricket has had, I suppose, fractionally faster bowlers than Dennis Keith Lillee. As I have written elsewhere, it is impossible to believe anyone, before or since, generated more speed than Frank Tyson did for three Tests in Australia in 1954–5. For subtle pace changes no one measures up to Ray Lindwall, the past master of the art. Keith Miller, Wes Hall, Peter Heine, Charlie Griffith and Andy Roberts all invoked plain fear. But Lillee emerges as one of the select few of the century able to bowl with a beautiful menace, venom and hostility, to make the bravest batsman afraid. He inspired universal admiration for his determined fight back to match fitness after a serious back injury which would have meant the end of a career for lesser mortals.

As I saw it, Lillee also became the archetype of aggressive Australian virility, which sometimes overspilled into the type of verbal assault the game should find intolerable. I find no amusement or excuse for an outburst which Dennis Amiss was once obliged to endure at Melbourne. For a time, too, there was an unhealthy excitement among Australian crowds when he bowled in partnership with Jeff Thomson. Lillee was clearly thinking of his image of the independently minded character going his own way when he flouted convention by asking the Queen for her autograph during the ceremonial presentation at the Melbourne Centenary Test. Dennis is far too intelligent not to know the Queen does not do such things, and his action highly embarrassed many Australians.

In the same match he bowled like a man possessed, and rightly became a national hero as the match-winner. I honoured his bowling triumph, and I would not become too heated in trying to disprove that Lillee and Thomson, with Max Walker as the back-up, formed the deadliest of all bowling combinations. Certainly England's batsmen in Mike Denness's ill-fated tour of 1974–5 would be inclined to support that contention. Of the 108 wickets falling in the series Lillee and Thomson shared 58; when Thomson was out of the sixth Test with a shoulder injury, and Lillee retired with a bruised foot after only six overs, England, who had been swamped until then, won by an innings and 4 runs.

I think the essential difference between the Lillee – Thomson and Lindwall – Miller spearheads could be found in a sustained physical aggression. Lindwall and Miller would have their bursts of bumpers and torrid spells, but the modern pair, particularly in 1974–5, scarcely let up. At Sydney even Geoff Arnold, the No. 11, almost had his hair parted by the first ball he received from Lillee. *Wisden* declared that Lillee bowled with a hostility bordering on savagery. I quote from John Thicknesse's observations in *Wisden*:

> When Thomson and Lillee were bowling the atmosphere was more like a soccer-ground than a cricket match, especially at Sydney, where England's batsmen must have experienced the same sort of emotions as they waited for the next ball as early Christians felt as they waited in the Colosseum for the lions. Passions were additionally roused by the fact that during the season Lillee had published *Back to the Mark*, a book in which he openly admitted that when he bowled a bouncer he aimed to hit the batsman and make him think twice about the wisdom of going on batting.
>
> No fast bowler had been as explicit as that in print (although it stands to reason that a bouncer has to be straight to be effective), and there was no doubt that the comment played its part in provoking the exultant chants of 'Lill . . . lee, Lill . . . lee' from the jam-packed Hill that accompanied him along the thirty-yard walk to his mark, and up the first half of his run-up . . . to be followed by an expectant hush as he neared the bowling crease.
>
> It would have needed umpires of much self-confidence to interfere with this Roman holiday, and Tom Brooks and Robin Bailhache did not possess it.

As would be expected Australia scornfully rejected all English complaints as 'Pommie wingeing' — much as England had described the bitterness of bodyline as 'Aussie squealing'. It is a curious commentary on human nature that the most strident and hysterical voices are always heard. The Aussies also declared that it had been England who had started a bumping war. I have but two observations to pass. One, I was, in common with many, surprised the Australian Board took no action (or at least made it public if they did) over Lillee's book; two, it has since often occurred to me that Kerry Packer's interest in cricket might have been aroused by the dramatic events and atmosphere created by Australia's unusually belligerent attack.

With a ninety-mile-per-hour missile flying towards the rib-cage, or leaping towards the skull, batsmen began to think in terms of self-preservation and gradually the helmet made its appearance. As I still believe the best defence to be counter-attack (assuming the ball to be within reach — if not it is logical it should be deemed a wide), nimble footwork and a resolution not to be intimidated come what may, I doubt if I would have taken to a helmet, not out of a foolhardy bravery, but because a bat is still the best weapon and I liked to be free from encumbrances. Helmets do strip players of their personality, and all tend to assume an anonymous similarity, like robots. What really surprises me is their use against medium-pace trundlers, whom the likes of the Don and Peter May could have played with a tram ticket. I suppose I betray a nostalgic, reactionary spirit when I say I cannot picture Jack Hobbs with a helmet!

It is also interesting to speculate whether umpires of the calibre of Frank Chester or Sid Buller would have controlled the type of inflammatory situation which has developed in recent years. I am inclined to think bowlers would have respected their high standing more, and 'tried it on' far less. There was more respect for authority, especially in Chester's day; if he had said 'cut it out' it would *be* cut out and no two ways about it.

If I am not wrong Lillee was not averse to controversy and promoting his image of an ogre on the field — all in the cause of cricket, of course! Any bowler gaining a psychological advantage over a batsman is obviously half-way to bagging his wicket. Trueman's ploy was to pay a bluff and hearty visit to the opposition dressing-room and, looking round, predict five wickets already in his pocket!

A leading Australian official once described Lillee to me as a gentleman off the field and a raging lion with toothache on it, a regular sporting Jekyll and Hyde. I also think Dennis liked to nourish the stories of his ferocious determination.

Subtract all the trimmings, real or exaggerated, and what is found? The answer is simple and conclusive: a brilliant fast bowler with a perfect action, who developed from a raw fifteen-year-old with Perth Cricket Club to the undeniable status of world class, and one of the greatest of the century. For me Dennis, born at Perth on 18 July 1949, stands apart from all other Australian fast bowlers since Lindwall and Miller, and even above his superb team-mate Thomson. How is it possible to separate the two? The margin may be slim and arguable, but I believe Lillee worked harder to perfect all-round skills. Thomson is an original. His strength and speed spring from abnormally powerful shoulder muscles, and he has the rare ability of making the ball leap like a cobra's strike off a length. Batsmen find the ball suddenly and unexpectedly 'takes off' with bewildering venom and pace. He does not need to 'dig it in' short of a length to make the ball rear — an almost frightening gift, particularly on a fast surface. Colin Cowdrey, from the experience of a record 114 Tests, said he had never known anyone able to make the ball rise so steeply. I well believe him. 'Thommo' is the type of character only Australia could produce. As a soccer player in Sydney he was suspended *sine die,* and he spends an enviable amount of time on the beach and deep-sea fishing! His laconic comment on seeing David Steele arrive at the wicket for his first Test at Lord's was, 'Cripes, they've sent in Groucho Marx!'

Life does not seem over-complicated for 'Thommo'. For Dennis, I suggest, it's been a harder battle if only to regain his strength and purpose in 1973 and 1974 when he had to overcome four stress fractures in the lower vertebrae. Obliged to be in a plaster cast for six weeks he was generally written off as a serious bowler of the future. Those who thought he had been cut off in his bowling prime, however, had not reckoned with the spirit and determination of an unusual man. His fight back took an arduous and gruelling path, starting as a batsman. Finally in 1974 he was ready to resume bowling. The rest is history. England's innocently begun adventure ended in destruction. A piece of pride was salvaged in the last Test, which served only to demonstrate what Lillee and Thomson meant to Australia. Two wickets were down when Lillee limped off, and the next three wickets produced 149,

192 and 148. Until then England had boasted of but one century stand in five Tests. Lillee and Thomson had sparked a side into inspired catching and fielding. They had put England on the rack. Yet without them both Australia (even allowing for a general easing off) and England were different sides. What more graphic evidence could be presented of the might and stature of a pair who are already a legend?

No cricketer can expect to get anywhere without drive, ambition, and the ability to ride hard knocks and disappointments. He must push himself beyond natural limits. There is no doubt that Dennis had from the start all the accepted requirements in abundance, plus height, strength, co-ordination and a perfect action. He never liked batsmen — at least, not until he saw their backs on the way to the pavillion — and aggression became his natural ally. Fired by the example (none better!) of Western Australia's own Graham McKenzie, a gentle giant, and inspired by Wes Hall, Alan Davidson and Freddie Trueman, he was always destined for stardom.

He entered Test cricket when John Snow ruled the roost and Australia were searching desperately for an answer to Ray Illingworth's success. In the State fixture at Perth he had delivered the broadest of warnings to England of the shape of things to come. In fact England's party could not fathom why Australia persisted with Alan 'Froggie' Thomson, a bowler they did not think in the same street as Lillee. Then Lillee inclined to a sprawling run and like most raw fast bowlers was obsessed with speed and little else. Cricket, however, is a wonderful freemasonry, and the advice of Lindwall and Davidson, among others, ironed out some technical imperfections. He had already been sent to New Zealand with an Australian 'B' side under Queensland's Sam Trimble — incidentally Lillee's first Sheffield Shield victim — and he topped the averages above 'Froggie' Thomson, Graeme Watson and Dave Renneberg. Perth's notoriously fast wickets were clearly not to Lillee's disadvantage.

In his maiden Test at Adelaide in 1971 Lillee had the wickets of John Edrich, Alan Knott, Ray Illingworth, John Snow and Bob Willis for only 84 — in a total of 470 — and though his contribution in the final match at Sydney was a modest three wickets he had placed the thorn in England's flesh. But few were prepared for his exciting impact in the following season. With South Africa's visit cancelled Australia met the Rest of the World, and in the second representative match on his home ground at Perth he had 8 for 29, including the astonishing spell of 6 for 0. Among his victims were Sunil Gavaskar, Farookh Engineer, Clive Lloyd, Gary Sobers and Tony Greig, which dispels any notion that the opposition was hotch-potch and of no consequence.

A turning-point — to use his own words — was the season he spent with Haslingden in the Lancashire League. As with so many overseas players grooming themselves for stardom, a spell in northern competition not only familiarized Dennis with English conditions, but essentially contributed to his ever-expanding skills. Above all he learned the value of accuracy — to bowl a fuller length, and to use the ball more adroitly. Sometimes he was obliged to slow down and just concentrate on direction and movement off the pitch. If it was a new experience for him it proved of immense benefit in 1972, under Ian Chappell, when he was Australia's principal bowler with 31 wickets at only 17.67 apiece. His outswinger was late and fast, and with his flowing hair and Mexican-style moustache he was a flamboyant figure as well as the quintessence of a rhythmic human bowling machine. His action and run-up were perfection — quite beautiful unless you were at the receiving end twenty-two yards away. As he loosened up in the dressing-room he started in top gear. Perhaps his manifest dislike for batsmen started there!

After the first Prudential Cup in 1975 Australia stayed on in England for four Tests, and Lillee and Thomson, though conceding the world cup to the West Indies, were the magnet, a compulsive and compelling twin force. Thomson was inclined to be erratic at times, and Lillee for once took a pasting from the little left-hander Alvin Kallicharran in the Prudential Cup at the Oval. Kallicharran, a diminutive five-foot-four and a veritable dwarf alongside the Australian, took 35 off Lillee's last ten deliveries, with a six and seven fours. Lillee dismissed him in the end, and during the onslaught there must have been a fleeting thought of the other occasions when he had been on the receiving end — Gary Sobers's 254 at Melbourne, an innings described by the Don as one of the greatest ever played in Australia, and Barry Richards's 356 for South Australia at Perth.

But in 1975 it needed the firmest resolution by England's batsmen to survive. Taking 21 wickets he was astonishingly accurate for his pace, and to make it hotter still he moved the ball either way off the seam. His 100th Test wicket was taken against the West Indies, who were equally punished, and in the nostalgic yet furiously contested Centenary match Lillee once more left the stamp of his genius and enthusiasm. In the first innings he wrecked England with 6 for 26, and when Derek Randall led an historic recovery with his innings of 174 it was Lillee, with 5 for 139, who took Australia to victory.

The Lillee – Randall duel will never be forgotten by those privileged to be on the ground. In a way it typified the struggles of the two countries for 100 years. The jaunty Randall, by no means overawed, answered one bouncer with a tennis-style smash which went like lightning to the mid-wicket boundary. Randall doffed his hat and bowed politely to Lillee after another short pitcher, and when knocked to the ground by a bouncer performed a defiant reverse roll to the delight of the crowd.

Randall was selected Man of the Match, but the real victor was Lillee, the man chaired off by the Australian players.

Happily we old players, drawn together for a misty-eyed occasion, and the cricket-loving public were blissfully ignorant of the clandestine negotiations to set up World Series Cricket. Unhappily, to my mind, Lillee was hired to the Packer camp. I cannot pretend to like or understand what was done as I was brought up in a different age with different standards.

But I salute Dennis Lillee the bowler. He stands high among the great fast bowlers of all time.

14

RAY LINDWALL

My old Middlesex skipper John Warr wrote in *The Barclay World of Cricket* that if granted one last wish in cricket he would settle for the sight of Ray Lindwall opening the bowling in a Test match from the Nursery End at Lord's. While appreciating his reasons, I doubt if his sentiments would be shared by those whose business it was to try and take runs off the greatest fast bowler I played against.

In my World XI from any era the name of Raymond Russell Lindwall would be the first to be entered as the bowling spearhead. Whether on the faster pitches of Australia or in the heavier atmosphere of England, where he did everything but make the ball sit up and beg, he was the supreme fast bowler, the quickest over a spell and the most controlled I ever faced. Having had considerable experience of his qualities both at home and overseas I find it hard to believe any age has produced a bowler of authentic speed with so many facets of the bowling art at his disposal, or able to conserve his energies so well. The late Sir Pelham Warner, whose experience bridged many generations, was moved to murmur 'sheer poetry' when he first watched Lindwall's majestic thirteen-pace run-up to the wicket. The description was exactly right. Lindwall was a poem of graceful movement and aroused in me the same emotions as a thoroughbred in full gallop, a cover drive by Hammond, a square cut by Rohan Kanhai or a dribble by Stanley Matthews on the soccer field. Just as Tom Graveney was a cultured sight at the crease so was Lindwall in his approach. Every fibre and muscle co-ordinated, and the gradual acceleration was in itself a threat. His pace was generated by the perfect synchronization of the strength in legs and back muscles, and his arm, as it should be, was merely the final instrument of his action.

His arm was lower than a coach would recommend, and it puzzled me that by 1950 he was able to add the inswinger to his repertoire, one which dipped in late and invited the hurried shot to his short legs. When he was in the Lancashire League his slip catchers understandably found it hard to take the lightning snicks off the bat, so he perfected the delivery moving in to the right-handed batsman. In the main his line was classically off stump, or around off stump, but he was perfectly capable of the restricting attack on the legs.

The position of his arm at the point of delivery was not only another example of the privileged unorthodoxy of the genius but had the effect of causing the ball to skid through at an awkward angle of flight. Yet it would lift off a length. Both his yorker, which swung late, and his bouncer should have been the exclusive property of the devil himself and not of a thoroughly likable and chivalrous opponent. His yorker would be slipped in when it was least expected, and I had a lot of sympathy for Graveney, who was unfairly criticized when Lindwall bowled him at Lord's in 1953. Tom had batted like a dream for 78, and was yorked first thing on the following morning before the new ball was available. No blame should have been attached to Graveney. Instead Lindwall deserved high praise for being able to produce a deadly swinging yorker before Graveney had a chance to settle in. It is a fiendish delivery to have to stop.

I followed Graveney and my partner Hutton and I had a torrid time against Lindwall and Miller, as redoubtable a pair of attacking bowlers as ever stepped on a cricket field. In the spell I did not get a 'sighter' or a single ball I could safely let alone from Lindwall, and the pressure never relaxed. It was speed bowling of a quality and dimension only they could turn on. Problems abounded when facing Lindwall, as his bouncer was delivered with precisely (or so it seemed to me) the same action as his slower ball, which was usually an outswinger. He disguised everything and had two outswingers — one starting early and the other late. At times Miller could produce a faster delivery, but his head-down charge to the wicket betrayed his intention to unleash a bumper. If too short it would fly harmlessly out of range, as if he had put on a display of mock anger for the benefit of the crowd.

Lindwall's bumper was different, deadlier and more accurate. It was pitched farther down the wicket, with a lower trajectory, leapt to between chin and throat height and was unerringly directed over the middle stump. The chance of evasive action was reduced to the minimum by the speed, length and course of the ball. A split-second decision had to be made, and it was not surprising so many batsmen were forced into hurried, ill-judged strokes. Its accuracy meant you had to be definite: either get out of the way, by ducking low, or hook. In the immediate post-war series English batsmen were new to genuine speed, and believe me, it could be a terrifying experience to face his bumpers. Pace variations — 'shades', as Sir Pelham called them — were another hazard, and in any innings against Lindwall when he was flat out in relentless pursuit of his quarry it was necessary to be prepared for speeds from around sixty to ninety miles an hour, blockhole swinging yorkers, in-dippers and outswingers, bumpers and the not so innocent ball going straight through. Under a cloud cover, or a heavy atmosphere, the ball would fizz and dip like a demented thing, and his use of the Keith Carmody umbrella field heightened the tension of the batsman who was taunted to drive into the empty spaces at almost half-volley length. But the ball swung and dipped in either direction very late.

During our first encounters in Australia in 1946–7 I soon realized Ray was far from a conventional fast bowler relying on brute force and sheer speed. He had the subtleties of a slow bowler's mind, inventive and constructive, forever probing for weaknesses, and generally raised what is considered to be the labouring force of cricket to an art form with his tactical shrewdness, control and variations. He could, of course, bare his teeth and show his hostility with a bumper barrage. In common with most batsmen I believe the bouncer to be overdone, but I had no complaints when I was hit by Lindwall in the Old Trafford Test in 1948.

This was the game for which Hutton, suffering from what might be termed shell shock, was controversially omitted — he returned to make 81 and 57 at Headingley — and we had lost his replacement George Emmett and Cyril Washbrook. Lindwall, without his partner Miller, tried to unsettle Bill Edrich and myself and I took a bouncer on an arm. Then I heard 'no ball' called off another bumper and tried to change my shot into a hook. All I did was to edge the ball on to my head, and I felt as if I had been struck by a sledgehammer. There is a moment of panic and shock after being hit, and I am not surprised when some batsmen after taking a severe blow on the skull are never quite the same again.

A few days later we were presented to the Queen at Lord's. Ray's bumper had left its mark, and I was much surprised when the Queen stopped and said to me, 'Mr Compton, how is your poor head? My husband and I saw what happened on television . . . You poor boy. I do hope it's better now.'

Rather as a crashed pilot is sent up again at the first opportunity, I think it is best to get back to the wicket as soon as possible, which after stitches, a rest and a brief knock in the nets, I was able to do, getting my revenge with a not-out innings lasting over five hours. *Wisden* records that I withstood some lightning overs of extreme hostility by Lindwall. I would not quarrel with those words! Between the third and fourth Tests my Middlesex colleague Jack Robertson was hit in the face by Lindwall, who also gave Hutton and me a real roasting in the last half-hour of the Saturday of the first Test at Trent Bridge. At the time the Nottingham crowd was still sensitive to the treatment of their hero Harold Larwood, and bumpers from Australians were regarded as singularly provocative. Keith Miller bowled five bouncers in eight balls to Hutton, but we still managed 82 runs in the last 70 minutes and had a drink together after stumps.

I was none too happy during the barrage to see Bradman at cover grinning his head off, and apparently deriving some amusement and pleasure at my endeavours not to get hit by the ball flying around my head and body.

As we walked off I went to him and said, 'I saw you were enjoying yourself just now. I can't really understand why and how you were. I thought you used to say this wasn't the right way to play cricket.'

Bradman, no longer smiling, seemed a trifle uncomfortable, and answered, 'You've got a bat in your hand, haven't you? You should be able to get out of the way of them anyway. I used to love it when I played against bouncers. I used to hook them.'

Before the resumption on Monday, however, the club broadcast an apology to the Aussies which must have privately appealed to their sense of humour. Ray has had plenty of stick in his time from home crowds for bumpers which he did not shirk from using against Bradman, Hassett and Co. in domestic cricket. I believe there were too many bouncers on that occasion at Trent Bridge and far from declining this form of intimidating attack has shown notable increase in recent years. While it is not, and should not be, possible to ban the bumper its use should be controlled and positive action taken at international level. At the same time the bumper would not be so excessively used at the present time if batsmen learned to hook properly and could trust the pitches. The current experiment to restrict bouncers to one an over has much to commend it.

Lindwall's answer to any criticism levelled at his use of the bumper was in the high percentage of his wickets bowled, leg before and caught at the wicket. No fewer than 145 of his 228 wickets from 61 Tests were among the first six in the order, including 67 openers. As with Alec Bedser he felled the big game with a striking rate of around 60 balls for a wicket — high considering the wickets in Australia were vastly superior to the surfaces Mike Brearley's team had in 1978–9. On twelve occasions he took five or more wickets in a Test innings, and at Adelaide in 1947 bowled Bedser, Godfrey Evans and Doug Wright in four deliveries. Tailenders perhaps, but it represented sharp and straight bowling.

My admiration for Ray extended to his dedication and determination to remain at peak fitness. A lot went his way. He was blessed with a beautiful action, and he had a wonderful partner in Miller and the perfect back-up in Bill Johnston — a brilliant left-arm pace bowler in his own right. He was not a Bedser bearing the brunt of a load, but he could never have become the first genuinely fast bowler to take 200 Test wickets without hard work and sacrifice. Only he knew what he had to go through to reach and maintain his exceptional fitness. Standing an inch under six feet he had a sinewy strength and an athlete's frame. A champion boy athlete he was capable of sprinting 100 yards in fractionally over even time, and as a Rugby League full back he was good enough to represent New South Wales — he always maintained fast bowling was more physically demanding than football. No one had a more gruelling training schedule than Ray, who was of Swedish-Irish extraction. Starting with limbering-up exercises in the dressing-room he went through a regular routine of toe-touching and flexing the hamstring muscles before his first ball. Out of season his road work would have made a boxer blanch; he thought nothing of thirty successive press-ups without touching the ground.

When everyone but Lindwall thought Lindwall's Test career was over he intensified his routine. Every morning he furiously pedalled a stationary training cycle, ran up and down a steep hill, and used a home-made rope and pulley to strengthen his left arm and improve his outswinger. Keith Miller, telling me about his partner's routine, was full of praise; certainly Lindwall's dedication was to pay off dramatically.

He had left the Army after service in the Solomon Islands and New Guinea in less than perfect health and atebrin tablets were needed to cure tropical illnesses and suspected malaria (though this was never confirmed). The war lords of Japan had interrupted his career at the age of twenty, but he resumed brilliantly. His luck was to have Bill O'Reilly as his mentor. O'Reilly, then a schoolmaster, used to make his way home through a street where Ray and his friends from the Darlinghurst Marist Brothers school played a coarse cricket with paraffin tins as wickets. If O'Reilly stopped for a brief chat, or gave a crumb of encouragement, Lindwall's day was made. Having watched Harold Larwood from the Hill at Sydney he had already decided to be a fast bowler. Eventually he joined the famous St George's club, whose captain was O'Reilly, and here I am obliged to think young Australians have an advantage over English boys who normally can worship their heroes only from afar.

O'Reilly knew there was an uncut diamond under his charge, and electric-eye photography was used to point out flaws in Ray's technique. They were together when Australia toured New Zealand in 1945 for Lindwall's first and O'Reilly's last tour. Lindwall was also fortunate to have Bradman as his Test captain, and a profusion of high-quality bowlers around him. Bradman used him properly. In the first series with England five bowlers, Lindwall, Miller, and the spinners Ernie Toshack, Colin McCool and Ian Johnson, took 11 or more wickets, and Bruce Dooland, a leg-break and googly bowler who could have walked into another Test side, had 8 in two matches. In 1948 when the new ball was available after only 55 6-ball overs it needed only Lindwall and Johnston (27 each), Miller and Toshack, who was the run-saver between the new-ball bursts, to destroy England.

Playing a long innings against an attack of this calibre meant intense concentration without the hope of easing off, the prospect of easier runs if Lindwall and Miller were held at bay, and the knowledge that the first mistake was likely to be the last. After the hostility of the Terrible Two came Johnston, of the Bill Voce school of fast-left-arm bowlers, and later in the series Sam Loxton came in. He wasn't in the same class as the others, but he was nippy, direct and needed close watching.

Around Lindwall and Miller was built a lethal attack. Though England in 1948 reached big totals by today's standards — 441 at Trent Bridge, 363 at Old Trafford, 496 and 365 for 8 declared at Headingley — Australia's bowling was seldom under strain. Every now and again the lightning strike would cause a numbing collapse, and the worst of all was in the final Test at the Oval when Lindwall really put England on the rack with 6 for 20. There were excuses — a sodden pitch, humid atmosphere and a weakened side. Hutton was last out for 30 out of 52, and when he went to field at long leg he turned despairingly to the crowd and asked, 'Are there any fast bowlers among you?' History does not record where Tyson, Trueman and Statham were on that fateful morning! For my part it would have taken a lot of persuasion to believe that Australia's legendary fast bowlers Cotter, McDonald and Gregory could possibly have been superior to Lindwall. I hear it repeatedly said that Jeff Thomson is the fastest of all. But is he a *better* bowler?

The freak spinner Jack Iverson and Johnston were the primary wicket-takers in 1950–1, but in 1953 Lindwall took 26 Test wickets in England to Miller's 10. Both enjoyed a fabulous visit to the West Indies in 1954–5, but in 1956, when the English pitches were all for spin, Lindwall, having missed the Lord's Test — the only reasonable one of the rubber and on which he might have prospered — with a strain joined the semi-employed ranks of the fast bowlers. Trueman (9), Statham (7) and Bailey (6) were the fillers-in for the spinners Jim Laker and Tony Lock. From a mere 100 overs Lindwall had 7 wickets, and was also dragged down with hepatitis. It seemed logical to assume he was not the bowler he was and the salad days were over.

The new Australian breed were Alan Davidson, Ian Meckiff and the leg spinner Richie Benaud, and in 1958–9 Ray slipped into the background, or so it seemed, while controversy raged over bowling actions, umpiring decisions and dragging — years before, on the advice of Bradman, Ray had merely started his run farther back. Then Meckiff was injured and Lindwall, having proved his stamina and fitness for Queensland with 7 South Australia wickets for 92 in a 100-degree-plus heat at Adelaide, returned to the Test side.

To be blunt he faced an England party weary and demoralized by one disaster after another. 'I am the last of the straight arm bowlers,' he proclaimed in a Red-Indian-style war-whoop. For that England, who believed they met one thrower after another, were exceeding grateful. It was a marvellous tribute to Ray's fitness that he should make a come-back after more than two years since his last Test, and at the age of thirty-seven, which Australian cricket normally regards as close to senility. He began by adding Peter Richardson to his collection of openers, and dismissing Trevor Bailey and Colin Cowdrey in the second innings, which left him with one wicket to pass Clarrie Grimmett's record of 216 wickets, then the highest-ever aggregate by an Australian.

Perhaps it was fitting that Grimmett should not concede the record at Adelaide. It came at Melbourne. The gods were with Lindwall. Benaud won the toss and put England in to bat on a typically first-morning Melbourne pitch with green patches; Lindwall's first ball kicked off a length and Bailey was held at fourth slip. Not many at the age of thirty-seven would merit a fourth slip. In the second innings Ray yorked Bailey for a 'pair', and one of his two further victims was Peter May with an out-swinger — a reminder of the lesson handed out to the youthful Surrey batsman at the Oval, where a six-ball over consisted of six completely different deliveries. Bailey's two noughts were an irony, for he had given his wicket away at Sydney in 1955 to enable Ray to get his 100th for Australia!

If Ray's leaning had not been towards annihilation of batsmen he might well have made his mark as one. Two of his five centuries from 5,017 runs were for Australia — 118 at Barbados in the 1954–5 series when he and Miller each took 20 wickets, and 100 off England at Melbourne in 1947. England had not been doing too badly until Lindwall and Don Tallon put on 154 for the eighth wicket in 88 minutes. Lindwall's 100 took only 113 minutes, and I recall thinking any No. 9 able to drive with such thrilling power had no right also to be the best fast bowler in the world. He was a mighty dangerous batsman to lurk in the lower order. His century against the West Indies was in the quick-fire time of 145 minutes, and what interested me was that in the same Australian innings Miller hit 137 and Ron Archer, their support bowler, 98. Imagine

Trueman and Statham sharing 40 West Indies wickets and scoring centuries in the same innings. Miller also had two more centuries in the two Tests in Jamaica.

In his last five seasons he captained Queensland with the same zeal which had prompted him as a boy to play in two matches a day on Saturdays. After a boys' game he would cycle to join in a men's match after lunch. The only opportunity to captain his country came in the familiar situation in India where Australia were hit by illness and injuries. He led his side to an honourable draw at the Brabourne Stadium, Bombay.

It goes without saying he was a fielder well up to Australian standards, which is as good an accolade as it is possible to give. He was the first authentic fast bowler to break the 200-wicket barrier in Tests, needed only 23 matches to take 100 English wickets, and ultimately had 114 at 22.44. He was a fearsome bowler to bat against, but in every sense he was an adornment to the game and has set terrifyingly high standards for all young fast bowlers to emulate.

In the ten years I batted against Lindwall I could never be exactly certain what he was going to bowl next. Everything he did was concealed in masterly style, and he never allowed a moment of relaxation. He made you play the ball because he was so straight and he made the most effective use of the new ball I ever encountered. Even when he had passed his peak he was still highly dangerous. While he appeared naturally hostile to batsmen he was too cool and tactically calculating to be provoked as Miller could be.

Lindwall — unequivocally the greatest fast bowler of them all.

Alec Bedser's classic action was not only absolutely right and a delight to the eye of the purist, but it helped him to avoid stress and strain and to be able to bowl for prodigious spells. In every sense he was a captain's dream of a brilliant bowler supported by a giant frame and the heart of a lion. At a time in the post-war era when England's resources were low he was a pillar of strength and a model professional. His stock ball was the in-swinger moving at the last seconds of flight, and his leg-cutter was tantamount to a fast leg break. After his playing days he devoted his time to administration and selecting, rising to chairman of Test selectors for a record length of time. He also managed England teams in Australia, where he is immensely popular.

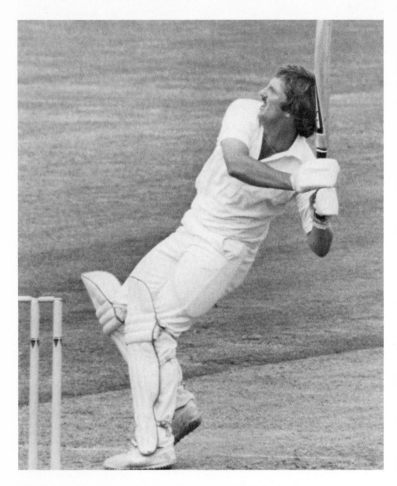

Above: All the powerful aggression of Ian Botham is shown in the completion of a savage six off the Indian fast bowler Kapil Dev in the Edgbaston Test, 1979. Now the indispensable all-rounder of the England side Botham completed the 'double' of 1,000 runs and 100 wickets in the record time of 21 Tests.

Opposite: This typical flying full-stretch leap reflects the vivacious, active, showman spirit of Godfrey Evans, one of the great wicket-keepers and characters of world cricket. When things were at their worst Godfrey could be relied on to rekindle enthusiasm and the zest for a fight. Godfrey, one of the line of Kent's famous Test wicket-keepers, played 91 times for England.

Above: Some insist Sir Jack Hobbs was better on all types of pitches, but the record of Sir Don Bradman defies comparison. On average he scored a hundred or more once on every three visits to the wicket. His appetite for runs was insatiable, and the game is unlikely to produce his equal. He had every batting virtue in abundance – eagle eye, swiftness of foot, balance, uncanny judgment, ruthless determination and a lucid brain. An unorthodox grip helped him to be a savage cutter and hooker. He firmly believed in attack, and he was one of the greatest captains. In short he gave a new meaning to the word genius.

Above: Few young batsmen have attracted such excited attention as David Gower, a left-hander with the priceless gift of timing and the spirit of challenge. In the words of Sir Len Hutton he can make batting 'look as easy as drinking tea'. Here he sweeps effortlessly to leg on the way to his maiden Test century against New Zealand at the Oval in 1978. Jock Edwards is the wicket-keeper.

Right: The bounding vitality of Wes Hall is vividly captured as, with both feet off the ground, he launches one of his famous thunderbolts. Blessed with a superb physique and strength, Hall could be frighteningly fast for long periods. With a gold cross and chain around his neck, a beautifully controlled approach and action, Wes was an awesome sight to the batsman. He ranks high among the great fast bowlers of all time.

'Our Len,' as he is affectionately known in his native Yorkshire, deservedly enjoys a distinguished place in the history of world cricket. Before the war he created a new individual Test record with an innings of 364 against Australia at the Oval. Despite a shortened left arm through a war-time accident, he continued to play a dominating role from 1946. He rates as one of the finest of all opening batsmen – correct, calm and technically near-perfect – and he became the first professional England captain. Oddly, his successes at international level, including winning and retaining the Ashes, never persuaded Yorkshire to give him their leadership.

Fast bowling is all about co-ordination and rhythm, and the athleticism and control of Ray Lindwall put him in a class apart. While able to mount a blistering bumper attack, such was his mastery of swing, swerve and subtle pace change that he lifted fast bowling to an art form. His run-up was exemplary. Gradually he gathered speed until he was at his fastest at the moment of delivery. Nothing was out of place, though his arm by purist standards inclined to be low. His alliance with Keith Miller was one important reason why Australia reigned supreme in the immediate post-war years.

Above: Deadly rivals in the middle and firm friends off the field Denis Compton, the non-striker, is probably grateful he did not have to face this express from Keith Miller in a Test in 1953. The dashing, cavalier Miller, war-time pilot, punter, fast bowler and first-class batsman, was a debonair personality and a truly magnificent cricketer – a big man of big deeds. The umpire is Frank Lee.

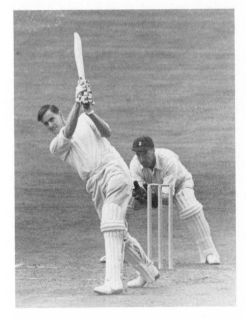

Right: Accepted by most as the finest of England's post-war batsmen Peter May had a masterly back foot technique. Here, in an innings for Surrey on a difficult pitch at the Oval against Derbyshire, he reveals the full majesty of the straight drive. George Dawkes is the wicket-keeper.

Not for nothing was the Irish–Aussie Bill O'Reilly dubbed 'The Tiger'. Standing 6 ft 3 ins tall he was an intimidating figure on the field, always on the attack and unwilling to offer any batsman the slightest respite. Despite his lumbering approach he was often described as 'the leg break bowler of the century'. His googly was apt to bounce like a tennis ball, and he had exceptional accuracy and control.

For a batsman to be the best in the West Indies he needs to be something really special. And Viv Richards, of Antigua and Somerset, is special – arguably the world's No. 1. Full of strokes, inventive and audacious, he is supremely gifted, and is pictured here in the course of his 138 not out which earned him the Man of the Match award in the 1979 final of the Prudential Cup. Bob Taylor is England's wicket-keeper.

15

PETER MAY

It will doubtless come as a surprise to the self-effacing Peter May that I rate him as the supreme English batsman of my era, which stretches back to 1936. I put him a shade in front of his own hero Sir Len Hutton because he was equally happy against all types of bowling and because he was the most brilliant player off the back foot I have ever seen, not excluding Sir Don Bradman.

May had more steel than the highly talented Colin Cowdrey, who played many notable innings but was inclined not to know his own mind. Geoff Boycott, another highly rated batsman and technician, is too complex a person for me to understand; and May punished the bad ball better than the prolific scorer Ken Barrington.

If May had been favoured with pre-war pitches, played under the old l.b.w. law, and been in the game as long, I believe he was capable of breaking all the records held by Sir Jack Hobbs and being acclaimed 'the New Master'. May's achievements came first in an era of dry turners — the so-called natural wickets — and then on green flyers. At the Oval he alone was consistently able to overcome conditions often grossly favouring bowlers.

He had both the consummate skills and the character to dominate on the worst of wickets and against the best bowling, and had no superior in the world. His wide range of gifts married elegance with controlled power, and despite a slightly unorthodox grip (according to the purists) he could play at will all shots in a wide ring from slip to fine leg. The majesty of his back play did not mean he was incapable of playing off the front foot with equal strength. He had a technique second to none.

He was unexcelled against genuine speed and in dealing with the delivery on the leg stump; and was equally skilful facing top-quality spin. Time and again he rescued England with a quality of performance unmatched by his contemporaries, but I am obliged to think the burdens of captaincy in a particularly difficult period affected what was basically a sensitive nature.

For me there was but one word for May — fantastic. I was delighted when he made 285 not out against the West Indies at Edgbaston in 1957 though it passed my 278 off Pakistan in 1954, which at the time was the post-war record score. May and Colin Cowdrey scored 411 for the fourth wicket, destroyed the menace of Sonny Ramadhin, who had taken 7 for 49 in the first innings, and saved a match which had appeared irrevocably lost. England went on to take the series 3-0.

May's 285 was the highest score by an England captain (Hutton's 364 was made long before he was captain), passing Wally Hammond's 240 in 1938. The day after his huge innings when Surrey were at Northampton a member went to Peter and said, 'Thank you for what you are doing for England.' Typically Peter was genuinely embarrassed by this tiny incident, which showed his innate modesty, a quality never to desert him.

He was truly one of cricket's blue blood, and from a tender age there was never any doubt of his destiny. At school George Geary, the old England all-rounder, then the coach at Charterhouse, told him, 'There's nothing much I can teach you, son. Just keep on practising and work hard.'

At twelve he made the school Under-16 Colts team; at fourteen he headed the first team batting averages; at fifteen, when considerably below the average age, he played for the Public Schools at Lord's; at sixteen he had occasional outings in the Minor Counties for his native Berkshire. Like his close friends the Bedser twins, Percy Chapman, Ken Barrington and Warwickshire's Tom Dollery, the first appointed professional captain, he was born at Reading.

Having established his cricketing pedigree at Charterhouse, May spent his two years of National Service as a writer in the Navy — he once heard a member at Lord's say he had served his time as a waiter! The fact that he was not commissioned led some to the mistaken belief that he lacked the essential qualities of leadership, but as a player under him I know this to be so much nonsense. If his period in the Navy taught him anything it was a better understanding of men, whom he inspired by example and comradeship and not by imposed discipline.

At Cambridge, where he scored a double-century against Hampshire as a freshman of twenty, he added his name to the distinguished list of England captains who were not captain at University — Percy Chapman, 'Gubby' Allen, Freddie Brown, George Mann and his father Frank, and Walter Robins. In his three years as a blue May played under Hubert Doggart, John Warr and David Sheppard, and it was ironic that he should be captain at his lesser sports of Soccer — all he lacked as an inside forward was pace — and fives. May was another example of the top cricketer with the eye and ball sense for all games.

Doggart, Dewes and Sheppard all played later for England, but it was evident that the jewel of the Cambridge crown was May, and I was privately pleased when he escaped selection for Australia in 1950–1. When he was twenty-one he announced his pedigree to the cricket world with a century in his first Test, against South Africa's strong bowling side. It was the first of thirteen centuries for England.

His reign as captain was crowded into six years: of 41 Tests as captain 35 were in succession. From 1956 to 1960 he carried an intolerable load which sadly ended in illness and his gradual departure from the game he graced. Not for the richly deserving Peter was there a nostalgic farewell, a public demonstration of affection for a master batsman, and as I write he is still the one great player without some decoration or proper recognition. There is no reason for such shabby treatment.

Captaincy was not a rosy path for him. He endured the more than difficult 1958–9 tour of Australia with its bitter throwing controversy, a dramatic loss of form in a series in South Africa, and finally a painful illness in the West Indies which forced his premature retirement.

It is no wonder that the strains of office overpowered him, and after the West Indies, sadly, he made only erratic appearances. Undoubtedly he was a victim of the intense pressures of top-level cricket, and cricket was immeasurably the poorer for his disappearance into the world of business.

Before the 1959–60 tour of the West Indies Peter had undergone an internal operation. Perhaps unwisely, he declared himself prepared for a tour which was seen as a peace-making mission after the eruptions of Hutton's visit in 1953–4. The wound re-opened before the second Test, a fact which Peter characteristically kept to himself. No one in the party was aware of his acute discomfort until he could keep the secret no longer and had to return home.

The only satisfaction Peter had was Cowdrey's success in holding on to the lead gained with a victory in the second Test. It was May's third and last disappointment as a tour leader. I shall never understand what happened to him in South Africa in 1956–7. Against provincial opposition he hit six centuries and could do nothing wrong; he was regularly hailed as the finest batsman in South Africa since Hobbs. Yet in the Tests he scored 153 runs, including one innings of 61, with a dismal average of 15.30.

It seemed inconceivable that such a brilliant batsman could fail in the way he did. I had particular sympathy for him, as I had the same collapse of form in the 1950–1 series in Australia. There was no logical reason for May's run of misfortune; it was one of those things that mock reputations and can bedevil any player.

Peter and I had one misfortune in common: we were each out to a fantastic catch in the first Test. I had gone to Brisbane full of confidence having taken a century off Victoria, who included the freak spinner Jack Iverson. In the first Test I went to a great catch when England were caught on a sticky, and from then on nothing went right for me in the Tests. The same fate befell Peter. He was going well enough when that superb catcher Russell Endean threw himself horizontally at square leg to hold a full-blooded shot which normally would have gone to the boundary.

When his expectations were at their highest Peter's scores in the series were 6, 14, 8, 15, 2, 2, 61, 0, 24 and 21, and England, two ahead after two Tests, only shared the rubber. If ever a game was designed to bring even a Peter May back to earth it is cricket.

South African hospitality is a byword among visiting teams whether official or private (as regrettably they have to be now), and I had a suspicion that the round of official functions and parties was not Peter's scene. He would, I am sure, have preferred quiet evenings with the boys. He showed a lot of tact both in South Africa, where the last Test was played on a poor wicket that would have provoked criticism from some captains, and in Australia. England went to Port Elizabeth after South Africa had won the fourth Test in a thrilling finish by 17 runs, and beaten England on a turf pitch for the first time at home. The Port Elizabeth authorities had attempted to relay the pitch in three months, and from first to last the ball kept low. South Africa squared the series in a strange and unreal match, but Peter was as dignified in defeat as he was in victory. Yet he was not free from criticism as a captain. In South Africa it was said his tactical attitude in no way corresponded with his pugnacity at the crease; that he was scared of defeat. The latter is an easy charge to make, and I believe it was most unfair.

May was singularly unfortunately to have been plunged into the maelstrom of cricket politics, and I do not think he could have handled the emotive issues other than by accepting the situation as it was. Both drag and throwing were matters for the administrators, and it was not until the series was over that authority tackled what were by then festering sores. It was no fault of May that, from the England point of view at any rate, everything went horribly wrong.

I think it is fair to say the cares of Test captaincy in that difficult period weighed heavily on him. At times I felt he kept a lot bottled up inside, and it might have been better if he had been a less gentle character and had blown his top to send his more hostile critics packing. Leading Surrey in the last two years of their seven successive championships was less exacting, with probably the strongest county side ever assembled — certainly in bowling — and must have give him enormous satisfaction.

By every standard I found Peter a super guy, without a trace of pretence or jealousy; he had deep reserves of iron-willed resolution and a keen sense of humour, and was modest and unassuming almost to a fault. Both as player and as captain it would have been unthinkable for him not to give a hundred per cent for his side. Indeed he did not know how to play any other way, and his first consideration was always for his team. I found him to be the most unselfish cricketer I have ever encountered, and you felt you just had to work hard for him.

Batting with him was a sheer joy. Apart from admiration and fascination for his technique his partners were grateful for the ready way he conceded the strike. If I was going well he would come down the pitch and say, 'Keep going. I can wait. You keep the strike.' Few batsmen, let alone the greats, are prepared to play second fiddle, and many dislike missing the strike for fear of going off the boil. Some batsmen were heartily unpopular for their habit of hogging the bowling, which, if you can count up to six, is not all that hard to do. I noticed the same players were also ready to concede the strike if the bowling was on top, or the pitch drying. The difference with Peter was that he actually encouraged a partner hitting form to keep the strike.

Another side of May to appeal to me was his ready appreciation and praise in the good times, and the comforting words in the bad. In contrast to Wally Hammond, Peter used to come alongside in the dressing-room and say, 'Marvellous, terrific,' or, 'There's always a tomorrow.' Every player is glad to have a cheering word from his skipper, and even if he was quiet he had an exceptional gift of communication, so that every member of the team was made to feel equal and important.

Tactically I would agree that he tended to be tentative and disinclined to take risks, but equally he often had to carry the major share of the batting, and it is all too easy to be a critic when one is not finally answerable for a strategic blunder. The essence of captaincy is knowing when to attack and when to defend, and Peter was not often to be faulted. Certainly opposing captains respected his judgement, and if at times he could be tough he never stepped outside the boundaries of fair play and sportsmanship.

Another attribute was his readiness to admit being wrong. In the 1956 series it was no secret that it took much persuasion by 'Gubby' Allen, then chairman of selectors, for Peter as captain to accept the recall of the veteran Cyril Washbrook for the third Test at Headingley. Having lost at Lord's England were one down and it was a crucial match. That splendid bowler Ron Archer made the ball move off the seam, and with only 17 scored Peter Richardson, Colin Cowdrey and Alan Oakman were out. May, then at the crease, confessed he had never seen a more welcome sight than Washbrook making his way towards him. The next wicket fell at 204, May made 101 — out, of all things, to a tennis shot off a high full toss — and Washbrook 98, and the whole course of the match and the series was changed. When May returned to the dressing-room his first act was to tell Allen, 'I'm glad I listened to you about Cyril.'

Just how much England owed to their captain in that successful defence of the Ashes was shown in the averages. May was top with 90.60, an average of 24 runs an innings better than David

Sheppard, and no less than 60 above Australia's top batsman, Jimmy Burke.

Temperament plays a big part in cricket, and Peter's was revealed with the very first ball he received in his first Test. Somehow he lost Athol Rowan's delivery in the background, which could be difficult around that time at Headingley. Many a young batsman of twenty-one would have panicked, but his sharp cricket brain told him to obey the old maxim of 'when in doubt play forward'. The ball found an inside edge and was snicked to the long-leg boundary. Had he made a 0 — and he wrote a chapter on making a nought in his *Book of Cricket* — I am sure he would have fought back twice as hard.

At Kingston, Jamaica, he found himself stretching too far to Gerry Gomez, but again instinct rescued him: he went boldly through with his shot and the ball sailed out of the ground over a sightscreen. Though it is not a big hit for a straight six at Sabina Park, Peter cleared a high wall by yards.

Courage of a stouter and different order was also needed after Lindwall's amazing over to him in Australia's match with Surrey in 1953 when Peter said, 'He gave me everything — including the kitchen sink.' Though it probably cost him his England place as he had failed in the first Test it was a lesson he never forgot. Indeed it perhaps formally completed his cricket education. He regained his place for the final Test and played his part in England's victory.

In all he hit thirteen centuries for England, and 4,537 runs in 66 Tests; his career record was 27,592 runs, with 85 centuries, and an average of 51.00. Statistics, however, tell only part of a story of a dynamic batsman. For a big-boned six-footer May was extraordinarily light on his feet, and I long for the sight of a successor with the ability to hit through mid-on and mid-wicket with even a modicum of his power ánd timing.

I shall always associate Peter with the attribute of true modesty, and with the genuine pleasure he showed at the achievements of his fellow players. When Hutton was at his best he would call the players out to the balcony and enthuse, 'Look at his cover driving. You'll never see anything better.'

The peaks of Peter's sadly brief career were against South Africa in 1955, when he averaged 72.75 against the formidable attack of Peter Heine, Neil Adcock, Trevor Goddard and Hugh Tayfield, and against Australia a season later. In the second innings at Old

Trafford in the South African season I had the good fortune to enjoy — the operative word — a stand of 124 in 105 minutes with Peter, who scored 117. From twenty-two yards away I recall saying to myself, 'If there's anyone better around than Peter then I haven't seen him.'

And that remains my firm belief. His freely given talents enriched cricket.

16

KEITH MILLER

Whenever I was due to play an important innings against my old cobber and fast-bowling adversary Keith Miller I checked on his social arrangements. Knowing him like a brother since we had met in India in 1945 during our Service days I could guess his options. He could be studying his constant reading companion, the *Sporting Life* — ask him to turn to his own records in *Wisden* and he wouldn't know where to begin! — he could be at the Festival Hall absorbed in a Beethoven symphony, hobnobbing with jockey or society friends, be at a party. Once he turned up for a day's play in a Test at Lord's still wearing his dinner-jacket.

If I realized it would be a case of 'the morning after the night before' I steeled myself for a particularly blistering onslaught. Keith's original cure for a hangover was to bowl flat out, faster than ever, in the belief that the more he put into it the quicker he would recover. His theory was effectively put to the test on more than one occasion to my cost.

Keith specialized in the unexpected, and I am sure he often had no preconceived idea what he intended to bowl even as he turned to start his run. One of his charms was his unpredictability, and as a batsman you never knew what was coming. It could be as fast a ball as anyone was entitled to expect on this planet, a slow leg-break, a bouncer or a fast back-break off an immaculate length, which would land outside the off stump and, if missed with the bat, would smack the legs.

If he tossed his head back it was usually a sign for real action. I used to wonder how he kept his unruly mop of hair so smooth after he brushed it back with his hand — a gesture thousands of spectators all over the world came to recognize. Then while batting one afternoon I discovered his secret. He held a tiny comb, no more than four inches long, in the palm of his hand, invisible to the crowd and players!

Service as a Mosquito pilot in the R.A.F. and a pancake landing after a raid on an airfield near Kiel left him with the legacy of a weakened back and a firm, clear philosophy. Hard as he played he never believed cricket should interfere with his enjoyment of life, his passion for the turf and happy comradeship with those who understood him best. To some he might appear wayward, irresponsible, happy-go-lucky, a cricketer of moods and fancies, but there was no better example of a man's man. Crowds adored his debonair, swashbuckling personality; he was everyone's friend on tour. He dined with the Mountbattens when Princess Margaret was a guest, was seen in the top-hat-and-tails enclosure at Ascot — and had at least one clash with his captain Don Bradman and, I suspect, with Ian Johnson, who succeeded Lindsay Hassett.

It was not so much a barrier of dislike or mistrust between them, but a meeting of opposites in outlook and temperament. I believe Miller had far better claims to the captaincy than Johnson. Clearly Australia played safe, with a guaranteed diplomat and a more 'reliable' personality, but Miller should have been captain in England in 1956.

Miller might have caused ripples of disapproval among the hierarchy (who happily accept the unorthodox on the field if it brings results), but his immense ability was something none could crush or under-estimate. Figures can tell but part of his impact as a bowler, batsman and fielder extraordinary. They cannot convey the excitement and impact he brought to every nook and cranny of a game, the genius able dramatically to turn the pattern of a match with one brilliant over, a breathtaking catch or a storming innings. Yet they are impressive enough. In 55 Tests between 1946 and 1956 he took 170 wickets at 22.97 each, and scored 2,958 runs, including seven centuries, with an average of 36.97. Only six Australians have taken more wickets, and thirteen have exceeded his run aggregate, and in the whole of Test cricket few all-rounders have comparable records.

Indeed comparisons are difficult because not all played in the same number of matches. Richie Benaud had eight more Tests, and though he took 78 more wickets Miller scored 757 more runs. Wilfred Rhodes in 58 Tests had 127 wickets and 2,325 runs; and

Trevor Bailey in 61 had 132 wickets and 2,290 runs. Sir Gary Sobers is way above all, but he had 38 more matches than Miller.

With Ray Lindwall he formed a fearsome fast-bowling partnership, at least the equal of Jack Gregory and Ted McDonald. In 1950–1 it was often said that the difference between Australia and England was Keith Ross (named after the famous Australian aviator) Miller, who, throughout his flamboyant career, played the major role in at least a dozen victories, and had a leading part in half a dozen more. His record in 29 Tests against England was 87 wickets at 22.40 each, and 1,511 runs, at an average of 33.57.

Since we were the best of friends Keith and I had our special private war and he spared no quarter. When I went in he had a standard greeting which dated from a match at Calcutta in 1945 when he was in the Australian Services side. I was batting when students rioted and, standing with bat raised prepared to defend myself, I was surprised to see the leader of the invading forces was my host (and Miller's) of the previous evening. As soon as he got within earshot he said politely, 'Good day, Mr Compton. You very good player. But you must go.' I went. For years Miller repeated those words when I arrived at the crease, and I knew he would do his level best to ensure I would go!

Keith, who christened his third son Denis Charles after me, always gave me everything he had, which meant the widest variety of deliveries possible, from bumpers to slower balls, swing either way off the pitch and even the occasional off break. At Lord's he once tested David Sheppard's faith by bowling him with a googly, and on the Brisbane sticky of 1946 he promptly adjusted his style to capture 7 for 60 with off-breaks. He also scored 79, the first 50 in 80 minutes. At the age of thirty-six at Lord's in 1956 he had five wickets in each innings — a feat he accomplished seven times in Tests — at medium pace.

There was no end to his versatility. Oddly, he was not rated as a bowler in his early days with Victoria in 1937–8; he hit 181 against Tasmania in his first match. Indeed he only turned to cricket and Australian Rules football (in which he was not surprisingly a top player) after his original ambition to be a jockey had been defeated by a sudden spurt in height and weight. Watching his athletic six-foot-two-inch frame spring into tigerish assault it seemed impossible that at fifteen he was a mere five feet tall and a paper-weight. His dream of riding the winner in the Melbourne Cup abruptly faded when he added a foot to his height with appropriate weight inside a year. Cricket was the lucky gainer.

Australia was agreeably surprised when Miller revealed his fast bowling potential in the Victory Tests in England towards the end of the war. Not only did he bowl fast and respond to the calls of his air-force friends assembled in front of the Tavern to bowl a bouncer, but he batted like a white Learie Constantine. In 1944 on a Bank Holiday he hit 85 out of 193, and in 1945, appearing for the Dominions against England, he had an eye-opening 185. At one stage he scored 124 in 90 minutes with cultured fluency, and he and Constantine added 117 in 45 minutes. Miller's special target was the Lord's pavillion, and a six over a dressing-room balcony was one of the biggest seen on the ancient ground. His average in the Victory matches exceeded 60 and was achieved with a style which made him compulsive watching. As he had been a leading batsman for Victoria until his departure to the R.A.A.F. in 1941 his run-scoring success was perhaps to be expected, but his emergence as a bowler of genuine speed and quality was a source of delighted Australian surprise. Bradman instantly recognized that he had a match-winning bowler, and no time was wasted in launching him on his international career in Australia's first-ever Test with New Zealand in March 1946. His opening bowling partner was Lindwall, and another famous partnership had begun. In that season Miller averaged over 130 for Victoria, despite persistent back trouble.

Keith has told me many times that he would have preferred to have been regarded and chosen purely as a batsman in his first series against England in 1946–7. Against his better judgement he bowled. He was a magnificent sight, using his height to full advantage and with his back arched like a bow with the arrow on the point of release. His arm turned a full circle, except when his quixotic spirit moved him to try a round arm. He seldom bowled off the same mark, which meant that if he suddenly turned round and ran off a few paces the batsman might not be mentally ready. The trouble was that he could be just as quick off a short run. If his charge to the wicket did tend to give his bouncer away it could be maliciously fast, as I found to my cost at Trent Bridge in 1948. I had made 184 and felt I could hook a short ball. But it came through much quicker than I anticipated, and in the scramble to get out of the way I trod on my stumps.

Fear of the unexpected was part of the problem he created for batsmen. The better the batsman the better he liked it. He took no satisfaction in a massacre of innocents or inferior opponents, as either batsman or bowler. On the day the Australians plundered Essex for 721 he allowed himself to be dismissed first ball, when for a batsman of his class a spectacular century was there for the taking. Arguments have always been not about whether Keith was great — this was an accepted fact — but what heights he might have reached if he had concentrated on one department of the game. Some maintain he was a batsman who should not have had to bowl so much, and others that he was a superb bowler and an over-rated batsman. All such questions are hypothetical, and my answer is that no player could consistently bowl and bat at Miller's peak form. One or the other had to give way every now and again.

At Adelaide in 1946 he had one of his few bowling failures, but he raced to a sparkling 141 not out which included a spell of 67 in 71 minutes when the bowlers could not contain him and Hammond could not set a field for him. His batting average for the rubber was 76.80, second only to Bradman, and he also had 16 wickets. In 1950–1 he was Australia's leading batsman, and in 1956 in England he was the leading bowler. In the West Indies he was second to Hassett in the batting and top of the bowling.

If Miller was on the opposite side the one certainty was that at any stage he could turn the situation inside out. A prime example was the third Test at Sydney in 1950. England began hopefully on an easy pitch, but Miller broke the opening partnership with a dazzling catch at slip to dismiss Cyril Washbrook. Len Hutton and Reg Simpson took the total from 34 to 128 when just before tea Miller was put on for what was thought to be a 'loosener' before the new ball was taken. At once he had Hutton leg before with a ball nipping back wickedly from the off. Three balls later he did exactly the same thing to me. He finished with 4 for 37, then proceeded to hit 145 not out, and by the time England batted again the wicket was ready to be exploited by Jack Iverson, who flicked his off-spinners with the middle finger folded down.

Miller caused Hutton some of the most anguished moments of his time as captain when England clinched the Ashes in 1954–55 at Adelaide. The stage was set for a display of brazen individualism, the streak of puckish fun which delighted in promoting the unexpected. England needed 94 to win with the wicket of no real use to the quick bowlers. A formality? Not with Keith around. When Miller's fiery burst accounted for Hutton, Edrich and Cowdrey in three overs for 12 runs, Hutton's spirits went to his boots and provoked his famous observation, 'The so-and-so's going to do us again.'

Hutton, in fact, left the room from which players watch at Adelaide, disappeared into the dressing-room and did not see another ball bowled.

When we had come off the field I felt the strain was really eating into Hutton, and I was very surprised when he came up to me and said, 'Denis, I don't feel like going in again. Would you mind going in first?' I said I would if he wanted me to, and I started to pad up when I reached the dressing-room. Looking up I saw Len was also buckling on his pads, and I asked him if he still wanted me to go first. 'Oh, no, no. I'll be going in first,' he replied. Far from being irritated I felt compassion for a captain who seemed so exhausted that he was oblivious of being on the brink of his famous captaincy achievement.

What a contrast was the jaunty Godfrey Evans, who arrived at the wicket grinning broadly, and bet me five bob he would make the winning hit! And he did.

When the total was 49 Hutton could have re-echoed his pessimism when who else but Miller should make one of his marvellous catches, this time at extra cover, to send back May. Fortunately Bailey and I held on and England won by five wickets, but Miller, in his element when presented with a challenge, had sent a shiver of apprehension through the dressing-room. That had been the type of situation to rouse Keith, a battle against odds, a challenge. The mundane bored him.

Lord's 1953 and Melbourne 1954–5 were other occasions when Miller's skills could hardly have soared to a higher plane. Taking advantage of some early dampness at Melbourne, Keith had nine overs before lunch — eight were maidens, and two scoring shots produced five runs for the wickets of Hutton, Edrich and myself. In 1950 there was a storm of protest when he was omitted from Australia's party to tour South Africa on the quite ludicrous grounds that he lacked temperament and did not concentrate. Ultimately he went as a replacement for Bill Johnston, injured in a road accident, which, considering the way he had been treated, proved what a big man he was. 'If I'm wanted I'll go,' he said, and by the end had easily the best bowling figures of either side.

As a batsman Keith probably lacked patience, and was none too bothered if his side was in a commanding position. He had a good upright stance, and brutish force in front of the wicket. I rate anyone who can take a century off Bill O'Reilly, as Keith did at Sydney after the war. Yet I think he found himself between the two stools of batting and bowling, and his batting was not disciplined enough at all times. He had all the strokes, a marvellous cover and straight drive, and physical strength allied to natural timing, but he was a creature of moods.

In 1953 he arrived in England with the firm intention of proving to all his batting class. He began with a Bradmanesque 220 not out at Worcester, 42 (run out) and 159 not out against Yorkshire, and was clearly a candidate for 1,000 runs before the end of May if he could sustain such form. The next fixture was at Fenners, and skipper Lindsay Hassett did the right thing and promoted him to open the innings. Here was a chance to plunder the university bowling. But Hassett was in happy ignorance of the fact that fourteen miles away at Newmarket a horse was running that Keith very much fancied, on the recommendation of his jockey friend Billy Snaith. After a quick innings of 20 he dashed to Newmarket, saw his horse beaten into fourth place, and hadn't enough cash left to invest in the best tip of all for a later race — Pinza, which was to win the Derby. Glumly Keith returned to Cambridge with an hour of play still to go, confident his team-mates would still be batting. Instead he was alarmed to see the Australian side filing out to the wicket! No music hall artist ever did a swifter change, and Keith had some explaining to do to Hassett.

Far from taking him to his 1,000, Keith's batting fell away to such an extent that he made only 39 more runs in the month. In the Lord's Test the flame was rekindled with 109 in the second innings. It would have been the match-winner but for heroic efforts by Watson and Bailey to save the game against all odds. At Leeds his bowling put Australia in a strong position, and England were rescued by Bailey's leg theory. Definitely not my happiest memory of England in a backs-to-the-wall situation.

The slow, so-called natural pitches of 1956 were anathema to Miller, as with all the Australians and not a few Englishmen, and while he bowled well enough and his ten wickets at Lord's at medium pace gave Australia a 1-0 lead, generally he had no technical defence to the spin of Jim Laker and Tony Lock. At Lord's the crowd applauded him affectionately all the way to the wicket, and there was a nostalgic hint of the Miller who had thrilled the war-time crowds. But on the turning pitch at Old Trafford he cut a sorry figure as he used his pads in a desperate bid to counter the spin. I was inwardly praying he would not be subjected to a similar ordeal in his farewell appearance in England at the Oval. Batting at No. 7 he top-scored with 61 after joining Neil Harvey with the total at a perilous 47 for 5 and the pitch far from easy after rain. As he had also taken 4 for 91 in England's first innings it was not a bad way to go, and if it was not one of his spectacular performances it saved Australia from the possibility of defeat.

The Cambridge incident would no doubt be seized upon by those who argued he could never have captained Australia. I don't agree. Behind the glamorous facade and devil-may-care attitude was an intelligent and thinking cricketer. For proof there is no need to research further than the development of his bowling after contact with English professionals who taught him how to cut and swing the ball. He may have tossed his hair, become involved with the crowd, caused feminine hearts to flutter, sent down all manner and types of deliveries from no settled bowling mark, but, believe me, as one who constantly batted against him, he knew what he was doing. The element of surprise was one of his prime assets, and behind all the fun and extrovert mannerisms and conduct was a thinking bowler and, in many ways, a sensitive character. His service as a pilot deeply influenced him. There is no doubt in my mind that his back complaint handicapped him and that he often ignored pain and discomfort to bowl flat out for Australia.

My sympathy was for him when he rebelled at Lord's in 1948. Though he told Bradman he could not bowl, the ball was tossed to him with the words, 'Have a bowl.' Miller turned away and Bill Johnston shared the new ball with Lindwall. Perhaps Keith was not clear enough in telling his captain how afflicted he was, but it was definitely not a case of temperament or of putting on a prima donna act. No doubt the incident went against him, but few of the Aussies harboured reservations that he was the most astute State captain in Australia when he took over the leadership of New South Wales. He had his eccentric moments — as at Brisbane, when the team was to be chosen from twelve and there was the little oversight of the captain failing to nominate the 'drinks waiter'. As he led his side onto the field agitated officials ran on and told him he had one player too many. Keith met the situation by turning and facing his charges and saying, 'One of you guys had better go off.' Miller was often an inspiring and humble leader, giving younger players key batting positions before himself, taking the burden of the bowling on unresponsive wickets, and generally proving he had the instinctive gifts of unselfish leadership. His idea of field placing was a general instruction to 'spread out'! The English public would have greeted him as a captain with enthusiasm, and I think he would have surprised many with the depth of his tactical knowledge.

Keith does not have one ounce of pretence in his make-up, but he is wise enough to recognize the human foibles of others. A pompous mutual friend of ours was introduced to Scobie Breasley. Sensing that our acquaintance was not over-impressed by the presence of a jockey, Keith added mischievously, 'The Queen's jockey.' The miraculous change of respect gave us a lot of satisfaction and amusement.

We have had some wonderful times together. Once in Calcutta we went to a race meeting, partly because I had been given the hottest of tips by a Maharajah, who we mistakenly thought couldn't be wrong. He was, and we were both well out of pocket. On another occasion in Sydney Keith introduced me to a well known bookie. I knew I was lucky at times to get generous odds, and when I asked if he would take a tenner on a horse I had taken a liking to he declined, rather to my surprise. With Keith standing at my shoulder he replied, 'You should put your money on so-and-so.' I took his tip, and I left the club later with my pockets stuffed with notes. It's the only time I have had a winning tip from a bookie, been given over the odds and been paid with a smile!

We were playing in a social match for the Writers against the Publishers at Vincent Square, London, on the day of the Royal Hunt Cup at Ascot. We had both backed the Queen's horse Pall Mall, and wanted to follow our hopes on television. Unfortunately there was no set on the ground. Boldly we knocked on the door of one of the flats overlooking the Square and asked an astonished elderly lady if we could use her television for a while. Understandably she was not over-keen on allowing two young strangers into her home, but eventually we were invited in, and while we were intent on the race she brought us tea.

Little Keith ever did could be condemned as dull. Yet he could be deadly serious when twenty-two yards away with a cricket ball in his hand. I never need reminding of his magnificent talents, or of his open-hearted generous nature. When he went to Buckingham Palace to receive the M.B.E. it was typical of his thoughtfulness that he should take with him the wife of an old family friend whose son was in hospital awaiting an operation. Just to cheer her up.

Keith rates very high as an all-round cricketer of any age, and as a manly man. In his playing days he was too big for some to understand his values. He has the satisfaction of knowing he left the game without a real enemy, and enough friends from all walks of life to pack Lord's.

17

ARTHUR MORRIS

Arthur Morris had just had time to announce his scorching ability when, like all his generation, he was engulfed in Hitler's war. When only eighteen he completed the unparalleled feat of scoring a century in each innings of his first Sheffield Shield match during Christmas 1940 for New South Wales against Queensland. For a brief time the Australian public was able to divert its mind from grimmer affairs and contemplate a star when peace returned. And Arthur remained true to his promise.

Morris's scores in that eventful game were 148 and 111. In the first innings he shared a second-wicket stand of 261 with the late Sid Barnes, later to become his first-wicket partner for Australia, and though he had set himself an impossible standard he ended the season with an average of 55.14.

For the next six years cricket was replaced by service life, much of which was spent in New Guinea with the Australian Army Movement Control, and he could not resume the game seriously until the M.C.C.'s tour in 1946–7. When I arrived with that side the gossip was usually centred on the Don's come-back and the comparison of the then-unknown (at least outside Australia) Morris with the other legendary Aussie left-handers, Warren Bardsley or Clem Hill. Both Bardsley and Hill were, of course, long before my time, but I was often subsequently left to ponder that they must have been very good indeed if they were better than the light-haired, composed Morris with the twinkling footwork and uncanny judgement. I cannot think of many batsmen able to make a decision on whether to play forward or back, attack or defend, as quickly as Arthur. He was in position in a flash.

His sunny, unruffled temperament and genuine friendliness —

which left him in the rare position of leaving the game without a single enemy — were priceless assets and had much to do with a career comparing with the best. In 46 Tests he scored 3,533 runs with 12 centuries and an average of 46.48. In all first-class cricket he aggregated 12,489 runs for only 242 innings, with 46 centuries and an average of 55.01. It is also a point worth remembering that the Australians with more centuries — Bradman excepted — like Harvey, the Chappell brothers, Doug Walters and Bill Lawry did not lose a sizeable chunk of their careers through the war.

Arthur's attitude of pure enjoyment to the game would pooh-pooh statistics, but they are useful to support his claim to be regarded as one of the titans of cricket. People were apt to regard him as one of Alec Bedser's bunnies, and while it is true that Alec had his wicket several times by brilliantly swinging the ball around his leg stump — perhaps Arthur's only area of vulnerability — honours were about even. If a great new ball bowler meets a great opening batsman in even conditions honours are going to be shared, and it is logical that there are going to be repeated dismissals by the same bowler. And an opening batsman is always liable to get a trimmer when the ball is new and shiny and bounces higher. The Morris–Bedser duels were the classics of the first post-war series. From them grew a deep respect for each other, as it should be. They spent a lot of time together off the field, and remain close friends to this day.

Neil Harvey had just as much trouble with Bedser, who got each of them out five times in the two rubbers of 1950–1 and 1953. Both Morris and Harvey said it was sometimes difficult — for no logical reason — to pick up the flight of the ball from Alec's hand. While it is possible 'there may have been something in Alec's natural action to present left-handers with a special problem, I think a more likely reason was the late swing away from the bat — a really wicked ball. As I write in my chapter on Bedser, the ball to a right-hander came arrow straight until it nipped in at the very last moment. The left-hander, committed to a stroke, would find the ball moving away just enough to contact the edge. Also the normal leg-cutter came into the left-hander like a sharp off-break. Both Morris and Harvey had also to be alert for the delivery which held its course and did not move either into or away from the bat. Enough, in my contention, for any batsman to have to face. Arthur as an opening bat had the extra hazard of a new, hard ball, bouncing high, particularly in Australia.

By the time Bedser was obliged to tackle Bradman, Morris and Co. virtually on his own Arthur had conquered his ambitious habit of driving just short of a length and he was indeed a formidable and elegant left-hander. (It's strange how left-handers are either unusually elegant or slightly clumsy-looking. There were no two thoughts about Arthur's style!) In analysing his methods I would stress his basic temperament, for he always seemed to be in perfect control of himself. If he had any nerves he hid them as well as any player I know. His was the perfect temperament, and his manner never changed whether the occasion was good or bad for him. As I have already said he had a marvellous capacity to decide early in the ball's flight what he intended to do. He watched the ball carefully on to the bat, rarely allowed a bad ball to escape punishment — which so often is the weakness of a defensive minded player — and had the skill to find the gaps in the field and to keep the ball on the ground. The on-drive was his speciality, which is the hall-mark of class, and he drove through the covers fiercely. He cut crisply and, in common with most left handers, he was exceptionally powerful on the leg side. Apart from his God-given serenity Arthur, to my mind, had exactly the right approach. He like to attack and believed it was a tactical victory to the bowler if he was tied down. The result was that he was for ever looking for the single and the two and keeping his score moving. Unlike someone I could mention he was an excellent judge of a run! Many times I have been in the field to Arthur and looking at the scoreboard been surprised to see how many runs he had accumulated without apparent effort.

Most of all, however, my professional envy was aroused by his tremendous footwork. He was as light and as quick as a Russian ballerina. If footwork is the basic of batting technique Arthur, it seemed to me, had a headstart on the rest of us. The prime example came in the 1948 match at Bristol, where the pitch had an awesome reputation for batsmen in that period. Sam Cook and Tom Goddard, the spinners, enjoyed sweeping successes and many thought they might end Australia's triumphant run and Bradman's well publicized ambition to be the first visiting captain to go through the tour unbeaten. Morris turned it into a gala occasion for himself, however, with 290, the highest score of his career, and a 6 and no fewer than 42 boundaries. He reached a century

before lunch, another between lunch and tea, and was at the wicket
for five hours — the standard time for a modern-day century. Poor
Goddard, whose eyes blinked at Arthur's nimble feet and audacity, had 0 for 186 in 32 overs and Cook 3 for 147 in 41. So much for
the unplayable Bristol wicket of the time . . . and an obvious
lesson for the leaden-footed, playing spin from the crease! His
deeds in England in 1948 surpassed even Bradman, with an average of 87.00 in the Tests against Bradman's 72.57. The son of a
Sydney schoolmaster, who was a fast bowler for the noted Waver-
ley club, Arthur began as a slow left-arm bowler. For a time his
family moved to Newcastle and he was a slow spinner in the school
side. Back at his home city of Sydney Arthur captained both his
school and the combined High School team, and he graduated to
St George's Club, then captained by Bill O'Reilly. The premier-
ship was won for three consecutive years. By now it was clear that
he was wasted as a tail-ender, and after taking a century off Sydney
University at the tender age of sixteen he was promoted to open
the innings. Even then his uncommon talent was shining through,
and, while still at school, he played for New South Wales 2nd XI
against Victoria 2nd XI.

Promotion was swift, and a century in each innings against
Queensland followed when he was eighteen. The war over and
with Hammond's team in Australia Arthur hit 98 off Queensland,
115 for an Australian XI against M.C.C., followed by 81 not out
for New South Wales in the state game with M.C.C. It was all too
evident that we were to see a lot more of Arthur Robert Morris.
His selection for the Tests was a formality, and after initial failures
he had 155 in the third Test at Melbourne and 122 and 124 in
the next match at Adelaide (where I also had a century in each
innings, the first time a batsman on each side had performed the
feat). Only one other Australian had scored a century in each
innings against England — Warren Bardsley, with whom Arthur
was so often compared. Arthur and I were photographed together
after the match, and the picture still adorns my wall as I write. I
remember the late Johnny Moyes, broadcaster, writer and a State
player, telling me that Morris had more strokes than Bardsley, but
that he regarded Clem Hill as superior to either. Well, I find it
hard to accept that any batsman other than Bradman could have
been much superior, if at all, and Morris quickly became recognized as one of a select band of players in world cricket in virtually

his first season.

He became captain of New South Wales in front of Keith Miller, and seemed next in the hierarchy to Lindsay Hassett, who followed Bradman. But Arthur was not the tough, uncompromising leader the Aussies favoured and this was his one failure. I sympathize with him as I had a similar experience. Some slip easily into leadership and it comes naturally to them as it did to George Mann, the best captain I ever played under. Though a magnificent driver and better than he modestly pretended to be, Mann was born for the captain's job. I feel that if the natural flair isn't there no amount of toughness, tactical know-how or experience can serve as an effective substitute. Bradman, given a head and shoulder start in the matter of the team's respect to him, had the computer type of brain to take in all situations. Hutton hadn't, despite his successes. Lindsay Hassett was always in firm control for all his impish ways and air of amused detachment, and if a vote was taken by the players, Mike Smith, with his ability to get his team solidly behind him in the Mike Brearley manner, would be classed superior to Peter May, though there could be no comparison between them as players. Ian Johnson, preferred to Morris as Hassett's successor, was very much the diplomat, and Frankie Worrell must be ranked as one of the classic captains of any age. To me the West Indies have slipped back into some bad old ways since his untimely death. I write of captaincy with some diffidence because I had my chance and was found wanting. In Morris's case I should say he was too self-effacing and too nice a guy to be marked out by destiny to crown his magnificent career with captaincy. And he was very unlucky. Controversy was aroused when New South Wales chose Miller for their captaincy, while the Australian selectors had Morris in front of Miller as vice-captain of the national side. Surely such a conflict of interests was avoidable with a little tact — a quality not all that common among Aussies — and, in the end, Miller, though still carrying the scars of his tiff with Bradman at Lord's in 1948, was appointed vice-captain to Johnson both in the West Indies in 1956 and in England a year later. Pardon my laugh at Miller being under Johnson.

Throughout the turmoil over the captaincy Arthur remained outwardly unruffled and commendably dignified. The Miller – Morris debate was a clear case of the extrovert in opposition to the introvert, and I am bound to say I always felt Australia passing over Miller did an injustice to a man who could have been a dynamic and fearless leader. In another era Morris might well have proved a quiet but effective captain. His second piece of bad luck was to be Australia's acting captain for Johnson when England won at Sydney in the second Test and reversed the course of the Ashes in 1954. I was injured and did not play, but I did see the pitch before the start and remember thinking I was glad not to have to make a decision about batting first had I been captain. The pitch was piebald and there were clouds about. Morris spent some time in consultation with Bradman, then Chairman of selectors, and put England in to bat. As England were still nursing the bruises of the crushing defeat in the first Test at Brisbane the decision was accepted as good psychology — that is until England won an amazing Test by 38 runs! Almost inevitably stones were cast in the captain's direction, which merely went to prove how thin the line can be between success and failure. Unless I am very wrong Arthur was tacitly removed from the captaincy contenders from that Test on, yet had Australia won the fluctuating struggle he would no doubt have been accepted as a shrewd tactician. Putting the opposition in first has become common enough, particularly in one-day cricket, but I recall a remark once passed to me by the wise old Surrey and England wicket-keeper Herbert Strudwick. When he was scorer for Surrey I suggested to him before the start of a match at Lord's that it might be a good idea to concede first innings. 'Denis,' he replied, 'I remember what W.G. Grace used to say — always take what the gods offer and bat first!'

If there were arguments about Morris's virtues as a captain there could be none over his towering ability as a batsman. Those of us who toiled to get out the leading batsmen of the finest side to come to England in my time will testify to his gigantic stature in 1948. In those days it is true to say England did not have much in the way of speed, apart from Bedser. But if all types of attack came the same to Arthur he really excelled against spin and with brilliant — almost cruel — disdain he and Bradman killed off England's only hope of victory in that series. We went to Headingley for the fourth Test two down and desperate for success. The public, too, longed for an end to Bradman's triumphant march. For four days Australia were held. Cyril Washbrook and my Middlesex 'twin' Bill Edrich scored centuries in a total of 496. Neil Harvey made a century in his first Test and in the end Australia wanted 404 runs in 344 minutes.

In the light of what happened it now seems the height of absurdity that Norman Yardley, the skipper, used a heavy roller on the last morning before the declaration after five minutes batting in order to 'break up' the pitch — something that in over forty years of playing and watching I have never actually seen happen! Even more strange was giving Hutton four overs to 'jolly' the Aussies on. He conceded 30. The Australian innings led by Morris is etched deep in my heart. The mere thought of what happened still chills me to the marrow because, for once, my left-arm spin and 'chinaman' bowling could have carried the day for England. The pitch took spin and lift and I was supremely confident that my unorthodox style taught me by that wonderful Leicestershire Aussie Jack Walsh could break through.

Unhappily Jack Crapp, normally the most reliable of slip catchers for Gloucestershire, could not read my googly, and he twice dropped Bradman off me after I had caught and bowled Hassett. To make matters worse Godfrey Evans had his worst-ever experience for England behind the stumps. Jim Laker was still learning his off-spinning trade — later the Aussies would have agreed he had reached professional status! — and anything Jim and I dropped short of a length or minutely off line was murderously dealt with. Morris made 182 and Bradman was not out 173 when the winning hit was made 12 minutes from time. Not much was said in the England dressing-room afterwards, but I was left with no two doubts about the genuine quality of Morris.

For too few years Arthur was a heavy scorer for country and State, and he passed his obvious enjoyment of playing on to the spectators. His exemplary character and pleasant personality are as well remembered as his batting. Eight years after his retirement he was persuaded to return for a brief unofficial tour of India and South Africa, and there is a story of Norman O'Neill rushing into the dressing-room at Bombay and saying, 'Come out and watch Arthur. You'll never see better batting.' Bradman had said much the same thing to his Australian players when Stan McCabe cut loose at Trent Bridge in 1938.

I can well believe any excitement at any revelation of Arthur's superb stroke-play and O'Neill's words could excellently serve the tribute I offer to a magnificent player.

18

BILL O'REILLY

Bowlers come and go, set new records, and strut their hour on cricket's stage. But significantly the reputation of William Joseph O'Reilly remains undimmed by time. Some sound judges insist only S.F. Barnes stands as his equal in this century. While it is inviting difficulties to compare the giants of different generations — even my time has witnessed vast changes in the game — the judgement on O'Reilly may well be right.

On the evidence of one season against him in 1938 I would heartily endorse everything said and written in his praise as a bowler extraordinary. From the Australian season of 1931-2 until the war O'Reilly made a deep impact on Test cricket, and with Clarrie Grimmett established a spin bowling combination which took 360 wickets in 64 matches. O'Reilly's share from a comparatively few 27 Tests was 144, including 102 against England at 25.64 each. It does not stretch the imagination to think what he might have achieved in figures alone if he had bowled regularly against some of the weaker countries in the international fold.

Before I first faced him I did not lack well intentioned advice, and if cricket had followed the modern trend of Soccer I could have been handed a dossier which might have read something like this:

O'REILLY	6 ft 3 ins Irish – Australian appropriately dubbed 'The Tiger' or 'Big Bill'.
BORN	20 December 1905. Played up-country cricket at Wingello N.S.W. against Bradman, with whom he was in the N.S.W. Second XI.
TYPE	Turns from leg, but cannot be categorized as an orthodox leg-spinner or googly bowler.

	Rolls rather than spins the ball.
SPEED	Near medium pace off 12-yard run.
APPROACH TO WICKET	Lumbering, awkward-looking with arms flaying and head lowered, but perfect co-ordination achieved in the final stride. Arm movements make it hard to follow the hand and to judge speed of ball.
VARIATIONS	Considerable. Googly can bounce like a tennis ball, and a straight ball at speed is an unsettling weapon. Will have two short legs, and pace will constantly vary. No two deliveries alike. Top spinner positively fizzes.
CHARACTERISTICS	Hostile, accurate, determined. Don't be put off by what he might say, as though he is forthright there is no malice. Relentless, unorthodox, fiercely intent.

After losing my wicket to him twice for M.C.C. and Middlesex — the second occasion not without some repayment — I learned that O'Reilly was capable of using about every type of delivery that can be bowled, and at a pace which defied the batsman to get out to the pitch of the ball. Hammond, Leyland, Hendren and others had told me they had received six different balls in the course of one over, and an attempt by Charlie Barnett on the 1936–7 tour to hit him into subjection was abandoned. Barnett, of course, had his hour when he made 98 before lunch out of 169 with Hutton in the first Test of the 1938 series at Trent Bridge.

By experience I found it was possible to spot O'Reilly's googly, which came fractionally slower and higher, but the eternal worry was his accuracy and ability to make the ball bounce; indeed the bounce he produced was positively unnatural. Like all truly great players he was different, an original, a law unto himself, and so presented complex problems unlikely to be solved by strictly conventional methods. It is an anomaly of cricket that the classical stylist can be penalized by his very technical perfection. The always accurate bowler is all very well, but after a while he can be classified and be played with the eyes half shut; the ultra-orthodox batsman can be pinned down because he plays in a set way as if he is afraid to break a rule. Some leg-break bowlers obligingly show their hand, either spinning too much or staying in the air too long, which is manna to the quick-footed batsman.

O'Reilly's sole concession to orthodoxy, it seemed to me, was his accuracy. He turned the ball enough to beat the bat. At the start of his grade and State career he rejected every effort to change him from a 'roller' to a genuine 'spinner'. The Don would not let coaches alter his batting grip and O'Reilly, who always knew his own mind, also firmly stuck to his natural methods. In hindsight it seems incredible that anyone should have tried to change them; or that Bradman and O'Reilly actually played as they did in 1926–7 in the same second eleven!

Originally a schoolmaster, O'Reilly had the advantage of an alert, straight-thinking, uncomplicated brain, and a character untrammelled by side issues. He eschewed all pretence, sham showmanship. When he was hit for runs he would snatch the ball back with,'Give me the bloody thing.' You never received any false congratulations for a shot. You knew you were up against a very determined opponent. Inevitably his down-to-earth attitude was hard to take by some who enjoyed a bit of light-hearted back-chat with the bowler, but Bill, with the Irish in his blood, was not that way at all. His appeals were demanding, but I never found him to have too much to say. To compare him with Trueman in this aspect is nonsense.

Batsmen were his natural prey, and he hunted with cunning, relentless resolve. His two short legs, Bill Brown and Jack Fingleton, appeared to me more as unfriendly predators than as fielders. He hated his first slip to 'hide' (as he said) behind the wicket-keeper, and any runs scored at the expense of the Tiger were hard earned. Groundsmen came in for some caustic comments if the pitch was too good, and Frank Chester told me that at the Oval in 1938 O'Reilly turned to him after completing his first over and demanded, 'Where does the groundsman hang out on this ground?' When Chester pointed out 'Bosser' Martin's hut he exploded, 'If I'd got a gun I would use it on him right now.'

O'Reilly bowled 85 overs in England's innings of 903 and dismissed the record-breaker Len Hutton, Bill Edrich and Eddie Paynter, for 178 runs. When Hutton was out and England's total was 770 for six he was to be seen stretched out on the ground oblivious to the excited scene around him. That was one side of O'Reilly — still superbly aggressive but economical in conditions to affront him. The other side was in the previous Test at

Headingley where he was Australia's match-winner on a worn pitch with five cheap wickets in each innings.

We in the England side knew we were in for it from Bill's first over. He bowled me in the first innings, and had me caught at the wicket off my wrist in the second when he had six close up on the leg side and not a man out to demonstrate his sublime confidence in his own accuracy in a tight-run situation. In the second Test at Lord's he also had me out sweeping — rightly given out by umpire 'Tiger' Smith. The truth was that on any pitch O'Reilly never allowed himself to be dominated. He took the attack to the batsman with an unflagging aggression and masterly control. I am told Lindsay Hassett successfully lofted him over mid-on. To do so needed oceans of skill and courage. Bradman hit him on his day, but few were his master for long.

Once Ernie McCormick reached his peak at the start of England's first innings at Lord's and swiftly faded, Australia's dependence on O'Reilly was acute. In the four Tests he took 22 wickets at 27.72. His erratic left-arm spinning partner Fleetwood-Smith had 14 at 51.92, including one for 298 off 87 overs in the 'bowler's nightmare' Oval match. O'Reilly *was* Australia's bowling, and it was therefore all the more remarkable that he should sustain his effectiveness. Four years earlier on his other visit to England he had 28 wickets for 24.92 in five Tests; Grimmett had 25 at two runs a wicket dearer.

At Old Trafford O'Reilly had a spell some of the old players talked about for years, and showed why he could never be taken for granted. England's openers Herbert Sutcliffe and Cyril Walters made 68 in an hour. During a stoppage for drinks Bill Woodfull complained about the ball and a replacement was made. With the game restarted Sutcliffe played a maiden to Grimmett. Then O'Reilly had Walters caught at short leg by Len Darling — one of the specialists O'Reilly recruited — and Bob Wyatt was bowled by the next ball. Now on a hat-trick O'Reilly, it is said, almost beat Hammond, but an edge went to the boundary. Hammond, however, was beaten by the next delivery and O'Reilly had three in four balls. England had gone from 68 for 0 to 72 for 3. In the end Hendren and Leyland scored 192 for the fifth wicket and O'Reilly finished with 7 for 189 in a total of 627 for 9 declared. In the two home series with England he was the leading wicket-taker with 27 and 25 wickets. In the age of Hammond, Sutcliffe, Leyland,

Wyatt, Paynter, Walters, Hendren, Ames, Hardstaff and Hutton he was the thorn constantly pricking the flesh.

Cheap runs against inferior attacks are all very well, but the real inner satisfaction comes from winning a battle when pitted against a foe of O'Reilly's stature, who grudges every hit, and comes back with even fiercer determination if he concedes a boundary. *Wisden* records that in the match between Middlesex and the Australians Walter Robins and I 'punished O'Reilly freely'. Well, I managed 65 out of 188 with O'Reilly bowling me for the last wicket.

'Cock' Robins, never lacking courage or confidence, twice picked O'Reilly's 'wrong 'un' and, going down on one knee, vigorously swept him into the old Tavern. As the pitch was set almost in the middle of the square and next to the strip reserved for Tests, both sixes were considerable hits — particularly the second, which went into the tea-room above the bar. Being at the non-striker's end I heard some huffing and puffing from 'Big Bill' and half-expected an outburst of ruffled pride. But, to my mild surprise, after calling for the ball his sole protest was, 'For a match as important as this I'd have thought they would have put the pitch in the middle.'

Punished or not, Bill still had 4 for 56, and Bradman (the so-called 'uncompromising' captain) declared only 58 runs on to give Bill Edrich his last chance to reach 1,000 runs before the end of May. There was only time for six overs and the skipper Walter Robins went into the Aussie dressing-room to tell them that on no account must Bill be made a present of the runs. I went in first with him; he hit 20 of 21 on the board and duly reached his target. Bradman had completed his 1,000 on 27 May, the second time he had performed a feat which is not possible for a domestic player in today's changed programme. In that year I was honoured by being one of *Wisden*'s Five Cricketers, together with Hugh Bartlett (Sussex), Bill Brown, then ranked second to Bradman in the Australian side, Ken Farnes, the fast bowler who was killed in an experimental night landing as a Pilot Officer in October 1941, and Arthur Wood, the Yorkshire wicket-keeper. In the same issue of *Wisden* Bradman wrote an article headed 'Cricket at the Cross Roads', and Frank Woolley declared that before the First War there were thirty batsmen in England as good as Hammond. Times have not changed all that much.

Grimmett's first Test partner of note was Arthur Mailey, who spun the ball almost square with a length sometimes as whimsical as his wit. Their association did not last long — it was the first Grimmett–O'Reilly combination which proved so effective, as fearsome as any slow bowling pair in the long history of the game. Unfortunately I never played against Grimmett, whose Test career went back to 1925 when he took eleven wickets against Arthur Gilligan's team at Sydney. He was in England in the following year. The little, gnome-like figure with the round-arm action did little on his first visit, but he was twice the bowler when he returned in 1930 to take 29 Test wickets. As Grimmett, who had started as an unlikely fast bowler, emerged as an international figure, O'Reilly was starting with New South Wales. It was an odd story, of the new bowler being dropped in mid-match. On Christmas Eve Victoria had lost two wickets, including Bill Woodfull, to O'Reilly. On that night the New South Wales team to play Queensland the following week was announced — without O'Reilly. When the game was resumed on Boxing Day O'Reilly embarrassed all by taking 5 for 22 on a perfect wicket. Clearly he was no ordinary recruit. O'Reilly's captain was R.H. Bettington, who led Oxford in 1923. With gracious timing Bettington suddenly found he was unavailable for the next match, and O'Reilly slipped into his place. Before the end of the season O'Reilly was playing Test cricket again against South Africa, in the 1931–2 series in which Bradman averaged a colossal 201.5.

The Grimmett–O'Reilly saga took off from then. In fifteen Tests their collective haul was 169 wickets. The only real failure between them was the axing of Grimmett after three Tests in the bodyline series, and if there was any doubt of the future the first Test at Trent Bridge in 1934 speedily put Australia's fears at rest. O'Reilly had a match aggregate of 11 for 128 and Grimmett 8 for 130, and Australia won with ten minutes to spare. O'Reilly had the last man Tommy Mitchell leg before and he always said that was when he learned to appreciate the impartiality of English umpires. By the last Test O'Reilly had 28 wickets, Grimmett 25 and the next highest tally was five! There was, by now, a theory (which still persists) that English batsmen are crease bound, unadventurous and particularly vulnerable to leg spin, but South Africa were equally fragile on their home wickets to the formidable pair in 1935–6. In the first Test they shared 13 wickets, 11 in the next, and then on to 15, 15 again and 17.

Grimmett's aggregate in five Tests was 44, the third highest in Test history, at a mere 14.59, but from then on O'Reilly effectively lost his partner, who was dropped in the series with England in 1936–7. There was a strong school of thought in Australia which held that a bad mistake was made in not sending Grimmett to England in 1938, despite his age. During the controversy I hoped he would be chosen if only to satisfy my curiosity, but in later years I had the compensation of many chats with him and was fascinated by his lengthy struggle for recognition. He made no headway in his homeland of New Zealand, or in Sydney, where third grade was about the best he could achieve. Going on to Melbourne he did get a few games for Victoria, but again he was ill considered. So he went to Adelaide for a final make-or-break try, and after ten years of rebuffs, was accepted. He was 32 when he was chosen for his first Test, and stayed in the side for eleven years before he was declared redundant — wrongly, many would say.

In contrast to O'Reilly's menacing charge to the wicket Grimmett had a shuffling six-pace run and like Lance Gibbs, the West Indies off-spinner, completed an over at top speed. He always wore his cap, to hide his bald pate, and English batsmen tell me the only complaint they heard from him was when he was taken off. Apparently he hated this — he liked to bowl and bowl, as even on the worst days he believed that he was on the point of out-thinking his opponent.

In appearance O'Reilly and Grimmett (known as 'Scarlet', after the Scarlet Pimpernel, because he was a bit of a mystery bowler) could scarcely have been more different — one of strong, towering physique; the other a short, inconspicuous figure, who would scarcely merit a second look outside a cricket field.

O'Reilly's other noted partner was Fleetwood-Smith, who had changed to slow left arm after breaking his arm. His stock ball was the off-break to the right hander, and his leg-break was the googly. I felt if you stopped his best ball there would be others to hit for he was often too wayward in length and direction. On his day he could be devastating, and his great moment was to bowl Hammond at Adelaide in 1937 and turn the tide Australia's way. Bradman had said to him, 'I want you to bowl the best ball you have ever bowled in your life.' And he did.

But it was always O'Reilly one feared. None had his control, venom and 'killer' instinct. After an hour against him you almost felt limp with the concentration he demanded, and every run you squeezed from him was an achievement.

As with Bradman, it can confidently be said that there will never be another O'Reilly.

19

GRAEME POLLOCK

At some future date when cricket is cleansed and freed of political hypocrisy, the recent era might well be dubbed the 'Sad' or even the 'Insane' Seventies. Tragically, when mediocrity and boring method-style technique flourished (in both batting and bowling) the precious talents of South Africans were left to rot and die on the international scene. When the game was aching for personalities and the true hall-marks of class South Africa continued the involuntary isolation begun in the black year of 1970. When lesser lights were parading their mechanical, stereotyped methods in a constant round of Test cricket for increasingly large rewards, the likes of Mike Procter, Barry Richards, Eddie Barlow and Clive Rice were denied the right to play for their country. That their talents were on display in English county cricket made the situation all the more poignant and baffling.

I confess my·South African leanings without apology. For my part, the Prudential Cup is a world competition in name only while one of the leading teams, perhaps the best of all, is outlawed by the complexities of politics. How much more compelling, gripping and strong the first two tournaments would have been for the presence of South Africa.

Treated as they have been, it is small wonder that Richards, Procter and other South African stars were attracted to Kerry Packer and his brand of commercial cricket. They could well have argued that if official cricket outlawed them Packer did not. The basic and illogical contradiction was that while the *players* of the West Indies and Pakistan apparently had no objection to the presence of South Africans in World Series Cricket — and presumably would have been of the same mind for the Prudential Cup —

their governing bodies blocked all efforts to end the situation. How can it be right for a Board of Control tacitly to sanction contact with South Africans in unofficial cricket and not at official level? And if they are really puppets of their governments, how can the governments justify such humbug? If the players contravene a government policy of non-contact, how can the same players continue to represent their country? To me the whole unhappy matter becomes a classic example of political expediency, with cricket very much the loser.

This preamble, which I am glad to get off my chest, is perhaps an unforgivable approach to what is intended as a tribute to Robert Graeme Pollock. But the fact is that he enters my gallery of immortals despite what has been done to him and his fellow countrymen. Here is a truly wonderful left-hand batsman in the mould of Frank Woolley, who gave infinite pleasure to countless millions, with a miserly record of 23 Tests and an international career starting in 1963 and presumably ending in 1969. The modern player crowds in as many Tests in a two-year period or so, and it is said that the Test coinage is not debased by too many matches! Nowadays there is no respite, as one feverish series follows another.

Graeme had to be a genius, a latter-day Woolley, to win universal acclaim in such a short stay on the world stage. I notice that modern writers, searching to praise David Gower, have compared him with Pollock. For me Graeme fulfilled every technical and temperamental requirement of examiner Compton which includes, as the reader must know by now, perfection in back-foot techniques.

Before I proceed in my undisguised adulation of Graeme, however, I admit to finding it a difficult decision to put him slightly ahead of the vintage New Zealand left-hander Martin Donnelly. In turn, Martin only edges ahead of the other distinguished Kiwi left-hander Bert Sutcliffe, who has a very high place in post-war ratings. Sutcliffe, Donnelly and the versatile John Reid formed a trio of talent any country would be proud to have.

Like all of his generation Donnelly's career was cut short by six years of war, in which he served as a Major in the New Zealand forces. I saw enough of him in Tests, and for Oxford University and Warwickshire, to become one of his most zealous admirers. He was only twenty and with the minimum of experience when he toured England in 1937 — the season I made my Test debut. Yet he finished second in the averages, and displayed rare ability with his driving, cutting and hooking of anything minutely short.

In 1945 he was stationed in England, and for the Dominions took 133 off England in an innings at Lord's which also included 185 from Keith Miller. The war over Martin went to Oxford and scored 142 against Cambridge. Also at Lord's in 1948 he was to score 162 not out for the Gentlemen against the Players — out of a total of 302 — and 206 in the 1949 Test. That 1949 double-century was the first for his country. Donnelly was also an international Rugby player, appearing as centre for England in Dublin, and was one of those fortunates able to excel at any game.

Pollock and Donnelly had much in common — immense natural aptitude, a wide stroke repertoire, invention, and nerve to go with a sense of adventure. While Martin was of moderate height, which probably helped his devastating hook, Graeme stands well over six foot and has a majestically powerful swing. His fault is the human one of a careless swish on occasions, and his running between the wickets has reminded some of Compton. As inventor of the triple call — 'Yes! No! Sorry!' — I am surprised at such a frailty, but I am sure he cannot quite be in my lonely class.

For a big man he is surprisingly light and nimble on his feet. Indeed he could not be otherwise, for footwork is the basis of batting technique. I first heard of the promise of Graeme and his brother Peter, the fast bowler, from that brilliant Sussex batsman and raconteur George Cox, who, at the time, was one of the dedicated band of English coaches. With the last ball of the county season bowled they migrate like swallows to the sunshine of South Africa to work in schools and clubs, promoting the game and putting young players on the right path.

South Africa owes much to these men. George Cox was coach at Grey High School, Port Elizabeth, and it must have been a joy for him to have the Pollock brothers under his wise control as their Scots-born father, who kept wicket for Orange Free State, had already instilled in both the rudiments of the game. They came from a sports-conscious family, and apparently at the age of three Graeme was holding a bat — left-handed, to the consternation of his parents. In everything else Graeme was right-handed.

Graeme also had the considerable advantage of elder brother Peter's bowling, and a back garden concrete pitch on which strokes could be made with confidence. The family, neighbours and fellow players soon discovered the young Graeme liked to bat and bat and bat. He was still only nine when for his school side he scored 117 not out and took 10 wickets for 25 runs. A budding genius if there ever was one! As he had been able to walk at the age of only eight months everything seems to have come to him easily and naturally.

At that early stage Graeme the bowler was fast like his brother, but he later developed useful leg-spin. It was Cox who shrewdly advised Peter to concentrate on bowling when his heart was for batting. 'You'll never make a great batsman, but you could be a great bowler,' was George's far-seeing and accurate prediction. But there was never any serious doubt that Graeme's precocious gifts entitled him to the status of a batting prodigy. As with many destined for later fame, ability burst from the seams. On his thirteenth brithday he was in the school team with boys four years his senior; chosen for Eastern Province, he scored 152 in the Nuffield Schools Week.

When a mere 16 years and 335 days old he became the youngest to score a century in the Currie Cup — South Africa's major domestic tournament — and at nineteen he was the youngest to hit a double century at first-class level. To complete his record he also scored his first Test century, against Australia at Sydney, in the 1963–4 series, when nineteen. Before then he played half a dozen matches for Sussex Second XI, when he accompanied his family on a trip to England, and I always think it a shame he could never be persuaded to play county cricket. Back home he made 209 not out at Port Elizabeth against a strong Cavaliers side organized by the late Ron Roberts, but it has to be admitted that he was not fully prepared for the off-spin — leg to him — of David Allen and Fred Titmus on turning pitches in 1964–5.

Revenge, however, was swift and complete. In the final Test, on his home ground, Pollock atoned with 137 and 77 not out. His driving past mid-on and cover could not be contained, and England's bowlers must have secretly feared what was in store for them in the return series in the second half of the summer of 1965. South Africa followed New Zealand in a split season, and it is now history that the Pollocks left an imperishable memory of dazzling batting and fast bowling. Such was the Springbok's impact as they won the rubber 1-0 that the two Pollocks, who virtually won the only Test to be finished, and Colin Bland were included in *Wisden*'s Five Cricketers of the Year.

Peter, the spearhead of the attack, took 20 wickets in the three Tests for only 18.30 each, and Graeme topped the batting averages with 291, including his famous 125 at Trent Bridge. South Africa had not won in England for ten years, and their victory by 94 runs with a day to spare was a singular triumph for the Pollocks. Perhaps there is no parallel case in contemporary history of two brothers playing such a historic role at international level. Batsman Graeme ended with 184 runs, held an outstanding slip catch and took the vital second innings wicket of Mike Smith. Peter had a match analysis of 10 wickets for 87 runs in 48 overs.

Graeme's 125 out of a total of 269 in the first innings, after the first five had gone for 80, was not merely a case of brilliant mono-poly. The crucial point was that he took on the English bowlers in their own conditions and in two hours and twenty minutes of glorious attack completely reversed the pattern of the match. The day with its overcast skies was meant for England, and in particular for Tom Cartwright, who took three quick wickets and indeed finished with 6 for 94, plus a broken right thumb which put him out of the second innings.

Graeme, then twenty-one, started with South Africa an unpromising 16 for 2. Understandably he felt his way until he was in the mid-thirties. Already he had shown remarkable defensive skill and application. Then, quite sure of himself, he suddenly cut loose, scoring 91 out of 102 in seventy minutes in a manner which still thrills me as I write all these years later. I have since heard that he 'slogged' and 'took his life in his hands'. If this be so give me more of it and less of the five-hour plod to a century in perfect conditions against bowlers no better than trundlers. In this so-called ultra-professional age a risk is condemned as a folly. The truth is that in the final analysis it pays to be aggressive. I see little merit in mere run-accumulation, which so often hides second-rate ability and sheer selfishness.

To me Graeme was sheer, undiluted genius on that memorable day at Nottingham, and he must have been in the same abandoned mood at Perth when he so deeply impressed Sir Donald Bradman. After an 85-minute century against a Combined XI including five Test men the Don remarked, 'If you ever score a century like that again I hope I'm there to see it.' Later, in the Adelaide Test,

Bradman was again the fortunate witness of another example of the grace, elegance and power of Pollock when he made 175 in a partnership of 341 for the third wicket with that chunky fighter Eddie Barlow, who did a great deal in a short time for Derbyshire. (I often wonder how far Derbyshire might have gone if he had been able to stay for another two years!)

In one over against Bobby Simpson's leg-breaks and googlies Graeme hit two sixes, two fours, and a two. I doubt if statistics meant as much to him as the exhilaration of challenge, the inner excitement and rising sap as formidable bowlers are overcome and the realization dawns that a big innings is in the offing. It can be an intoxicating emotion. I would also have given much to have been at Scarborough when he scored 101 in 52 minutes, or to see his 203 not out at Canterbury with five sixes and twenty-eight fours. To quote *Wisden*, he 'reminded many of the elderly spectators of the grace and charm of Frank Woolley, whose style he so much resembled'. Could the citizens of Kent have offered a higher accolade?

Then there was his supreme achievement of 274 in 420 minutes against Australia at Durban, in the second Test of the amazing series when Bill Lawry's side was whitewashed in four Tests. Graeme reached 100 in 170 minutes against an attack consisting of Graham McKenzie, Alan Connolly and Jack Gleeson; his 200 took 307 minutes. The remarkable feature of this innings, which some of his victims later described to me as murderous and the most dazzling they had ever seen, was its merciless and constant attack. Even the great innings normally have periods of 'breathers' and defensive overs. Bradman was, as always, the exception, and here was Graeme doing much the same thing.

In the same match Barry Richards, an opening batsman of the highest quality, ranking with the best of all time, and Pollock utterly demoralized the opposition. I always felt watching Graeme that he was a giant in every respect, with the rare capacity to make even his finest contemporaries look modest by comparison. There have been precious few batsmen in my time who aroused such feelings within me . . . Bradman, Hammond, Hutton (when he let himself go) and the W's, and certainly Pollock.

Graeme had the unusual facility of being equally strong on both front and back foot. He was amazingly adaptable, which I accept to be part of genius. Different conditions did not defeat him, as has so often happened even to the very best, and those in South Africa in the 1966–7 series have told me how he attacked off the front foot in making 90 in 90 minutes at Johannesburg, and a week later on a slower surface at Cape Town made 209 off the back foot. Like all the masters his placing was of the highest class. In other words he found the gaps in the field and could never be tied down.

During his famous Trent Bridge innings Graeme became the youngest player to reach 1,000 runs in Test cricket, and heavens knows what his aggregate might have been but for the cruel ban on his talents. The same can be said of Richards, Procter and other South African victims of the accursed modern politics.

Graeme's exploits must be linked with those of his brother, who bowled at authentic pace and began to exercise subtlety in England where the conditions helped him. At the time he was comfortably the fastest bowler in the side, but he had learned to pace himself and to bowl within himself when it was patently absurd to burn up energy going flat out. On no fewer than six occasions he had five wickets in an innings, and he was head of the averages with 50 wickets for only 17.02 each.

Peter had the average fast bowler's natural aggression, and the right physical strength from a frame over six feet two inches tall. For my part he was one of the most impressive fast bowlers of the post-war years. Whether he would go in front of Cuan McCarthy, Heine or Adcock would be a matter of debate, but to be in their company is no small recommendation.

The Pollock brothers are a significant part of South Africa's cricket history, and I particularly salute Graeme, a magnificent batsman by any standards and a consistent attacker.

20

VIV RICHARDS

Before the arrival of Viv Richards and Andy Roberts the Leewards island of Antigua was famous only as a naval base of Horatio Nelson. With no disrespect to Britain's most famous seaman or to history, I suggest that many an atlas has recently been searched to locate the speck in the Caribbean Sea which bred two of cricket's immortals.

I first played at Antigua when Richards and Roberts were toddlers, and I remember its golden sands, a steel band named 'Brute Force' (did the quaint titles of pop groups originate in the West Indies?) and 'trusty' convicts from the adjacent prison preparing the pitch. I congratulated one on the excellence of the wicket and he replied feelingly, 'I've been at it long enough!'

Though teams from the Leeward and Windward Islands have achieved first-class status and compete in the two major competitions in the West Indies, it is nevertheless remarkable that such a comparatively tiny island should produce a fast bowler of Roberts's stature and a batting titan named Isaac Vivian Alexander Richards from a population of under 70,000. It means that natural aptitude stands for everything; the size and population of an area counts for little.

The big advantage the West Indies have lies in the perfect climate, a bubbling infectious enthusiasm for the game and a complete lack of inhibitions. Richards is a typical product — superb, almost animal-like grace and athleticism, perfect balance and eye, and a thirst for runs at any level. I was not surprised to learn that his father Malcolm was the best fast bowler in Antigua for many years, and that brothers Mervyn, a batsman, and Donald, a fast medium bowler, also represented the Leeward

Islands. Nor that Viv was a crack soccer centre-half playing for Antigua in his teens — though later he failed a trial with Bath City!

No doubt we could swap a few football yarns. Once I was about to go on to the field at Villa Park for Arsenal when George Cummings, the Scottish international full back, came alongside. 'I hear you can crack 'em through the covers,' he said, 'Yes, I suppose I can,' was my innocent reply. 'Well, if you still want to, keep away from me this afternoon!' he warned.

Viv played football the afternoon he and Roberts left for the much publicized coaching scholarship at Alf Gover's 'academy' in London, and he arrived at the airport just in time. Richards and Roberts were sent to London in 1973 by the local Cricket Association by public subscription, and there can be little doubt that the wise instruction by the genial former Surrey bowler had a marked effect on their careers. Viv was taught to hit straight and to curb his natural instinct to clout every ball for a six or four — though many bowlers will insist Alf failed in this aspect — and the transition from St John's to Somerset was eased.

There was a season in Taunton club cricket before Viv joined Somerset, and experience for Roberts in Southampton as he prepared for Hampshire. (Later he was to be engaged only on the casting vote of chairman Charlie Knott, a fine off-spinner in his day!) Viv was earmarked for Somerset by chairman Len Creed, a Bath bookmaker, who sagely noted some comments in the *Cricketer* by Colin Cowdrey on a young West Indian batsman. Creed went out on holiday and saw Richards play against a touring team called the Mendip Acorns. When he left Bath I wonder what odds Creed would have offered against spotting — and securing for Somerset — one of the greatest batsmen in the contemporary game.

I have been told, moreover, that Richards was well out in that particular innings before he so deeply impressed the bookmaker from Bath. Of course his ability was such that it would have come out, despite an astonishing two-year ban which delayed his progress towards first-class cricket.

From the beginning Viv, both as footballer and cricketer, was the idol of his native island, and his very popularity got him into serious trouble in 1969. During an inter-island game against St Kitts — and all such games arouse considerable excitement and passions — he was given out caught at short leg off bat and pad.

Richards immediately signalled that he had not snicked the ball and stayed put at the crease while addressing a few words to the umpire. After an uncomfortable delay he strode off. But a riot was sparked off, play was suspended and spectators chanted in unison, 'No Vivi, no match.' Two hours elapsed before play was resumed with the ridiculous concession that Richards should continue his innings.

If that was not a bad enough decision Viv's agreement to do so was even worse, and was not made right by his allowing himself to be stumped at once. In a sense the young Richards was made the scapegoat for official foolishness, though he would now be the last to condone his own behaviour.

Knowing a little of the pressures and jealousies a sportsman in the limelight is obliged to endure, I have been much taken by Viv's general demeanour. His crown sits lightly on his head. So much is always expected of him that it speaks highly of his temperament and general outlook that he is seemingly so cool and outwardly detached. There was an incident at Old Trafford which shows how careful a player in his position needs to be. Annoyed with himself at getting out (and who isn't?) he smashed a dressing-room window. One newspaper devoted the whole of its back page to the incident, though Ian Botham was breaking a world record on the same day in a Test at Lord's. I suppose, in a way, it is a back-handed compliment to a player's status that one minor outburst should provoke such a blaze of reaction.

The effect of the Antigua row meant that Richards was twenty before he could be selected for Leeward and Combined Islands. He made up for lost time with 82 against the touring New Zealanders, but too often an undisciplined Richards, for all his ability, got himself out with careless strokes when the hard part had been done. Oddly, for one who appears to score at will, he had still to reach a first-class century before he was chosen in front of Rohan Kanhai for the 1974–5 tour of India and Pakistan. It has since been described as an inspired selection. Maybe, but I think even with a low score a man with half an eye would see he is way out of the ruck. Such unhurried strokes! If Hammond was the master of off-side play, Richards and Peter May may be described as supreme on the leg side. And the way Richards can merely lean on the ball to send it scorching through the covers is possible only by perfect timing, positioning and balance. To me Viv has it all. A little over-confident at times? Maybe, but he fits exactly my conception of the truly great batsman with the right approach. A little gamble with fate now and again, like taking the ball pitched middle and leg to the mid-wicket boundary, and a little impatience to get on with it. If that be a fault please give me more with similar defects!

The path to glory was first trodden at New Delhi with an innings of 192 not out, and in the first eight months of 1976 he scored no fewer than 1,710 runs from eleven Tests, including 829 in four Tests against England — a record aggregate for a year and the fourth highest aggregate for a series. Perhaps if Bradman had played as many times in a calendar year he would have set up figures none could have touched, but there was no denying the prodigious achievement by Richards. His sequence began in Australia against the best fast bowling of the day with scores of 44, 2, 30, 101, 50 and 98. Against the renowned Indian spinners in the four-Test series at home he made 142, 130, 20 (run out), 177, 23 and 64. In England his average was 118.42 and the only relief the bowlers had was when he was injured and missed the Lord's game. His Test scores were 232 and 63 at Trent Bridge, 4 and 135 at Old Trafford, 66 and 38 at Headingly and 291 at the Oval.

Only Bradman (974 in England in 1930), Hammond (905 in Australia in 1928–9) and Harvey (834 in South Africa in 1952–3) have a higher aggregate in a Test series. Richards, whose final figure for the year was 1,811 (from the first Test in Australia in November 1975), and Bradman had only seven innings against nine by Hammond and Harvey. Watching him that summer I often wondered if he had a magic wand rather than a bat of willow, and as *Wisden* said, 'Mere figures cannot convey his perfect style and stroke play. His cover driving was superb and with his feet always in the right position the way he flicked the ball on his leg stump to square leg had to be seen to be believed.'

In addition to his mammoth Test innings he took 176 against Hampshire, 121 off Glamorgan, 113 at Lord's against M.C.C. and 119 not out in a match at Scarborough not granted first-class status. In 25 innings he aggregated 1,724 runs, and one was often left wondering why lesser mortals made batting appear so difficult. Always he had plenty of time to make his shots, and all the hallmarks of the master batsman were paraded with an almost languid and casual air. It could be argued that England's attack was undistinguished, but it contained John Snow, Bob Willis, Derek Underwood. Mike Hendrick and Chris Old among the twenty-one Alec Bedser's harassed selectors called up during the series.

When one reflects on the quality of the West Indian batsmen who have toured England, George Headley (who had 3-match series), the W's, Basil Butcher, Conrad Hunte, Rohan Kanhai, Clive Lloyd, Gary Sobers, it seems incredible that Richards should compile a record number of runs despite missing one Test. In Australia in 1975–6 Richards was in less trouble than any of his compatriots, and a decision to put him in first made him a more responsible batsman. The move was made partly because the West Indies had an opening problem, and partly to help him conquer his habit of getting out when set, and it worked like a charm. His course was set for the stars.

Unlike some I could mention Richards clearly enjoys every minute he is at the crease, or indeed in the field, and whether batting, fielding in the covers or occasionally bowling his tidy off-breaks he adds gaiety and impressive individualism as well as consummate and effortless skills to the most important occasion. I find it fascinating that a player should come from the quaint and picturesque little town of St John's, so far from the sophisticated world, and not be a little overawed. Here is the son of a prison officer, who started working life as a waiter and was about to be sent to New York to study electrical engineering, able to take the cricket world by storm from Sydney to Lord's, from Kingston to Bangalore. He remains a typical 'small islander', enjoying late nights, jazz and the rest, and one of his richest private jokes was the story that he had gained five 'A' levels at school. The truth is that he didn't get one, which puts him on my own level of scholastic attainment.

Apart from his God-given talents Viv, I contend, was particularly lucky to have the early advice of Gover, a coach at Somerset of Tom Cartwright's calibre — shrewd enough to let him go his own way and learn of English conditions by bitter experience — and a no-nonsense captain in Brian Close. I know there were mixed opinions about Close's handling of young players, but undoubtedly he helped Viv to change his attitude and bring some steel into his play without putting on manacles. In 1973, for instance, Viv hit 73 sixes, and won £250 for the most boundaries in the Test Series. Armed with such statistics some have it that Viv hits the ball harder with less effort than anyone in this or any age. But it is beyond argument that he makes batting look simple. His century in the Prudential Cup Final of 1979 which, with an economical spell of bowling, won him the Man of the Match award, was classical, a joyous exhibition which none who saw it will ever forget. He toyed with the bowling, made light of all Mike Brearley's attempts to block the recognized scoring lanes — improvisation being one of his prime assets — and, despite every effort to prevent a last telling shot, put the final delivery by Hendrick into the crowd. The Don at his best could not have been more impudently superior.

In the first Prudential Cup in 1975 he atoned for a rare failure with the bat by running out three Australians — a contribution almost as decisive as Clive Lloyd's century. Yet he felt obliged at one point of his first tour in Australia to call on the help of Arthur Jackson, the doctor who has been of immense psychological benefit to Bob Willis among others. Viv declares his concentration improved after his visits. For all that he seems to me so relaxed at times as to be almost languid.

Richards's arrival at Taunton coincided with Somerset's spurt to the top. Any side with Richards, Ian Botham — Viv is godfather to his son Liam — and the six-foot-eight Joel Garner has to be strong. In my days the Somerset fixture was not exactly one to send apprehensive shivers down the spine, but now they are one of the powers of the land, ambitious and with a large partisan following.

Off the field Viv has had his moments. His car had a seventy-mile-an-hour blow out on the M4 and plunged twenty feet onto concrete; and he made a late start to the 1979 season while he recovered from injuries suffered at gunpoint in an incident outside a post office in Antigua. The orthodox, staid life it seems is not for him.

Viv is one of the few modern batsmen whose emergence from the pavilion causes a hum of expectation to sound from the spectators. A few drinks are hurriedly downed, and he certainly makes me sit up and take notice. Hampshire's Gordon Greenidge, the West Indian who learned his cricket in Berkshire — what a difference he would make to England's strength! — is another, and when I was asked at a quiz in which order I placed the two

Richardses I admitted to being caught, bowled and stumped with one question. Both, in modern terminology, are superstars, as good batsmen as has ever been known. In the hindsight of reflection I still hesitate to separate the especial gifts of Viv and Barry, but my vote would have to go to Viv for the simple reason that he has had the chance to splatter the Test record books cruelly denied the superb South African.

I have little doubt that if South Africa had not been hounded out of the international scene Barry would have smashed record after record. His talent shone through for Hampshire, South Africa and Natal. But Viv has the advantage of the figures in the book and proof of his greatness at the highest level. Long may he continue to flourish. The ancient game needs him.

21

SIR GARY SOBERS

If the life story of Garfield St Aubrun Sobers had been the invention of a novelist's fertile imagination it would have been laughingly dismissed as too fanciful by half.

Who could possibly accept the character of a superman cricketer able to bat in the style of Frank Woolley, bowl fast-medium at least as well as Alan Davidson, turn the slow-left-arm orthodoxy of a Bishen Bedi on the googlies and 'chinamen' of a George Tribe, and catch like Wally Hammond in the slips and Tony Lock at backward short leg? And with the captaincy in 39 Tests thrown in for good measure.

Any attempt at realism is so far abandoned that our hero is able to confuse a technician of the order of Geoff Boycott with the new ball, and as an opening batsman smash 43 in fifteen violent minutes off the holy terrors Ray Lindwall and Keith Miller. To his outrageous talent is added the improbable romance of an under-privileged boy from a tiny Caribbean island surviving two heart-stopping personal tragedies and eventually being knighted by the Queen. A likely tale indeed!

Yet the unique gifts and career of Sobers stand as a living testimony to the old adage about truth being stranger than fiction. One's mind reels at his accomplishments. One record tumbles over another and one is left simply to wonder at the saga of the finest and most versatile all-rounder in the history of the ancient game. From 30 March 1954, when I played against him in his maiden Test at Sabina Park, Kingston, to 5 April 1974, Sobers created his own history in 93 Test matches — the highest number of appearances after Colin Cowdrey and Alan Knott. His record aggregate of 8,032 runs include twenty-six centuries and the biggest individual Test score of 365 not out against Pakistan at Kingston in 1958; and his three-style bowling produced 235 wickets, with five or more in an innings six times. As either batsman or bowler he has irrefutable claims to immortality. There is the bonus of 109 catches, many little more than half-chances at leg slip on behalf of the off-spinner Lance Gibbs.

Add his runs for the Rest of the World on his visits to England in 1970 and Australia a year later — both as captain — and his record at international level swells to 8,961 runs with twenty-eight centuries, and a lift in average from 57.78 to 58.18, with 265 wickets and 116 catches.

In all first-class cricket for his native Barbados, nine tours for the West Indies, Rest of the World, eight seasons with Nottinghamshire in the English county championship and three for South Australia in the Sheffield Shield, he made 28,315 runs, and it would need a computer to calculate his full aggregate in eight years in the northern Leagues, several private tours and regular matches for the Cavaliers before the advent of the John Player League on Sundays. No fewer than 89 of his 93 Tests were consecutive, and it was scarcely surprising that his energies and enthusiasm began to wane. It has to be said that there were days with Nottinghamshire when I thought he gave the impression of being on compulsory overtime.

The penalty of his lavish talent was to be in the thick of every game, the centre-piece of strategy and performance, and like Bradman and Hobbs he was deemed a failure unless he played to his maximum capabilities. I experienced something of the strain in 1947, when I began to bowl googlies as well as bat for long periods, that Gary endured for twenty-one years. Whenever cricketers talk of him I notice one telling point — the discussion begins on the premise and acceptance of his pre-eminent status and dwells on possible comparisons. Some Australians loyally put Alan Davidson in front, but there is no comparison between them as batsmen. I would place Keith Miller closer, and his case becomes stronger if his flaws against the spin of Lock and Laker in 1956 are ignored. Miller, Wally Hammond, Mike Procter and Frank Woolley in his hey-day as batsman, slow-left-arm bowler and slip catcher, must be in the same exalted company without achieving the range of Sobers's attainments.

I have named only the superlative all-rounder performers of

my own playing and watching days, but it is impossible to ignore
Dr W.G. Grace, with his 54,896 runs and 2,876 wickets. His
bearded figure might raise a smile in our sophisticated age, but he
was without a shadow of a doubt a very considerable cricketer. In
1906 the Yorkshireman George Hirst scored 2,385 runs and took
208 wickets. Wilfred Rhodes ended a 32-year career with 39,802
runs and 4,187 wickets — figures to roll around the tongue — and
from batting at No. 11 rose to partner Hobbs in a first-wicket stand
of 323 at Melbourne in 1911–12, still a record in England-
Australia Tests. What a player he must have been! But even the
great Wilfred did not reel off centuries in Test matches, and would
I imagine have been insulted if he had been told to bowl fast with
the new ball. Sobers must be the supreme virtuoso of cricket. Even
the greatest musicians are not masters of four instruments.

Sobers first played for the West Indies as an orthodox slow left-
arm bowling replacement for an injured Alf Valentine at Sabina
Park in 1954, when he was seventeen. He came in at No. 9 with the
total 110 for 7, a time of crisis for the match and the series. I
remember a slim, shy youngster betraying not the slightest nerve
as Len Hutton, thirsting for the kill, surrounded him with an
attacking field. All the senior batsmen, Weekes, Worrell, Walcott,
Stollmeyer and Gomez, had been defeated, but Sobers not only
survived an awkward fifteen minutes before tea but did not make a
mistake. Already the basic technique and temperament were
there. Nor was Sobers perturbed by an interruption for rain, and
his first scoring shot was a beautiful wristy square-cut boundary
off Jim Laker. He and Frank King took 11 off an over by Trueman, and Sobers was not out for 14. His first wicket was Trevor
Bailey, later to be his ardent admirer and biographer, with a faster
ball which went with the arm, and he added the wickets of Wardle,
second top scorer to Hutton's wonderful 205, Lock and Laker for
75 in 28.5 overs, a performance in a total of 414 which would have
done much credit to a seasoned bowler.

In the second innings Sobers was last out for 26 — caught by
Compton off Lock — and it did not need much gumption to see the
West Indies had made an important discovery. A crystal ball,
however, would have been necessary to predict the glittering path
he was to tread. His prospects had already been glowingly forecast
by Vijay Hazare, whose Indian touring side the previous year had
yielded seven wickets to a sixteen-year-old spinner for 142 runs. In

those immature days Sobers's main attributes were control and flight far in advance of his years, rather than turn of the ball.

He developed his googly and 'chinaman' (the off-break to the right-hander) in the sixties after watching George Tribe, who played for Australia and Northamptonshire, Wardle, and — I was flattered to hear — myself. Tribe gave him some lessons. I in turn had been shown the unusual art by Jack Walsh, another Australian who did so much to lift the once depressed Leicestershire off the floor. I had frankly become a little bored with bowling the same way, and I induced the generous Jack to let me into some of his secrets. Bowling the unorthodox version expanded my interests and added to the fun.

Sobers turned to the new ball and fast medium at the request of Frankie Worrell and challenged Davidson as the best of his type at world class. He took less time than Alan to realize that the most dangerous form of this attack was to swing late either way on and around the off stump. The late dipper from a fast left-hander of the calibre of Davidson and Sobers was a nightmare to early-order batsmen. If Alan had the slight edge as a pace bowler he was no match as a cutter or spinner of the ball.

There must have been at least a dozen Tests which Sobers virtually won, or on which he exercised the major influence as batsman or bowler or both. He had ten centuries against England, eight off India, four in Australia, three off Pakistan in the 1957–8 series when he passed Len Hutton's individual record, and one off New Zealand, against whom, strange to relate, he was not conspicuously successful. For series after series Sobers was the fulcrum, the inspiration and the power of West Indies cricket. As Bradman observed he consistently hit harder than any of his contemporaries. Further, the Don described the 254 Sobers made for the Rest of the World at Melbourne in 1971 as probably the best innings ever seen in Australia. Now that was some assertion, and knowing his critical but fair judgements and respect for words I would, were I Sobers, value Bradman's evaluation more than the individual record established at the expense of a weakened Pakistan attack.

Fortunately the Melbourne innings was recorded on film and there cannot be a better example of the aggression, the free rhythm and graceful free swing of Sobers to hand down to posterity. The backswing was long and straight, the footwork swift and neat, and

Sobers was in position so quickly that stroke adjustments were always possible. Many a bowler's heart was broken when, with one magical movement, or a flick of those steel-strong wrists, he turned a wicket-taking delivery into a breath-taking boundary. At Melbourne Gary played every shot in the book, patented a few more and finished with three sixes and thirty-three fours. The strokes to excite me most were his square cut and almost nonchalant drive wide of mid on, while a variety of improvisations off his legs were so perfectly timed that their execution seemed child's play. Gary never wore a thigh pad — neither did I — unlike some current batsmen who seem so heavily armoured that it surprises me they can run between wickets. I always felt my best protection was my bat. Gary also took the fast bowlers on by hooking the bouncer, and I cannot recall him being forced into hurried evasive action. Frankly he was so quick and positive that I would not relish bowling spinners at him.

Six feet tall, lithe, athletic and beautifully balanced, he could not be categorized as essentially a front- or a back-foot batsman. His improvisations were so instinctive and stunning that he would find a stroke for almost every type of delivery. Nor do I think many realize how combative he could be. When he hit the maximum of six sixes in an over from Glamorgan's left-arm Malcolm Nash at Swansea in 1968, Tony Lewis, the home captain, was quoted as saying, 'It was not sheer slogging through strength, but scientific hitting with every movement in working harmony.' Nottinghamshire were 300 for 5 when Sobers (at No. 7!) went in to bat, looking, as *Wisden* put it, like a black panther eager to pounce. Straight drives and pulls put the ball out of the ground, and the last six was not recovered until the following day. It is now to be seen in the Trent Bridge Cricket Museum.

The killer instinct was epitomized by his destruction of Pakistan, who virtually had only Fazal Mahmood and Khan Mohammad as fit bowlers. A.H. Kardar started with a broken finger in his spinning hand. It took Sobers, then twenty-one, ten hours and eight minutes to break a record which had taken Hutton three hours twelve minutes longer to set up almost twenty years before. Sobers overshadowed even Walcott, Weekes, Hunte and Kanhai, and followed his record score with a century in each innings of the next Test at Georgetown. His aggregate of 824 was only three short of the highest for a West Indies player, made by

Walcott against Australia in 1955. Those who dismiss Pakistan's bowling as second-rate should remember the concentration and discipline demanded of a young batsman, and the fact that he attacked for most of the time.

Lord's 1966 was as good an innings as I ever saw from Gary in England, at least in the context of the West Indies, then regarded as world champions, being in the unfamiliar position of being up against it. For once he saved the match instead of the winning it, and his century and record partnership of 274 for the sixth wicket with his cousin David Holford not only thwarted England but proved, if proof were necessary, that there was not a chink in his defensive technique. England, with a lead of 86, had Conrad Hunte, Joey Carew, Rohan Kanhai, Basil Butcher and Seymour Nurse out for 95 in the second innings when Holford joined Sobers without much batting to come. Five hours twenty minutes batting time later Sobers declared — a simple fact to present the bare bones of a heart-breaking experience for England, which began with Sobers successfully counter-attacking skipper Colin Cowdrey's tactic of a close-set field. Attack was the life blood of his cricket.

On his first tour of England in 1957 *Wisden* earmarked Sobers as a stroke-player who should go far. His 219 not out at Trent Bridge, where he was later to return as the Prince of Nottinghamshire, was the highest individual score of a tour on which the West Indies were not seen at their best. In 1963 Sobers furthered his cricketing education under Frankie Worrell and was almost automatically named as one of *Wisden*'s Five Cricketers of the Year. By 1966, now captain and with consistency in all departments, he was the dominant personality in a series which, until the final Test, was the West Indies all the way. As batsman, three-styled bowler, superb catcher near the bat, and a tactical captain able to drive home his big advantages, Sobers enjoyed triumph after triumph in his best-ever series. Until he came an unexpected cropper against the new captain Brian Close he seemed like Alexander of old, seeking new worlds to conquer. Sobers collected a duck in the second innings, which, with respect to all concerned, was regarded in the same miraculous light as England's last three wickets adding 361 runs! Until then Sobers had notched 722 runs, including 161 at Old Trafford, 163 not out at Lord's, 94 at Trent Bridge, 174 at Headingley and 81 in the first innings at the Oval. His aggregate bettered the record of 709 against England he set up in the home series of 1959–60. To his 722 runs were added 20 wickets, one fewer than Lance Gibbs, and in all matches he had 60 wickets, more than any other bowler, and 23 catches, the highest for an out-fielder. At Canterbury, on a good pitch, he became the first West Indian bowler to capture nine wickets (for only 49) in an innings in England. And he won all five Test match tosses! It is hardly surprising his reputation as the infallible cricketer grew. His name is associated with no fewer than five of the West Indies record partnerships against England.

In the memorable Worrell tour of Australia in 1960–1 Gary made a century in the Brisbane tied Test, and another, the highest of the series by the West Indies, at Sydney where he was fighting a bad patch in the only way he knew — intelligent attack. There was a familiar ring to the praise showered on him at Brisbane. Some hardened critics wrote that it was the best innings they had ever seen. It took him just two hours to score 132 against Davidson, Meckiff, Mackay, Benaud and Kline.

Sobers the attacker was always an awesome sight — so much ability given to one man. Sobers also demonstrated at Lord's his contempt for a crisis. In 1967–8 at Sabina Park he made 113 not out when England were anticipating victory, but England had some cause for grievance. On the third day they looked like winning comfortably and were halted by a bottle-throwing mob. Though he was badly missed at slip when seven Sobers played magnificently for over six hours on a distinctly sporting pitch — sporting, that is, unless you are the batsman when you would call it a fiery menace. In the end Sobers and Gibbs almost span England to defeat.

I was in the West Indies as a commentator and saw the Port of Spain Test which ended in a miscalculation by Sobers giving victory to England, and with it the series. Strange were the events of that match. The West Indies scored 526 for 7 declared and England 404. In three overs, however, Basil Butcher, an occasional leg-spinner, seized four wickets; and he finished his ten overs with 5 for 15. Sobers was presumably persuaded that Butcher had found the English weakness, and declared at 92 for two, leaving a target of 215 in two and three-quarter hours. I saw Colin Cowdrey, the captain, and begged him to go for the runs. As I saw it Sobers had miscalculated and given England a golden opportunity. So it proved to be, and with Geoff Boycott pacing his 80 runs as if his mind was a slide rule England won by seven wickets with three minutes to spare.

Much of the hysterical criticism of Sobers was manifestly unjust, as few on the ground anticipated that England could manage 78 an hour over such a long period. Gary had always been a bit of a gambler, and perhaps too fond of the gee-gees, but the asking rate was almost double England's average scoring progress during the series, and if Boycott and Cowdrey had not performed so well Sobers might well have won and those same critics lauded his imaginative aggression. Sobers succeeded Worrell, which was hard in itself, and after beating Australia in his first series he had his successes and failures. To have the responsibility of captain as well as being the leading player is an enormous strain. In a winning side the load is bearable, but it becomes intolerable if things go wrong. He did not always find it a smooth path, particularly in Australia in 1968–9 when his side were generally in difficulties. Surprisingly he lost at home to India, and was held to a draw by New Zealand.

I would rate his captaincy as instinctive rather than shrewd or that of the text-book tactician. He was anything but a disciplinarian like Douglas Jardine, and missed many of the details which would have been apparent to the Don, Hutton or Ray Illingworth. His major inspiration to his players was his own performances. If ever a Test captain led a team by example of what he personally did with bat and ball it was Gary. His warm-blooded nature would not permit him to regard Test cricket as an extension to a funeral parlour. Combative, yes; over-serious, no. I would regard him as a captain at his best when there were not too many problems tactically and he was at liberty to go ahead as an uninhibited member of an uninhibited team.

Sobers's gifts were amazing, and he had the fortune to be raised in a cricket-mad island of sunshine and true wickets. Apart from cricket he played soccer for Barbados as a goalkeeper, he drives like a top golf pro, and excelled at basketball, lawn tennis, table tennis and athletics. Cricket, indeed, could have been invented for Sobers's personal enjoyment, and like Neil Harvey he was part of of a sports-mad family. One of his four brothers Gerry played for a time in the northern Leagues of England, and even his two sisters played in the family games of cricket.

In January 1941 Gary's father, a merchant seaman, was drowned when his ship the *Lady Drake* was torpedoed and all hands perished. Gary was possibly too young to absorb the full implications of the death of his father, but the loss of his best friend, Collie Smith, was a numbing blow. Life had been particularly good for Gary in that fateful year of 1959. He was already the acknowledged master batsman, holder of the world record, and scorer in the previous winter of three consecutive centuries off India. The cricket world was in his hands.

Collie Smith, another young West Indian batsman of huge ability and attractive personality, was the back-seat passenger on a night drive to play in a charity match in London on the following day. A third West Indian League cricketer, Tom Dewdney, sat beside Sobers, the driver. There was an accident and Smith, who could have climbed the stairway to the stars, died in hospital. A shattered Sobers took time to conquer and live with his sorrow. The seventies were not kind to him. He got involved in a political row when he went to Rhodesia for a double-wicket tournament. He was crucified. His days as captain were numbered. A knee began to play up, he was out of the Test side for the first time in nineteen years, and played in only three Tests in England under Rohan Kanhai. In 1974 he announced his retirement, and it seemed that a light had gone out of cricket. No doubt he was weary in body and mind, and I end my judgement of Sobers as I did of Bradman: I doubt if we shall see his like again.

22

FREDDIE TRUEMAN

Fast bowlers are a breed apart, and Freddie Trueman was apart from the breed — an incorrigible extrovert, compulsive talker, Yorkshire to the core, and with 307 wickets for England to stake his claim in history and to damn any critic of his filibustering style.

I suspect he would have played in more than 67 Tests, and taken even more wickets, but for the reputation he earned for himself on his first overseas tour, to the West Indies in 1953–4. There can be little doubt that Fiery Fred talked himself out of favour for England turned to Frank ('Typhoon') Tyson to partner Brian Statham in Australia in 1954–5 despite Trueman's 134 wickets in the English season.

In fact Trueman did not play in a Test again until Tyson was injured and withdrew from the Lord's Test against South Africa in 1955. Between 1958 and 1963, however, Trueman revisited the West Indies, where he took 21 wickets in the series — 11 more than the next best by Statham — and went twice to Australia. After his second tour there in 1962–3 he returned with his Test tally extended to 250 — a figure no bowler in history had reached at that time.

As a team-mate on the turbulent tour of the West Indies I much admired his stamina, his willingness to bowl until he was fit only to drop, and his potential, but I could well understand the shocked reaction of the home batsmen. In a calmer atmosphere it might not appear too dreadful for a batsman to be told he would be pinned against the blankety sightscreen, but the atmosphere became anything but calm. Trueman did not learn that what might be acceptable in Sheffield was regarded as an insult in Jamaica, and if in the course of time invented rumour and apocryphal anecdote were linked with his name he only had himself to blame. In the end I fancied his captain Len Hutton and manager Charlie Palmer gave him up as a bad job; but he remained intensely popular with the crowds. Whatever authority might think of him he was always an engaging personality and a crowd-puller wherever he played.

As a player I always thought Freddie grossly overdid the brash aggression act. He was too great a bowler to need to resort to verbal intimidation; as with Keith Miller, I expected the unexpected from him. He had pace, hostility, and a glorious outswinger, but I was often bored by his non-stop comments and gestures which were not always intended for the entertainment of the ring.

If anything one of his verbal broadsides, delivered in his rich South Yorkshire accent, had the effect of strengthening my determination. I could well understand batsmen tiring of the glare down the pitch, and if one played and missed there would not be a spectator left unaware of the fact. Without doubt he expressed more resentment of fate and his immediate opponent than any I knew, and there were times when I thought his captain should have stepped in and put an end to the chat show.

What right has a bowler to abuse a batsman? None at all! Towards the end of his career Freddie seemed to be trying to live up to an image he had created of the pipe-smoking, earthy, ale-supping Yorkshireman, full of salty wit and candour, with a warm heart under a bluff, rugged exterior (which I would be the last to dispute). While he might have scared some young players and visiting Indians with his blustering threats, I vouch for his sense of humour and genuine love for the game — few can catch him out with his memory for facts and figures. He is a veritable walking *Wisden*.

His wit on the field could be pungent and shrewdly penetrative, and like that of his old Yorkshire colleague Johnny Wardle it was well timed and spontaneous. The solemnity of a Test at Adelaide was once shattered by a ceremonial salvo from the guns of a near-by parade ground. Freddie, who was in the middle of his run-up, threw up his arms in a pretence of being shot. The ground collapsed. Near the close of a home Test with India he asked an umpire, 'Can I claim the extra half an hour to get 'em out?' The less belligerent Fiery could be very funny indeed.

But his antics, funny or not-so-funny, did not disguise the fact that he ranks among the great fast bowlers, pre-eminent in my judgement in the English ranks of my experience, though I have seen faster — Tyson, who for two years must have been as quick as any in the history of the game, and Ken Farnes in the pre-war Gentlemen versus Players match at Lord's.

Trueman, like 'Gubby' Allen, had a glorious action, which led to his lethal late outswinger. Batting against him held some of the terrors of picking a path through a minefield. You dreaded the unexpected. Before he began his walk back to his mark you might have had the Glare, the Cold Stare, the Mutter or the Full Treatment. His hair was a dark dishevelled mop and he moistened one side of the ball from the sweat of his brow to gain swing.

His run, the length of a pitch, was controlled perfection, with every movement co-ordinated and rhythmic. In the split second before delivery all you could see was the pointed left shoulder, and then a ninety-mile-an-hour ball would be on its way.

I put Trueman in front of Statham because he was more often capable of producing the type of delivery to defeat the best batsmen, no matter how well set. No other English fast bowler had a similar gift. You never felt completely on top. You were always looking for something to come out of the blue — a real trimmer against which there was no real defence. With his wonderful action, and his stamina, he was able to keep going in the most exacting of conditions.

Trueman could not have had a better partner than Statham, known as 'Gentleman George', in his international career. Their styles were complementary, and I am sure Freddie would be the first to agree that he owed many wickets to the unflagging support and persistent accuracy of Statham. It is in the perverse way of things that Brian was inclined to be too accurate on a true pitch. You had a fair idea where the ball was likely to pitch. Statham was terribly good for Trueman, and later for Tyson; I remember when Tyson was the cynosure of attention after his 7 for 27 at Melbourne in 1955, Sir Don Bradman made a special point of going to Statham and saying, 'It wouldn't have been possible without you.' In the first innings Brian had taken 5 for 60, and in the second he bowled eleven economic overs when the 'Typhoon' blew Australia to pieces.

There was in fact little between Trueman and Statham. I would not quarrel with the contention that comparison between them is futile. But while Brian's attack was a relentless, ordered pursuit,

Trueman could vary his bewilderingly. Batsmen tied down by Statham felt there was a better chance of runs off Trueman and often lost their wickets as a result. More mistakes were made against Trueman than Statham, and Freddie had the gift of producing the great delivery.

Both could be extremely fast, but I cannot believe there can have been faster bowling than by Tyson in 1954, at least for three Tests in Australia. To be in the slips was almost as much as an ordeal as it was to face him with the bat, a thought which was one compensation for my being injured in the famous Sydney Test of that series when he had a downwind from Botany Bay to add to his natural speed. Bob Wyatt told me it was the same with Harold Larwood on one occasion at Sydney when he was one of the slips obliged to retreat farther and farther back — not through apprehension but as a tactical necessity.

Tyson was not fully fit and going off the boil in the home series in 1955, but he was still as quick as anything I saw in the first Test at Trent Bridge against South Africa. After the first ball Trevor Goddard let out a heartfelt, 'Blimey!'

The Ken Farnes exhibition at Lord's in 1938 was little short of terrifying. The game was notable for the fact that Wally Hammond, who had captained the Players to victory in 1937, now led the Gentlemen. Frank Woolley, in his last season, was captain of the Players and was given a remarkable ovation, and Hugh Bartlett, the Sussex amateur left-hander, hit 175 not out in three hours, with four sixes and twenty-four fours. Two of his sixes went on the roof of the grandstand and the other two high up on the Mound stand. I was shivering in case I would be put on to bowl!

It was an unforgettable innings, but what concerned me more at the time was the fast bowling of Farnes, who had been left out of England's side. His attitude was plain for all to see: 'They don't think I can bowl fast enough. Right, I'll show 'em.' The Players went in just before the close, and Bill Edrich was immediately knocked out by a wicked riser via his glove and was caught at backward point.

Before the innings started Woolley had looked around the dressing-room for a 'nightwatchman', and, as he did so, I tried to melt away. His eye fell on Fred Price, the Middlesex wicket-keeper, who stammered a little, and didn't fancy his prospects either. I remember his protest: 'But F-Frank, I have a wife and k-kids to keep.'

Fred went in and was caught at slip to Hammond, and I was one of Farnes's eight victims for 43 runs. I was young and impressionable, but it remains a vivid memory of how terrifying really fast bowling can be. Farnes was killed in the war in an R.A.F. accident.

For some time after the resumption of first-class cricket in 1946 England laboured under the severe handicap of no genuine fast bowling, while Australia had Lindwall and Miller, who could bowl bouncers at will without the threat of retaliation. Trueman, the young Yorkshire miner with shoulders like a battleship (as Hutton used to say), was the first to emerge with Yorkshire in 1949.

Statham, making a spectacular transition from county cricket to Test, was in the England side before him. They formed a superb fast-bowling combination over nine years, and there is no doubt that Trueman as well as being fast was a subtle and clever bowler. There was far more in bowling to him than propelling the ball to the opposite end of the pitch at the utmost speed — and there are plenty who do just that, hoping that holding the seam upright will do the rest. He had already appreciated the value of bowling straight with his successes against India in 1952, and with experience came control and variation, and the realization that on slow pitches the bouncer was effective only if used sparingly. For all that I think the general criticism can be levelled that he overdid the bumper. To me, on occasions, it appeared as a gesture of defiance to the world at large.

Apart from nature's generous bonus of physical strength and self-confidence Trueman had, like Godfrey Evans, a priceless flair for the big occasion. The bigger the better for Fiery Fred. His youthful leg trouble, which started when he was hit on the thigh by a ball and meant constant attendance at Rotherham Hospital, was never evident in his later career. Those bowed legs carried him through twenty gruelling years and over 16,000 overs, including many in Australia and the West Indies where the bone-dry surfaces can be cruel for fast bowlers.

On leaving school Freddie worked in a factory, and established himself as a terror in the local Leagues before going for a trial with Yorkshire via Sheffield United (the cricket club, not the football one against which, I cannot resist saying in passing, I played in an

F.A. Cup final!) The coaches of the day were Arthur Mitchell and Bill Bowes. Bowes reported he had the three major assets he looked for in a young fast bowler: a smooth cartwheel action, a good physique, and a love of fast bowling.

By then Trueman had a new job in the pits, and it used to fascinate me to see him rest briefly squatting on his heels, miner-fashion. One old bowler eyeing him predicted that a winch would be necessary to haul him back on his feet, but Trueman would be up and ready to go again.

For once Yorkshire caution was set aside and at eighteen he played against Cambridge without the formality of a second team outing. He went on to play in nine games, but he was passed over for the month of August, a fact which he didn't like and which could explain his general attitude towards the game's authority. As cricket took him away from the mines he had to do his National Service, and as A/C2 Frederick Sewards Trueman played for England with the kind permission of the Commanding Officer of his unit. Freddie was a sports storeman.

I fielded in the slips when India lost their first four second-innings wickets without a run on the board at Headingley to Trueman, in his first Test, and Bedser. Trueman took three, and had 29 wickets for 13.31 each from the four Tests in the series. It was all too easy. At Old Trafford the Indians were totally demoralized, with Trueman taking 8 for 31. To this day he can recall in detail the dismissal not only of those first wickets but of his entire 307 for England, 229 of which were on home wickets.

It is a stupendous feat for any bowler to end with 2,304 wickets, including 1,488 in the bread-and-butter county championship. For a fast bowler it is a miracle of consistency, skill and physical and mental endurance. Statham can match Trueman's overall record, and indeed his wickets cost only 16.36 to Trueman's 18.29, but to exceed 2,000 wickets is a rare and brilliant feat.

Trueman took five or more wickets in an innings no fewer than 126 times, and ten or more in a match 25 times, twice taking 14. He also hit three first-class centuries, and held 438 catches, mainly at short leg. If he was dispatched to the boundary — his most solemn punishment was to go to a position out of talking reach to player or spectator — he revealed an effortless long throw with either left or right arm.

He never gave anything but his best for England, and he was

rightly proud of his achievements. One story, which is true, was of Trueman en route to Australia by ship in 1961. On board was the athlete Gordon Pirie, who took the players in P.T. Pirie rashly told Trueman that his legs needed strengthening. 'What!' replied an indignant Freddie. 'Let me tell you they held me for over 1,000 overs last summer. And they've never let me down for England, which is more than a lot of sportsmen can say!'

There can be no answer to that cutting reply.

23

CLYDE WALCOTT

Built like a champion heavyweight boxer — inevitably he was dubbed 'Jersey Joe' — Clyde Leopold Walcott scored many a spectacular knock-out on the world's cricket fields. Everything about him suggested sinewy strength, allied to the balance and instinctive movements of the natural games-player. Standing six feet two inches tall, with a proportionate frame of fifteen stones, Walcott commanded attention, and his deeds as the third member of the immortal 'W' triumvirate matched his physique. A big man of big accomplishments, he was the most powerful batsman off the back foot I have ever seen.

In the two successive home series against England and Australia in the mid-fifties, when he scored eight centuries and aggregated an astonishing 1,525 runs, it came as a shock to recall that he kept his place in the West Indies side at one lean period only by keeping wicket! Both Walcott and my brother Leslie, who did so well for Middlesex, gave the lie to the widely held theory that a wicket-keeper must be small, or at least not in the heavyweight class.

Members of the 'Gubby' Allen team to the Caribbean in 1947–8 returned with stories of a big fella who thought nothing of driving straight sixes off the back foot, could bore holes through fielders at cover, extra and mid-off and had a blacksmith's strength in his forearms and wrists. Apart from 120, for Barbados, when he cut and drove with breathtaking power, he did little as a batsman in the Tests, with a top score of 45 and a No. 8 position in the final match of the series.

All the assessments of his potential, however, were substantiated in the first post-war tour of England by the West Indies, when he hit seven centuries (the same number as Weekes). The most important was his 168 not out at a crucial period of the Lord's Test. He proceeded to keep wicket expertly to Ramadhin, which could not have been easy even if he was a party to the little spinner's subtle secrets, and Valentine, and Walcott played a large part in the famous West Indies first victory on English soil — so exuberantly celebrated by the supporters, including a mass invasion of the Long Room! In addition to his ferocious driving on either side of the wicket Walcott stumped Cyril Washbrook and caught Bill Edrich and 'Roly' Jenkins, and his 211 with Gerry Gomez was then a record for the sixth wicket — Sobers and Holford later passed it on the same ground. Only George Headley's 169 not out in 1933 was at that time a bigger score for a West Indian in England.

For all his cavalier treatment of county bowling and his Lord's Test century Walcott tended to fall in the shadow of Worrell and Weekes, but he had already announced his international claims with the first two of his fifteen centuries for the West Indies, in India at New Delhi and Calcutta. Much was expected of him and his side in Australia in 1951–2, but not for the first time talented visitors found how hard it is to succeed in Australia. Walcott had a broken nose and a slightly displaced cartilage in his spine to contend with, as well as Miller and Lindwall, and he was so defeated by pace, bumpers and spin that his six Test innings produced only 87 runs, of which 60 came in one knock. His back trouble cut short his wicket-keeping activities, and with all his thoughts concentrated on the one objective of scoring runs he now began to show what he was really made of.

At one stage he would not have his name talked of in the same breath as Worrell and Weekes. He once said to me in all modesty, 'If my name hadn't started with the letter W nobody would have thought of putting me in the same class as the other two.' By the end of the 1955 rubber with Australia there was no possible doubt that he had earned his place alongside his two fellow countrymen.

Like all youngsters from the idyllic island of Barbados, which is a mere 166 square miles in area and has a population roughly that of Croydon or Coventry, Walcott took to cricket as naturally as a duck takes to water. From a plane Barbados seems to consist of the one town of Barbados, coral beaches, palm trees, sugar plantations and cricket grounds. With its permanent sunshine and true pitches no youngster could have a better environment, and they tend, like Pakistanis and Indians, to emerge at a very early age.

Walcott was only sixteen when he first played for Barbados, who are often the strongest non-Test team in the world, and he went in as an opener against Trinidad. An elder brother Keith played in the same club side and for Barbados, and Clyde was in the school side at the age of twelve, in the same team at Combermere School as Frankie Worrell. At the same age Walcott moved on to Harrison College, the premier school of the island, and became a wicket-keeper because there was a vacancy and he found runs hard to get, a difficulty not very evident when two years before the visit of Allen's M.C.C. he and Worrell made a record stand of 574 on the Trinidad mat. Worrell made 255 not out and Walcott 314 not out.

His upright and correct stance suggested orthodox coaching, but, as such, he had none — good advice from seniors was all he needed to perfect a technique which was much helped by intelligent use of his long reach. For a large man he was extraordinarily nimble and light on his feet. Anything within reach of driving was murdered. He would open his broad shoulders and that would be that. If the bowler countered by dropping his length he would soon discover Walcott's square cut, or pull and hook to leg. He had all the accepted strokes and, as with all the top West Indian batsmen, a few of his own.

When freed of the wicket-keeping chores he was a top-class slip and was a respectable bowler, as befitted a successful League pro with Enfield. In short Walcott was one of the West Indies breed born to the game and capable of performing better than well in any department.

The Australian-inflicted wounds rapidly healed in the recuperative atmosphere of New Zealand with three centuries in four matches, including a Test. By 1953, Hutton's tour, Walcott was on the threshold of his major achievements, which, in the words of *Wisden*, challenged Hutton for the title of the world's leading batsman. For me no true comparison was possible between two players of such obvious contrasts in method and outlook, but for at least two years the performances of Walcott put him into the highest class of post-war batsmen.

I used to think when Clyde went to the wicket that he was a giant carrying a toy bat, and that I wouldn't care to be in the same boxing ring with him. At first I wondered if he might be heavy-footed, and vulnerable to spin. It was a fair supposition, but one of the characteristics he shared with Worrell and Weekes was his dancing feet against the slow bowlers. All would pulverize spin on normal wickets. Jim Laker and Tony Lock *did* get Worrell's wicket in 1954, but he scored 698 runs, with a double and two single centuries and an average of 87.25. His 220 in the second Test at Barbados was his highest for the West Indies and was celebrated by a rhyme, written in the local idiom by Cuffle de Poole Junior, and appearing in the Georgetown *Advocate*. One verse ran:

> Jeff got run owt, nought. Worrell too got a 'globe',
> VM WUZ 25 for 3 when y'ung TEDDY HOBE —
> Hoi! MUH MOWT slip AH really meant HOLT,
> Lef' afta' mekin' eleven. DAH was helluva jolt,
> To the Windian SOIDE;
> Then came in CLOYDE —
> Two hunned and twenty he dash in deh robe.

Clyde's success naturally caused much jubilation on his home ground, coming as it did after a second-ball dismissal in the colony fixture and the bad start with Holt and Stollmeyer going cheaply. True to character he resolutely refused to allow his side's delicate position to alter his natural aggression, and he met skipper Hutton's attacking field with a massive counter-assault. The gaps left in front of the wicket to reinforce the slips and crowd the bat on the leg side could have been an invitation to disaster for the less gifted. For Clyde they were there to be exploited and he did so superbly. Even the good-length ball was forced at bullet-speed past the bowler or in the direction of mid-on. The strength in his forearms seemed superhuman. The last thing I wish to do however is to suggest Clyde was all brute force. Nothing could be further from fact: he had the most delicate of leg deflections and could place the ball precisely. His long innings were a blend of violence and touch skills.

There was an amusing sequel to this magnificent double-century, containing a six and twenty-eight fours, when M.C.C. reached British Guiana. Hutton was asked by local journalists to comment on Walcott. With his dry humour Hutton replied that England had discovered Walcott's weakness — a reference to his dropping me in the slips in the second innings of the Second Test. A very difficult chance I might add! Unfortunately Hutton's remarks were reported as coldly factual, much to the surprise of the team's bowlers reading the papers the next morning.

Clyde was immensely popular with all teams, and kept well apart and aloof from the squabbles of that unfortunate tour. In the Barbados game Jim Laker bet him he would get off the mark with a stroke past Walcott at slip. Jim was out for a duck, and had to pay out a second time for an equally ambitious gamble — he bet Peter May he would score more runs of the pair. Both made 0, so Jim was again the loser.

The third Test at Georgetown, which marked the turn of the tide in England's fortunes, and produced the first of the now-familiar riots in West Indian grounds, represented Walcott's only failure of the series, but on the Trinidad mat he made 124 and 51 not out and took the wickets of Willie Watson, Tom Graveney and Dick Spooner, who had a good record for Warwickshire as a wicketkeeper-batsman, for 52. Early in the tour Spooner, the reserve keeper, had given No.1 Godfrey Evans a piece of coal for luck, which in the heat gave off a distinctive black mark on the hip pocket of his trousers!

Spooner, deputizing for Evans at Trinidad, was to experience at first hand the impact of the W's. Weekes made 206, Worrell 167 and Walcott 124 out of 681, which as I write in 1979 remains a record in Tests between the two countries. Long before the final Test at Kingston, when he made 50 and a truly brilliant 116 in the face of defeat, England's players had agreed that of the W's Walcott was by far the hardest to get out and the most difficult to contain. As Walcott went from strength to strength, Weekes suffered from sinus trouble and Worrell, despite two big scores, was vulnerable to speed and appeared stale.

High as his reputation was after the Hutton tour it grew even taller with remarkable exploits at the expense of the Australians a home series later. Walcott's aggregate of 827 runs was the highest in a series for the West Indies, and he created a world record by scoring two separate centuries in a Test twice in one series. He made five altogether in ten innings, and his scores were: 108, 39, 126, 110, 8, 73, 15, 83, 155 and 110. In the second Test at Trinidad Weekes too was only thirteen runs short of hitting a century in each innings, and yet Australia comfortably won the series 3-0. I cannot imagine what my thoughts might have been if I had managed five centuries and the best part of 1,000 runs off an attack consisting of Lindwall, Miller, Johnston, Archer, Benaud and Johnson, and finished on the losing side. Walcott, daring, dominating but discriminating, by then had a record of twelve centuries from twelve Tests, and his elevation to the vice-captaincy for 1957 under John Goddard was deserving and forward-looking. Unfortunately there was a vast difference in the wickets and Walcott pulled a leg muscle in the first Test at Edgbaston when in scoring 90 he gave every impression of maintaining his run-making records.

I always thought Clyde had the bearing and tactical know-how as well as the performances to have made a first-rate leader, and he might have had the chance to prove it but for the misfortune of being injured at the same time as Goddard. Worrell took over and gave the first evidence of his gifts for captaincy. It might so easily have been the other way round, as he demonstrated when he became captain of British Guiana. Walcott's own form was blighted by Laker, but in the county matches he was as devastating as ever and only May, Worrell, Cowdrey and Graveney finished over him in the full season's averages. Batting was not easy in that era of so-called natural surfaces, and it was particularly hard for stroke-making West Indians.

Back home against Pakistan he took a dazzling 145 at Georgetown, where he then lived and worked, and scored 62 on a turning pitch at Trinidad. One of the best tributes ever paid to him was to call him out of Test retirement during Ted Dexter's tour in 1959–60, in an effort to boost the West Indies scoring rate, which was not entirely due to the accuracy of England's bowlers. In three Test innings Walcott made 84 with a top score of 53, and he took part in a stand of 87 with Sobers. The ploy was not entirely a success, but, to my mind, it was asking too much of him at a time when cricket had entered a period of ultra-sophistication. Later as a manager Walcott won renewed respect for his tact and courtesy and added to the considerable service he had rendered his country at all levels. His overall Test record was 3,798 runs at the very high average of 56.68. On figures alone — with eleven wickets and 65 victims as wicket-keeper — he is entitled to a respected position among the all-time greats, but only those who bowled and fielded against him can really appreciate the power and majesty of his batting. He is one of Barbados's noblest sons, and truly fit to be in the company of his fellow W's — whatever he might have felt to the contrary.

24

EVERTON WEEKES

As colourful as his name and his native Barbados, Everton de Courcy Weekes flashed across the international cricket firmament with the brilliance of a meteorite. Seldom failing to attack and exhibiting all manner of exotic strokes and improvisations he was vastly entertaining, though, as he showed on a Lord's flyer in 1957, he could be the brave and skilled defender. Of the W's he was probably the most ruthless run-compiler, and his compact build and high-scoring performances inevitably invited comparison with George Headley.

Many would argue Headley to be peerless, the master inspiration and the foundation of the modern success of West Indian batting. The W's modestly insisted they merely stood in Headley's shadow, but having played against the two generations I can testify that the W's, Sobers, Rohan Kanhai and Headley shared a common genius and flair. Sir Pelham Warner placed Headley in the class of Bradman and Hammond. He had two tours of England: in 1933 he scored 2,320 runs in a side able to win only five times in 38 matches, and in 1939 he carried the batting. Going in at No. 3, he knew that if he failed the West Indies would fail. I fielded when he became the first to score a century in each innings of a Lord's Test in 1939, and again at Kingston in 1954 when he was imprudently brought out of the Birmingham league for a Test.

In the face of such ability is it fair to bracket Weekes with Headley? A real comparison would only be possible if some magic time force could whisk Weekes back to the struggling pre-war West Indies side, and put Headley in the talented post-war teams.

On the odd occasions they were together, in India in 1948 and against England in 1947 and 1954, Headley was the revered but fast-fading star and Weekes was rising to the top like a rocket. In India injury restricted Headley to one Test when he made 2, while Weekes averaged 111.28. In 1947 Headley's two innings of 29 and 7 not out compared with Weekes's average of 48.83, while the one-match return at the age of 44 against Hutton's side was almost a tragi-comedy.

Over £1,000 — a fair sum at the time — had been subscribed by his admirers to bring back Headley to Jamaica to play against England, but I am afraid the enthusiasm was misplaced. Even when he practised at the nets his shots provoked roars of appreciation from the considerable number of onlookers. The selectors were placed in an invidious position, and to make the situation even more difficult there were threats to boycott the match, or even dig up the pitch, unless he was chosen. In four innings up to the Test his scores were 1, 12, 5 and 53 not out — the latter including two missed chances and taking four hours. Moreover he had been struck on the arm during the first match, and it was clearly evident to all but the purblind that Headley was being exposed to an ordeal.

Unhappily the forebodings proved right and the great George was dismissed for 16 and a single. I confess to being sad at the sight of his stumps being shattered by Lock with one of the fastest deliveries I have ever seen from a slow bowler. To me it was nothing short of a tragic and undeserved exit for a batsman of such distinction, who should be remembered for his vast achievements at the zenith of his powers.

Unlike Weekes, Headley, in his prime, was seldom in a position to take risks. He developed a powerful back-foot defence. Most of his shots were off the back foot, and, as with Bradman, he was an astonishing cutter and hooker. He did not always drive straight, and he did not always use his feet to go forward. Aussie bowlers of the 1930-1 tour rated him as the finest on-side player they had seen, which I would not dismiss as an exaggeration. What impressed me most in the 1939 series was his timing. He was also a model for all to copy in the way he watched the ball — none of the modern fox-trotting at the crease — and he had the gift of beating the field no matter how carefully it was placed.

Older players told me he was not always an essentially back-footed batsman. The technique developed as the years progressed, and whereas Weekes, who had the handicap of injury, failed on his one tour of Australia, Headley hit two of his four centuries in Tests. He scored consistently whether at home, on the faster wickets of Australia or in England — no doubt helped by his experience in the Leagues.

The Headley story is quite fascinating. Only a delayed passport kept him in the game. He was born in Panama where a large West Indian labour force helped to build the Canal. As a boy Spanish was his natural language and his mother, a Jamaican, sent him back to her island primarily to become fluent in the English tongue. While he was there it was decided he should go to America to study dentistry. But he had already become hooked on cricket, and after watching the fluent Yorkshireman Percy Holmes his ambitions were stirred. Still, the plan to go to America was unchanged and he was awaiting passport clearance from Panama. Headley, then only nineteen, hit 78 and 211 off Lord Tennyson's side. His sights were now firmly on cricket. Dentistry was forgotten.

Despite the early evidence of his outstanding natural gifts the myopic selectors of the day passed him over for the 1928 tour of England. In 1929–30 against the Hon F.S.G. Calthorpe's M.C.C. the young George scored 21 and 176 in his maiden Test, 114 and 112 in his third, and 223 in his fourth — an aggregate of 703 runs from eight innings with an average of 87.8. To notch a century in each innings and a double century was stupendous. In 1932 another English team led by Lord Tennyson visited Jamaica, presumably for Headley's own special amusement, for in a month his scores were 344 not out (which included the world sixth-wicket record of 487), 84, 155 not out and 140.

Lord's also became his playground. In 1933 he hit a century on his first appearance there, and on the next tour he made his 106 and 107 in the same match. In 1933 he hit 169 not out in the second Test at Old Trafford, and in the home series of 1934–5 Bob Wyatt's England were taken for 270 not out at Jamaica. Not always was the best England side available for the early West Indies tours, though it was still representative and contained some of the foremost players of the day. But George was able to prove himself the master in England, against the full strength, and eight of his ten centuries in only 22 Tests were off England. As No.3 he totalled 2,190 runs with an average of 60.83, and had he consistently played against some of the weaker countries it would have surely been even better — I made the same point with Bill O'Reilly's bowling figures.

Weekes in 48 Tests scored 4,455 runs with fifteen centuries and an average of 58.61 compared with Walcott's 56.68, Worrell's 49.48 and Sobers's 57.78. In 1950 both Weekes and Walcott equalled Headley's West Indies record of seven centuries on an English tour, and Weekes with 2,310 runs was only ten short of Headley's record aggregate. Weekes had five fewer innings.

For all his flamboyant attack and aggression Weekes was fundamentally correct in defence, and was quite superb off the back foot — my hall-mark of the really top player. He was probably straighter and a more classic driver than Headley, who could claim a marginally wider range of strokes. Many a bowler was confounded by the extraordinary power with which Weekes drove both off the back foot and in the direction of mid-off and cover. He also had a savage pull to mid-wicket and a whipcrack square cut. Even when defending he seemed (as with Bradman) to accumulate runs, and he did not allow himself to be bogged down. The main fear of his rivals was for him to settle in. If he did it often meant he would not stop after the first hundred but continue to make a mountainous score.

The summer of 1950 was wet, but by 3 July Weekes had 'done a Bradman'. All his three-figure innings were doubles except for a treble — 304 not out against Cambridge. The other scores were: 279 v Nottinghamshire; 246 not out v Hampshire; 232 v Surrey; 200 not out v Leicestershire. The first hundred runs at Leicester took 65 minutes, and was the fastest century of the season. Among county bowlers there was a positive dread of Weekes's improvisation: more than likely he would crack their best delivery to the boundary. One took a long time to recover from the shock of seeing his opening ball, a fair off-break of a good length, square cut for four while both the batsman's feet were off the ground!

Weekes followed his massacre of the counties with 129 in the first Test at Trent Bridge, and at Cambridge and Leicester he and Worrell had taken part in stands exceeding 300. Undoubtedly Weekes was *the* batsman of 1950.

His Test career opened modestly enough against Allen's 1948 side with a top score of 36 in his first three matches. In fact it was only one of those quirks of fate controlling our lives which set him on the path to fame. He would not have made the team for the last

Test but for an injury to Headley, and he might not have made the party for India in 1948–9 if he had been taken in the slips before he had made his first run. Having survived he went on to reach 141 — the first of a record five centuries in succession.

India beckoned, and he hit 128, 194, 162 and 101 and missed a sixth century when he was run out for 90. In his seven innings of the series Weekes accumulated 779 and his average of 111.28 was achieved without the help of a not out innings. At Calcutta in the third Test — the first time the West Indies batted twice — Weekes was the second West Indian after Headley to score a century in each innings of a Test. It is all too easy to denigrate performances on the slow Indian pitches, but there are factors like the intense heat, which dulls concentration, and the arts of the Indian spinners, and the artful controlled swing of Phadkar. Weekes had to conquer Vinoo Mankad and Ghulam Ahmed, two very fine slow bowlers. In all Weekes had nineteen innings in India and Ceylon, and scored 1,350 runs with an average of 90.00. Walcott had sixteen more runs from three more innings, but the quickness of Weekes's eye, wrist and foot enthralled the cricket-mad Indians.

Hopes were high for the West Indies when they went to Australia in 1951–2 but Australia's plain dominance proved a poor anti-climax to a series claimed to be for the world's unofficial championship. Weekes figured among the failures, averaging only 24.50, and 70 of his 245 runs came from one innings. There were valid excuses. Weekes was not properly fit, and by some strange arrangement of the itinerary the West Indies went into the first Test with only one first-class match behind them. Weekes had some revenge, if not his team, with 469 runs, an innings of 139, and an average of 58.62 in the home series against Ian Johnson's 1955 Australians. He was, indeed, distinctly unlucky not to have scored two centuries in the second match at Port of Spain where he followed his 139 with an undefeated 87 before the close. Walcott scored a century in each innings and Weekes was 51 with forty minutes to go. But the Aussies rightly did not willingly concede a run and despite a magnificent assault he played out the last over thirteen runs short.

Later Weekes went off to New Zealand with a young West Indies side and opened with a string of five centuries, failing by one to equal the record set up in 1901 by Charles Fry, and since equalled by Don Bradman and Mike Procter.

Everton was less impressive on his second tour of England in 1957 when he was bedevilled by sinus trouble and bad pitches. His aggregate of 1,096 was less than half his total in 1950, and he had to wait until the last fixture at Scarborough to have the satisfaction of a century. Yet, by common consent, his 90 in the second innings of the Lord's Test was one of the finest knocks seen in contemporary cricket on the ancient ground. There was a ridge at the Nursery end and only the best technicians and the stout of heart survived for long. While England had exactly the attack to exploit the conditions with Statham, fast and consistently on a length, Trueman and the highly intelligent Bailey, who routed the West Indies in the first innings with 7 for 44, their opponents ignored the reputation of the pitch. England left out Laker and Lock, and the West Indies brought in Valentine, whose slow-left-arm spinners were no more use than a parasol under Victoria Falls. In an England total of 424 he contributed three overs. Gilchrist was the only speed bowler in the West Indies attack.

The facts of the match are necessary to emphasize the full splendour of Weekes, who went in after Kanhai, Collie Smith and Walcott were out for 45 and England, over 250 ahead, were able to concentrate the full fury of their fast attack on Weekes and Sobers. With the ball rearing spitefully, particularly at the offending Nursery end, knocks on the ribs and fingers were commonplace. Everton became a casualty with a cracked finger in his right hand.

I suppose it is one of the clichés of cricket that the finest batting is displayed in the face of adversity. But how well Weekes and Sobers underlined its truth. Instead of tame surrender of a lost cause they added 100 in 95 minutes. For almost three hours the handicapped Weekes attacked the eager bowling with such devasting effect that he hit sixteen boundaries. When he was caught at the wicket off Bailey there was an audible groan of disappointment from 30,000 throats for never was a heroic batsman more deserving of a century.

In every respect it was the innings of a genius, and I am prepared to wager it gave him infinitely more satisfaction than the slaughter of an innocent attack at Fenners, or for that matter his double century off England at Trinidad in 1954. In those days Port of Spain's lovely Queen's Park had a mat, and the poor old bowlers had a thin time. Some tell me that the mat provides the fairest of all cricket as the pitch does not change and the winning of the toss is less important. But over the world I discovered the mat can be tightened or slackened, and at Trinidad on this occasion the re-start was delayed one morning because a wet patch was found in the base under the mat. Early each morning the mixture of clay and sand under the mat was rolled and watered to iron out the indentations made by the ball during the previous day's play.

Barring an earthquake or a loss of morale a draw seemed certain. The West Indies made 681 for 8 declared, and England 537, with 206 from Weekes and centuries by Worrell and Walcott — all three W's had also hit centuries in a Test against India the previous year — plus May and myself, while Graveney was only eight runs short. Weekes, then twenty-nine, had torn fibres of the thigh muscles which caused a visible ridge; he was well below full fitness during that series and his average of 69.57 was all the more commendable. Had he been blessed with the physique of Walcott his unbridled genius would have been even more apparent. I think it was generally accepted that Everton gave bowlers what could be described as a sporting chance because he chanced his arm on and around the off stump. I do not mention this possible weakness in an uncomplimentary sense, but to offer an insight into his person-ality. On Hutton's tour the attack was directed at his off stump and he was caught at slip or even bowled attempting to cut after being tied down for a while. He always wanted to get on with it, and I find that very much in his favour. It would be fair to say he was England's most feared opponent during that period.

The first Weekes I played against was a cousin, Kenneth, a dashing left-hander, who made 137 in the Oval Test in 1939. Everton was one of the Barbados breed destined to play cricket with transcendent skills at the highest level. He was in his school side at St Leonard's at an absurd age — at least by English standards — but it was not until he came under the notice of the former West Indies player E.L.G. Hoad that he was given his chance for Barbados.

At the time he was serving in the Barbados battalion of the Caribbean Regiment, and while I helped to pull the roller in my formative years at Lord's he was engaged in the same chores at Barbados. There are worse ways to start a cricket career. Little formal coaching was necessary. He progressed by listening to others and in the course of time he was able to pass on his experi-ence as captain of Barbados after his retirement from Test cricket at the age of thirty-nine.

In the northern Leagues, and on Commonwealth tours, Weekes was a prolific scorer and was deservedly popular. His overall first-class career ended with an average in the middle 50's and an assured place among the game's most distinguished batsmen. First as a cover and later in the slips to the bowling of the Calypso spinning twins, Ramadhin and Valentine, he was a delight to the eye in the field.

All the W's were good enough footballers to have represented Barbados, though Weekes had to refuse his invitation as he was already committed to a cricket tour. Worrell was a forward and the hefty Walcott a full back. Football, in fact, was one cause of Worrell the bowler becoming a batsman. Worrell and Walcott went for training one evening and decided to climb over the wall instead of going through the entrance gate. In doing so Worrell cut his left hand on some broken glass and was unable to bowl in his next cricket match.

It stretches the credulity that three players of such ability will ever come from one small district again, even in the West Indies. As someone once said it was as if Bradman, Hobbs and Hammond were born within eighteen months of each other at Pudsey, or in an up-country town in Australia. But there, it happened, and the game of cricket was immeasurably enriched.

25

SIR FRANK WORRELL

Fielding on the boundary at Georgetown, British Guiana, during Len Hutton's tour of the West Indies I became conscious of a persistent voice trying to attract my intention. When I was able to turn round I saw the very black face of a very old man. 'Massa Compton,' he squeaked, 'Massa Worrell, Massa Weekes and Massa Walcott come first and de Lord above He come second.'

When on that gloomy morning of 13 March 1967 Frankie Worrell died of leukaemia at the age of forty-two, my thoughts went back to those words. For much more than a cricketing hero had died. Frankie, the first black captian, had by his dignified demeanour and example unified the far-scattered islands and won from the world a new respect for the West Indies. Through cricket he had brought the islands together, which the most vociferous campaigning politicians had singularly failed to do. There may have been better players, though very few, but none was better respected or loved than Frank Mortimore Maglinne Worrell, who was knighted in the New Year Honours of 1964.

A master batsman, athlete, ambassador — that sorely hackneyed word had true meaning for Worrell — entertainer, he was a captain who made the mercurial but often undisciplined players of the West Indies believe in themselves. The teams under him would do anything for him. At the end of a playing career of 51 Tests, in which he scored 3,860 runs at an average of 49.48 and took 69 wickets, he had a seat in the Jamaican Senate, and was in turn Warden in the University of the West Indies at Kingston, and Dean of Students for the branch of the University of the West Indies in Trinidad.

His death only three years after leading the West Indies in

England and a month after returning from India cruelly ended a career set fair at least to equal the attainments of his distinguished predecessor Lord Constantine. Three weeks before it was discovered he had leukaemia. He died at 10 a.m. and by midday every flag in the West Indies was at half-mast, and the son of a steward on the Royal Mail Line was remembered at a service in Westminster Abbey. Never before had a cricketer, black or white, been so honoured at the Abbey, a fact which he might have thought justified his dream of a non-prejudiced society.

Frankie Worrell was both a remarkable man and a remarkable person. At the height of his powers he read optics and then social anthropology at Manchester University and was polished, educated and articulate. He was handsome and courteous, with a fine sense of fun, and it came as a distinct surprise to find when I first went to Barbados a curious antipathy between the island and one of its most illustrious sons. When he was three, so I was told, his parents were so frustrated by the lack of opportunity in Barbados, that they went to America, leaving Frankie to be brought up by a grandmother. There was an incident, trivial in retrospect, which hurt him badly. At the age of thirteen, the youngest in his school team, he was No. 11, and not anticipating the need to bat for some time (shades of Keith Miller at Cambridge!) he asked leave to go to a cinema. Half-way there he was confronted by the Headmaster striding in the opposite direction. Much affronted by his slow-left-arm bowler's absence from the cricket field he condemned the young Worrell to a severe wigging in front of the whole school. The same master accused him of batting too long at the expense of his team-mates! One evening Frankie told me the story with a laugh, but he lived with a reputation he did not deserve for a long time. Eventually he deserted Barbados for Jamaica. Barbados thus lost one of the three W's who were all born within a mile of each other within a time space of eighteen months.

The sad reconciliation came when his body was returned to Barbados and the island was awash with tears.

Worrell was a man before his time, a missionary with a conception of the West Indies far transcending the stifling insularity so often to be found in the small islands and the arrogance of 'big brother' Jamaica. He was too big for the petty rivalries and jealousies which abound at all levels, and neither before nor since has a West Indies captain succeeded in knitting together so many opposed factions. He would never have his teams neatly parcelled into groups from Barbados, Jamaica and so on. He banished, at least temporarily, the factions and cliques, and to my mind this was his greatest achievement. Unless you have been to the Caribbean it is difficult to appreciate the distances. Sometimes Middlesex and Yorkshire seem a world apart, yet Lord's and Headingley are divided by a paltry 190 miles. From Jamaica, whose nearest neighbours are Cuba, to Barbados, it is no less than 1,300 miles, and Guyana, on the South American mainland, almost another 500 miles farther on.

Miraculously Frankie did what was always said to be impossible — cut through the cultural differences and assembled a team. If that could be done almost everyone agreed that the West Indies, with their bubbling talent and effervescent spirits, could be well nigh unbeatable. They have the abilities, the weather, the wickets, and the public enthusiasm to dominate the world of cricket. To achieve his aim Frankie used not the rod of discipline but an easygoing charm, which was helped by a complete absence of affectation. To the players he became a paternal figure, a person to trust implicitly, and to obey. If he ordered a batsman to 'walk' before an umpire could make a difficult decision, he walked. If he failed to walk, it would only happen once.

The one human trait, from either black or white, he could not stand was arrogance, and indeed he incurred some wrath in Barbados by writing to a newspaper criticizing the decision to celebrate the island's independence with a match against the Rest of the World. By an unhappy coincidence the news of the seriousness of his illness broke during the game. I do not know whether Frankie's stance on what seems to me to be a comparatively innocent issue was justified, but I do know he was prepared in his own way to take up the sword on his people's behalf. He was less outwardly emotional and more clear thinking than most West Indians, and thought all matters of philosophy out for himself. No second-hand views and stereotyped opinions for him.

Frankie's calmness in all situations partly sprang from the fact that he was a fatalist. Once when we talked well into the night he much surprised me with the flat statement that the result of the match we were currently playing in (on opposite sides) was already decided. Until he expounded his theme I thought it a passing idle remark made in half-jest, but he insisted that the outcome of every game was predestined. If that be so the knowledge must have helped Frankie no end, as he was perhaps the most relaxed cricketer I have ever encountered. The Don might have been nerveless, but he was never less than intense and determined when it mattered. Basil d'Oliveira was a marvellous 'waiter' before he went into bat, but Frankie had the knack of sleeping at the most critical times. Before his first Test innings in the series with England in 1947–8 I am told he slept peacefully and was woken up when it was time to bat. Some said the more important the game the sleepier he became, and I remember talking to one of his team after the West Indies had suffered a collapse in a Test at Lord's. 'What did Frankie think about that?' I asked. 'Oh, he was asleep on the massage table,' was the reply.

Even the bumpers of Lindwall and Miller left him completely unmoved. Not being a hooker — though he had every stroke — he merely moved out of line and ducked with unhurried dignity. All his batting was stamped with dignity, an almost noble and regal quality, and there cannot be a serious argument against the widely held view that he was by far the most graceful and technically light of the three W's. For that he was none the less exciting to watch.

At least I can share one experience with Worrell and Sobers. We were all slow orthodox left-arm spinners who started in the position in the batting order from which there is only one way to move — and that is upwards! I began as No. 11 against Sussex, and was given leg before for 14 after Middlesex had scraped a first-innings lead. 'Gubby' Allen, my captain, was my not out partner and told the umpire Bill Reeves I was not out. Bill, a noted character, was unabashed. 'I know it,' he replied. 'But you had your lead and I was dying to spend a penny.'

Worrell's first outing for Barbados was in 1941 at the age of seventeen. A year later, while still at Combermere School, he was sent in as a nightwatchman and stayed to make 64. His story as a batsman is almost a set-piece script in the West Indies, and from that innings his advance was rapid and uninterrupted. In the same season he reached 188, the first of his 40 centuries, against Trinidad. It often happens in the Caribbean that fledgling batsmen make huge scores. They seem early conditioned to going on from the first century, an attitude which comes harder in the colder English climate. When nineteen Worrell went on to score 308 in an unfinished stand with his future Test captain John Goddard, then a record for the fourth wicket. Two years later he improved on the figures when he and Clyde Walcott scored 574 against Trinidad. Again it was an unbroken partnership.

Worrell's technique stemmed from his feather balance, and ability to get into position very quickly. A clear brain and nimble feet worked in harmony and he had a very straight and correct bat. It was always said he could not have played across the line of the ball with a crooked bat if he had been paid to do so, and he always appealed to me as the ultimate in correct and orthodox technique. He gathered runs with painless ease, being equally facile on both off and leg sides, able to drive with genuine power and cutting with exquisite charm. His late cut, or back cut as the Aussies have it, was profitable. It is not a stroke to be risked often with the modern posse of slips, but Frankie seemed to charm the ball away from the bat with an almost imperious wave. Perfect timing, selection and positioning were, of course, the secret. When it came to the art of placement — that is, beating the fieldsman — Worrell had few superiors. Behind the seeming languor, the composed detatchment and adamant refusal to be hustled was the polished professionalism of skills deliberately fashioned and toned in the northern Leagues. He had all the basic gifts of a good eye, balance, trusted judgement, supple but strong wrists, the defence and all the shots, plus very sharp little grey cells. Primarily self-taught, he knew exactly what he was doing.

The Leagues were in fact his cricketing university, as they have been for so many overseas players. In 1948, having emerged as an outstanding Test batsman against England, he became pro at Radcliffe in the Central Lancashire League for £500 a year. He was pitted against his friends Weekes and Walcott, the tough and brilliant Australians Ray Lindwall, Ces Pepper (perhaps the finest all-round cricketer never to play for his country), Bill Alley and Jock Livingston and the Indian all-rounder Vinoo Mankad. The requirements of the League necessitated a bowling change from slow to fast-medium, which was to serve him and the West Indies on tours of England. In the right conditions he could move the ball off the seam and there was a deceptive pace off the pitch. He could, if needs be, effectively seal up one end with tight economic spells. Radcliffe thought so highly of him that a street there was named Worrell Close and the town officially mourned his death. Later he played for Norton and Church and with his daughter born at Radcliffe and his years gaining his B.A. (Admin.) degree at Manchester University he became so anglicized that a rather unfair attack on English cricket and cricketers in 1961 seemed widely out of character.

Allen's weak and injury-ridden side in 1947–8 was ideal opposition to establish a reputation, and with two centuries and a 97 in three Tests Worrell averaged 147.00. Clearly he was a formidable batsman worthy of the highest class bowling and in 1950–1 when the West Indies won for the first time in England he led the averages with 539 runs at 89.53, and balanced the attack with his fast-medium bowling. His impact was immense. After taking three key wickets in the Trent Bridge Test he followed up with 261, which, at the time, was the highest by a West Indian in a Test in England. To allay any suspicion that he could do it only at the expense of the struggling post-war English sides Worrell had a fine tour as an all-rounder in Australia in 1951–2, and was opening batsman and opening bowler in England when John Goddard's team took a hammering.

Also at Trent Bridge in 1957 Worrell, pressed into service as No. 1 because of the failure of the younger openers, carried his bat for 191 out of 372 against Statham, Trueman, Laker, Bailey and Sussex's Don Smith. When the Ramadhin bubble was burst by May and Cowdrey in the first Test at Edgbaston Worrell responded by topping the bowling averages. At Headingley, the West Indies then in disarray, he had 7 for 70, and it is interesting to recall that Frankie took the second new ball at 3.45 pm when England, in reply to 142, were 179 for four wickets. Worrell continued to bowl until stumps at 6.30 pm, his only relief being a ten-minute shower and a thirty-minute tea interval because of rain. In that period he bowled 22.2 overs taking 5 for 42, and England's lead was eventually restricted to 137 runs.

The greater Worrell glories were, however, just around the corner. He had seen the cancer of internal strife and the unhelpful postures of senior players add to the anxieties of the white captain John Goddard. For him the lessons were painfully clear. Wisely he stepped clear of the internal politics which led to his appointment as the first black captain of the West Indies, in Australia in 1960–1. Nowadays all would seem natural. Then it was a momentous break with tradition and there were acrimonious rumbles. He knew he could not afford to be a failure, for the sake of his ideals, his race, and the future of West Indies cricket which had gone through an unfortunate period.

If he had contributed nothing else in this career Worrell left a sublime memory for cricket in every corner of the world where the old game is played during the Australian tour of 1960–1. Richie Benaud did his share, of that there can be no question, but Worrell will be for ever in the hearts of the Australian public. Never has a touring side anywhere been accorded such affection and esteem and an uplifting series, which included the Brisbane tie, restored faith after seemingly non-stop bickerings over throwing, slow over-rates (still unfortunately with us), bumpers and downright dull and unattractive cricket. When the highly acclaimed Worrell and his players left for the airport and home in a motorcade of open cars the streets of Melbourne were crowded with cheering enthusiasts. The most popular of monarchs could not have had a more royal send-off, and public sentiment was faithfully reflected by the setting up of the 'Worrell Trophy' for series between the two countries. It can be said that no side in the history of cricket was more popular than the West Indies were in Australia during that astounding series.

Worrell had brilliant entertainers and dazzling stroke-makers, including Kanhai, Hunte, Sobers, Nurse and himself; and Wes Hall was a thrilling bowler. He gave his batsmen their heads, and argued that in a policy of attack at least two should come off. Invariably they did. They scored fast and lost wickets . . . and the series 2-1, with one tied, one drawn, and only a two-wicket margin for Australia in the final match. This was the match in which Wally Grout was believed to have been bowled but was given 'not out' as the umpire was unsighted. No fuss was made, another tribute to Worrell, who was backed up by a splendid manager in Gerry Gomez. At the start of the tour Worrell had pledged acceptance of umpires' decisions, and neither he nor his team put a foot wrong. From the fence it was difficult to understand the deep inspiration of a new captain. His gestures were few, and the bowlers got on with their jobs without those lengthy discussions which suggest captain and bowler are on the field for the first time together.

Defeats did not seem to worry him. Twice the West Indies lost to New South Wales by an innings, and in the first first-class game of the itinerary they went down by an innings to Western Australia, a defeat which most touring sides would have regarded as nothing short of a calamity. They just bounced back without a tremor. I think only the ebullient West Indies could have played in such a way, and only Worrell could have held them on his course. By the end Worrell had assumed a god-like status with his team. His own batting was of the classic school, oozing confidence to all around him. In every sense he was a remarkable man and leader.

With ample justification cynics might point out that the euphoria lasted only as long as Worrell's reign. In the return series three years later the countries were at loggerheads over the bowling action of Charlie Griffith, and Benaud, armed with a camera, was a leading prosecutor. It is also true that some of the bad old habits returned, and the West Indies lost caste and sympathy when a monstrous bumper attack on John Edrich and Brian Close was unhappily permitted to go unchecked one evening at Old Trafford. Not for one fleeting second could I imagine Worrell permitting such an onslaught. For one thing it was bad cricket tactics; and, firm though he was, he stopped far short of ruthlessness. As for the players withdrawing in mid-series, as the captain Clive Lloyd and others did over Kerry Packer issues, it is unthinkable that Worrell with his high-minded principles could have taken such an action. The much harassed West. Indies Board of Control accused the players of being 'under the dominance of World Series Cricket'. Again I cannot believe Frankie could have allowed himself to be dominated by an outside promoter.

At least England had the chance in 1963 of seeing Worrell's cavaliers. Now he was rising thirty-nine, without Weekes and Walcott, and it would be idle to suggest that time had not stolen some of his skills. But he was still distinctly useful as a batsman and fielder, and his captaincy was quite outstanding. If he had not scored a run, taken a wicket or held a catch he would still have more than pulled his weight. In the first Test, aiming for a declaration, he gave more than a glimpse of his best days when he made 74 not out from twenty-nine scoring strokes, with fifteen fours and fourteen singles, and his runs came out of 103 in ninety-five minutes. Alas, such form was not repeated, but his two primary objectives were comfortably achieved — to win the series and the Wisden Trophy, and to make such an impact that England would invite the West Indies to tour again before the scheduled visit in 1971. Arrangements were at once put in hand for another visit in 1966.

The conquering hero returned to a tumultuous reception at Kingston, where the side played two matches.

Short of another tie, the second Test at Lord's could not have been more of a cliff-hanger, with Colin Cowdrey going in with a broken left arm and England ending six runs short with the last pair David Allen and Cowdrey together. The result could have been victory to either side, a tie or a draw, and in the last over with excitement at boiling point Worrell, ice-cool and efficient, was probably the least affected on the ground. Racing in from short leg he ran out Derek Shackleton by beating the batsman to the bowler's end off the fourth ball, which meant Cowdrey's entrance for two balls. He did not have to face a ball, but had he been obliged to do so he would have batted left-handed. And against Wes Hall too!

At the start of that momentous over Worrell nonchalantly strolled over to Hall and instead of heightening the tenison with a chapter of instructions merely drawled, 'Man, make sure you don't bowl any no balls and give them the match.' Worrell never missed a trick.

Sir Frankie was taken from us far too young, and when there was still much for him to do, not only for the West Indies but in the wider sphere of world cricket and human relationships. We may be consoled by the imperishable memory of him as a stylish and great batsman, as fine a leader as the game has known, and as a person held in esteem and affection in all things and by all men.

INDEX